ON TURNING SIXTY-FIVE

ON TURNING
SIXTY-FIVE

Notes from the Field

John Jerome

Random House New York

Copyright © 2000 by John Jerome

All rights reserved under International and Pan-American Copyright Conventions. Published in the United States by Random House, Inc., New York, and simultaneously in Canada by Random House of Canada Limited, Toronto.

RANDOM HOUSE and colophon are registered trademarks of Random House, Inc.

Library of Congress Cataloging-in-Publication Data

Jerome, John.

On turning sixty-five: notes from the field / John Jerome.

p.   cm.

Includes bibliographical references.

ISBN 978-0-812-99233-5

1. Jerome, John.   2. Aged—United States Biography.   3. Aging—United States Case studies.   I. Title.

HQ1064.U5J47 2000

305.26′092—dc21

[B] 99-42761

Random House website address: www.atrandom.com

BVG 01

Book design by Mercedes Everett

146484122

For Janet and Fritz, who have been there and done that—and for Marty, who is on his way.

ACKNOWLEDGMENTS

My particular gratitude to John Henry Auran, the late Marion Boggs, Dr. and Mrs. Alfred Decker, Dr. Norman Gahm, Dr. Theodore Grand, Paul Jamieson, Dr. David Kaufman, Bard Lindeman, Michael McCall, William H. MacLeish, Dr. John Raycroft, the late Richard R. Ruopp, and to my literary agent, Denise Shannon, who, when I said I was going to take out the embarrassing stuff, told me not to take out too much of it.

Some of what follows appeared in different form in *Men's Journal* and *The Complete Runner's Day-by-Day Log and Calendar.*

Contents

ON TURNING
SIXTY-FIVE

NOVEMBER: *The Dumpster Project*

"Says I to myself" should be the motto of my journal.

—Henry David Thoreau,
November 11, 1851

As a sixty-fourth birthday present to myself, my plan was to rent a Dumpster, park it in the driveway, and clean out the house and garage. Toss in the accumulated clutter—unwearable clothes, dead appliances, bicycles, skis, car tools, decades of abandoned projects. A ton of paper. It struck me as an appropriate way to start off my sixty-fifth year: as if preparing for a move, although we weren't going anywhere. It's a foolish dream, I suppose, to catch up with the mountain of stuff we seem to keep pushing ahead of ourselves. Clearing out the trash of youth and middle age. I'd yearned to do it for years.

It was the birthday, of course, and not the clutter that was driving this extravagant if not hysterical plan. I'd recently watched a friend turn sixty-five, receive his first Social Security check, and sink into depression: the government had officially declared him an old man. Seeing him struggle was instructive. It had entirely sneaked up on him. I hadn't given sixty-five much thought either. I don't like being blindsided any more than the next guy.

Not that age wasn't already landing the odd sucker punch. I had begun to find winters, for example, harder to take. A writer's days are insidiously sedentary, and in winter it becomes far too easy just to sit still. Brooding ensues. The previous winter had been a severe one in New England, not in the least conducive to physical activity other than perhaps shoveling snow. I couldn't run, or didn't want to, and vegetated instead—and took a serious hit from the aging process as the price.

Sitting still is the specific winter problem: how to obtain sufficient movement? I used to ski, and have known skiers who continued into their dotage, but the thought of a ski slope now makes me shudder. I guess I got tired of being really cold. Age does exacerbate that. ("When you're old, you're cold"—the late Dr. Benjamin Spock.) I swam through several winters, in indoor pools, and really enjoyed it, but overdid it, developed overuse injuries, and had to quit. It's a quandary, lack of movement. By the time last spring arrived I was startled to find myself feeling, for the first time in my life, positively frail.

Well, I thought, I'll get *that* right back, and plunged into a hashed-up exercise program, almost immediately reaggravating the bum neck that had made me quit swimming in the first place. Weak spots do have a way of quickly turning painful, particularly as we age. Getting strength back took longer than seemed right, and it didn't all come back. My wife, Chris, and I love wilderness canoe trips, but the previous summer's expeditions had been shockingly hard. Ordinary household tasks seemed to leave me unnecessarily tired and sore. I was suddenly not so bullish. A lot of plans, professional as well as personal, looked due for revision—downward.

The high point of the summer, on the other hand, had been some exquisitely enjoyable lake swimming in the Adirondacks, after my neck had quieted down. I decided I'd try swimming again as winter exercise. If I eased into it maybe I wouldn't have problems. Only a couple of days a week, swim a quiet thirty minutes or so, and see if I couldn't manage to keep moving a little more consistently over the winter to come.

A friend, hearing of my Dumpster plans, referred me to *Walden*. Thoreau attends the auction of a deacon's estate, and, not uncharacteristically, is mockingly aghast:

> As usual, a great proportion was trumpery which had begun to accumulate in his father's day. Among the rest was a dried tapeworm. And now, after lying half a century in his garret and other dust holes, these things were not burned; instead of a bonfire, or purifying destruction of them, there was an auction, or increasing of them. The neighbors eagerly collected to view them, bought them all, and carefully transported them to their garrets and dust holes, to lie there till their estates are settled, when they will start again. When a man dies he kicks the dust.
>
> The customs of some savage nations might, perchance, be profitably imitated by us, for they at least go through the semblance of casting their slough annually; they have the idea of the thing, whether they have the reality or not.

Aha, casting our slough—that's what I had in mind. (And look, they seem to have had the equivalent of garage sales back in the 1850s.)

Digging out the Thoreau was an entertaining exercise. He's long been an interest of mine. Another of the winter's projects was to read his journals, all two and a half million words of them. I'd bought them in a two-volume set years before, but had lost momentum about a quarter of the way through. Maybe, I thought, I'd get going on them again. Whatever he wrote, his entire life, concerned the one central question: how to live. I figured I could still use advice on that subject, even in my sixty-fifth year.

I love the journal form. I keep one myself, for practical rather than literary purposes. Thoreau used his mostly for observation of the natural world. You don't find much detail about his daily life, except for where he walked and when. But he did sprinkle his pages with new understandings, new awakenings, from his ongoing self-education. He was certainly obsessed with that—*Walden* is in a sense a record of his own development—but he usually chose to conceal this self-involvement. Occasionally he let it slip. "I should not talk so much about myself if there were anybody else whom I knew as well," he famously says at the outset of *Walden*. Much later, in 1860, he wrote his friend Harrison Blake a more mature version: ". . . whether he wakes or sleeps, whether he runs or walks, whether he uses a microscope or a telescope, or his naked eye, a man never discovers anything, never overtakes anything or leaves anything behind, but himself. Whatever he does or says he merely reports himself."

That's what I'm doing here. What follows is not a journal, exactly, but a record of a year nonetheless. Actually, like *Walden*—to which in no other way does it bear the slightest resemblance—it is two years compressed into one: the year in which I turned sixty-five and a year of attempting to assess that turning. Thus I write of one November while experiencing the next, a handy reminder. Thoreau's journals cover twenty-four years, giving me roughly an additional twenty-four Novembers to refer to, if more are needed. So broad a reference seems appropriate in talking about age. In a sense I'm trying to cram as many years' experience as possible into one—the object of the aging game being, as well as I can judge, to acquire as many years as possible. Make that good years.

If you have no interest in what it's like to grow old, what follows is not for you. However, if it's going to happen to you (and it is), and the outcome is ultimately going to be negative (and it is), then finding a way to make the process as bearable, even as enjoyable, as possible might be worth a little attention.

According to the World Health Organization I'm already "elderly," a category I find insulting enough. WHO considers that category to span ages sixty to seventy-five. I'd prefer just to be "old," but don't reach that designation until seventy-six. Most geriatricians consider their practice to start at seventy-five. Over ninety, according to WHO, is "very old." At the end of the year, on my sixty-fifth birthday, I can actuarially expect fifteen more.[1] That will put me well into "old," the last category I have much interest in.

If I make it into "very old," I hope to do so with my sense of humor intact. We have a ninety-four-year-old friend who writes, "The event of the week is that, passing the vision test, I have a renewed driver's license for five years. I would need the genes of a swan to live that long."

Call him Pierre; he is senior in my cohort of ancients, the other old men I know, from whom I am trying to learn about aging. By "aging" I am really saying "aging/dying," but will try to avoid saying that as long as possible. Mention either aging or dying, however, and you get my attention. It comes with age. Pierre has prostate cancer but doesn't seem to be dying of it, at least not in any great hurry. A

---

1. Or maybe more: the Department of Commerce says today's average healthy male of sixty-five can expect to live to eighty-one.

retired professor, he claims to derive wry amusement from stead-
fastly outliving his remaining faculty colleagues. There are two still
to go, whom he visits in a nursing home regularly.

He lives alone—he nursed his wife through Alzheimer's—and is
self-sufficient still. A lifelong outdoorsman, he took care of a couple
of nature preserves into his eighties, until he could no longer perform the trail maintenance. As a postretirement project he took on
a massive legal battle for the public good, and won it. He doesn't
want to be identified, so I won't say what that battle was, but it will
be his very nice monument.

I am trying to ask him and my other older friends about their
aging, but I'm not sure I know what the questions are. A while back
I did ask Mike if he'd been noticing any physiological changes from
aging. Mike is Chris's adored and adoring eldest brother, a year and
a half my senior. He's a former Canadian naval aviator who, with
fifty-four-year-old mate Jo, recently built a house—I daren't call it
a "retirement" home—in Nova Scotia. He's an avid birder, a fellow
canoeist who has cycled all over Europe, a vigorous person.

"I certainly don't have any physical problems," he cheerfully denied by return mail.

> The old body just ticks along doing whatever I want it to,
> when I want it to. It's just as serviceable as it was thirty years
> ago. Well, except for the right shoulder. There is a more or less
> constant ache in the upper arm and shoulder area which pretty
> well prevents me from throwing anything overhand with any
> force. I buzzed a small rock at a red squirrel on the feeder two
> days ago, and the stabbing pain is now receding slightly. This
> minor ache also causes me to wake in the night when I roll
> over onto my right side. But that's the only problem I have.
> And I guess it's the same problem which makes driving in re-

verse painful. Turning my head to get a good view out the rear window hurts like hell. Frustrating . . . but lots of younger people have this, so I don't think it's an aging thing.

Really, my body is just what it has always been. Except perhaps for my right knee. The orthos had a go at it three years ago, and I've kept recurrent soreness at bay with medication, not daily but whenever it flares up. Which is usually following a day with lots of stooping and lifting, or when I overdo it in the running line. Which I haven't done now for months, have I?

Actually, though, apart from those few minor items, I hum along perfectly. Though I have begun to enjoy afternoon naps. But look, even kids take naps. I'll look upon it as an age thing when I drop off and miss the official cocktail hour. And I don't suppose it has anything to do with the body, but my lower jaw and my brain do get out of sync after one good, stiff belt, which is why I very rarely ever have more than one martini anymore. But that's just an exhibition of the common sense I have had since youth but didn't bother applying. Nothing to do with the aging body.

As for jiggy-jig, I do have to confess to a falloff in frequency. But that has absolutely nothing to do with my body, mind you. It has to do with having a partner with whom I am in complete harmony, thus making it unnecessary to leap into the sack at every opportunity. Nothing to prove pretty well sums it up, I think. And in my view it's better than it ever was, probably because one learns to be less frantic and to take one's time. I do note that the member has altered as well. I was never one of those guys with a real hose, who liked to walk around the locker room on display; I suppose it was average. But in its relaxed state these days it is a piddly, odd, insignificant, almost comical item. I note that young guys peeing into a toilet produce a near thunderous sound. My stream is closer to your classic tinkle—no authority in its tone.

So I guess this answers your question, but the answer is probably disappointing. I'm sure you were looking for signs of diminution of activity and wear and tear on the body. Since I haven't experienced any, apart from a couple of small non-events I've mentioned, I guess you'll have to find some real old guys to ask. Sorry to disappoint. P.S.: Don't let my sister see this. She doesn't even know I've Done It.

Aging isn't *all* loss. The Dumpster project—a lust for throwing things out—is only the latest of a set of rapidly developing new appetites, which we began discovering when we gave up media for a year. That was a rich, if flawed, experience. Our rather lofty notion was to imagine the house and land as a kind of yacht, which we would sail on a one-year voyage around the sun: one year out of reach of the buzz. It was a noble plan, although we couldn't resist peeking now and then. (It did, however, allow us to skip the O. J. Simpson matter almost entirely.)

One of its surprises was to show us how much else in our lives we preferred, upon examination, to do without. That too is probably an effect of aging. We noticed a certain urge toward divestiture—of goods, obligations, capacities, not to mention an acquaintance or two. We began talking about gutting the interior of the house, remodeling for space and light. We were looking for ways to get a little more air into our daily lives.

"Withdrawal" sounds negative, and that's the opposite of how this feels, but I suppose it's what it is. It is admittedly easier for us than for most. We're longtime urban dropouts, working at home, living extremely quiet lives at the end of an exceedingly rural dead-end road. Our families are scattered, our social obligations minimal to nil. As writers we've tried to keep up, electronically, but we are not, for example, cn-line. Tried it, didn't like it: ate more time than it saved. We're not that heavily engaged in day-by-day intercourse with contemporary culture anyway. What was most startling about giving up media was not the loss of information and entertainment but the gain in time. We had no trouble filling it.

That in fact was the most impressive thing our media experiment had to teach: that the quality of our lives depends on the quality of our time. It's a simplistic little truth, but not so easy to live by, and it too is exacerbated by age. As time becomes more precious, one tries to slow it down. Curiously, this makes you more patient. It's a development I seldom think of when old folks—older folks, I should say—are impeding my progress in store aisles, parking lots, on rural roads. Maybe the patience thing is what makes them so poky.

Improving one's time is a concept right out of the Victorian Age, but it is infectious. We began thinking harder about how we were spending our days. We planned an extensive Adirondack canoe trip for our thirtieth wedding anniversary, and another for northern Canada the next summer. The truth was, we could begin to see an end to larks like that, and figured we'd better stock up on them. It was time, in other words, to start planning an endgame.

The prospect of swimming again stimulated me more than I can easily explain, but the previous summer's enjoyment surely fed into it. We have a swimmable pond at home, although it hadn't gotten much use in recent years. One fine late-summer Sunday afternoon, though, I strolled down and went for a long, slow swim that seemed to restore everything I'd lost in the several years since I'd been able to swim freely. I was stunned with pleasure. Water *is* the unconscious, where you go when you dream. Last fall those dreams took a disturbing turn; I'd be swimming but couldn't complete a stroke, could not somehow get my arm over the top of its arc. It was as if some neuromuscular linkage, at least in my unconscious, had gone awry. Something needed reconnecting.

It was time for a checkup anyway, always recommended before resumption of exercise. During the blood-pressure formalities I mentioned to the attending nurse that I planned to resume swimming. Where, she asked, the Y or the Aquatic Center? I hadn't heard about any local aquatic center. Oh yes, she said, they'd built a new pool at the junior high in Florence. Just opened. There would be public hours. The school was on my way home, so I swung by to investigate, and found a brand-new state-of-the-art pool, open for lap swimmers at 6:30 A.M., with a special $65 membership rate for nonresident gaffers such as myself. Cheaper than the Y, a better pool, only fourteen back-road miles from my driveway. I felt like a city-links golfer who had been given a membership at Pebble Beach.

So a few days before my birthday I slipped quietly out of the house in the predawn dark and drove down into the valley, where, in a reassuringly familiar routine, I slipped on a wispy little tank suit and goggles, got into the pool, pushed off, and began slowly stroking toward the other end. (What a weird feeling it is to be grinning underwater: making a private face, for no one to see.) As I approached the far wall I realized I was about to make my first flip turn in more than ten years. I *love* doing flip turns. I rolled under, relishing the underwater tumble, and pushed off again, stretching tight to streamline, feeling the swirling rush along the length of my body. Something was dampening the inside of my goggles. Glorious. I conceived that I might survive another winter after all.

"Lives based on having are less free than lives based either on doing or on being," says William James, in *The Varieties of Religious Experience*, "and in the interest of action people subject to spiritual excitement throw away possessions as so many clogs." I'd never realized I was subject to spiritual excitement.

Lucky, lying Mike: watch the rest of us change as we shuffle along, belts racing toward our armpits. Crumpling, deflating, imploding. The insidious thing about gravity is its stunning and relentless attention to detail.

My own height is now an inch less than in college. It is predictable enough to lose length in the trunk, from shrinkage of the vertebral disks, but we actually lose length in the extremities as well, mostly from changes in the joints and flattening of the arch of the foot. (Since I turned forty my shoe size has seemed to go up one digit per decade. Doesn't everyone's? Or do we just begin to prefer more room?) Arm span, on the other hand, doesn't change much: thus at eighty your reach still gives a good indication of what your height was at maturity.

We *look* narrower, particularly across the shoulders, from loss of muscle. Jackets begin to feel larger. Pelvic diameter increases, making pant sizes go up even when there's no weight gain. (Sure, that's what it is, pelvic diameter.) Chest size actually increases front to back, from changes in lung elasticity, but the side-to-side measurement decreases. Hat size decreases until age sixty, then starts increasing again. Nose and ears get longer and thicker—and remarkably hairier, to the fascination of grandchildren everywhere.

Men generally gain weight into their fifties, then begin to lose it again, reduced activity replacing muscle with fat. "Replace" is misleading: muscle fibers just shrink, and fat cells expand. Our specific gravity drops for the same reason, which is why immersion is the best means of measuring percentage of body fat. The losses aren't all muscle: other organs lose mass too, whether you're active or not. Liver and kidneys may lose a third of their weight between maturation and extreme old age. Not the prostate, however; its weight usually doubles. Its significance—its capacity to get one's attention, so to speak—quintuples, or worse. But its function, unfortunately, declines.[2]

And so on: a change of dimension here and there, with resulting disorientation; as with adolescence, a series of small, clumsy adjustments required by, or in accommodation of, a changing body. The changes take place at the level of the cell.

It's loss of subcutaneous fat, incidentally, that's behind Dr. Spock's observation about sensitivity to cold. You also lose significant amounts of active cell mass generally: "In the old," as one physiologist puts it, "the body is housing a smaller engine."

Okay, maybe I'm age-obsessed, but it's no surprise that sixty-five represents a psychic watershed. (The term "shitstorm" also comes to mind.) Turning twenty-one or any of the other symbolic numbers didn't seem to require a great deal of forethought; sixty-five is different.

Fortunately in my case it carries with it no wrenching change, at least in objective circumstances. I am unretirable, and therefore don't face the prospect of stopping work, with all that that frightening step implies. Traditional retirement's threat of loss of identity, authority, personal power, is not on the horizon, at least not yet.

2. Most of these general observations about aging, and a lot of the details to follow, are from *Aging, Physical Activity, and Health,* by Roy J. Shephard (Champaign, Ill.: Human Kinetics, 1997). It's the best general text I've found on the physiology of aging, and I've drawn heavily on it throughout these pages.

Still, age sixty-five is assumed to mark the formal beginning of decline, physical if not mental. I'm not the one to judge the latter, but now must begin dealing with the former. That's the crux.

Make no mistake, the body is the vehicle that age will use to get your attention. I make my living with my head, *in* my head. I'm clearly guilty of an obsessive interest in the human body, but it's an intellectual interest; I place far greater value on mental than physical accomplishment. The life of the mind, however, is not enough: you also have to get around. The most important intellectual problem the aging mind must deal with may just be what to do about the body. "After seventy," said the late Jimmy Stewart, "it's patch, patch, patch."

What you're patching is the physical self, and you patch it—or, in some cases, become obsessed with it—because it brings you the *real* news. The most immediate and crucial daily update on current affairs we ever get has to do with future pleasures and pains. We can ignore this news, in fact we all do, for remarkably long periods of time—usually with distressing results.

The odd thing about this whole age-sixty-five matter is the significance assigned to a completely arbitrary number—which governments even change from time to time. Betty Friedan claims we wouldn't presume to date the onset of childhood, adolescence, or adulthood, but we do: see drinking, voting, the draft. Certain numbers—sixteen as well as twenty-one, thirty, forty, fifty—hold considerable psychological if not regulatory import. Sixty-five happens to be, in society's definition, the moment when geezerhood kicks in. A certain amount of despair, even panic, can be expected to follow—not to mention hair transplants, convertibles, trophy wives. We don't deal well with sixty-five in this culture.

Note how we're perceived by the young. Sitcoms about young adults and, presumably, written by at least reasonably young adults, are sprinkled with aging parents who parody the state, with their cranky tastes, stone-dumb insensitivity, weird personal habits. Almost all of them are younger—as characters, not necessarily as actors—than I am. The live-in dad on *Frasier,* for example, is a gimpy retired-cop widower whose role is to be a thorn in the main character's side. He's supposed to be sixty-three—usually expressed as "He's *sixty-three,* for God's sake!"

Other cultures are kinder. In the perennial wisdom there are four stages to life, with symbolic acknowledgment of the points of transition. In India, for example, upon reaching the fourth stage one changes one's style of dress, one's diet, even one's name. The French refer to it as the Third Age, perhaps having learned to ease off a little earlier than the rest of us. (In England there's something called the Third Age University. Offering what, a degree in getting old?)

Ceremonies embarrass me, but I see the Dumpster project as a practical rather than a symbolic one. I can use more of those. I tend toward the contrarian approach anyway, but then everyone knows old people get cranky. My evidence so far is that loss of function aside, everything else about aging is a gain. And I suspect that it is specifically the mortality part—enforcing finite discipline, perhaps eventually replacing panic with a certain philosophical calm—that gives the fourth stage the possibility of being the richest and most rewarding time of all.

To think of aging that way requires acknowledging that it exists, which has proved difficult for our consumer society. Most of my male contemporaries would rather drop in their tracks than admit they're even tired. A lot of this attitude comes from the geriatric press, which is constantly haranguing us to think young. You're as young as you act, hang on, don't give in. Aging is all in your mind, they like to say. It's an arguable concept: don't let it happen and it won't.

Cleopatra's barge is loaded with clichés, and we all know the name of the river on which it floats. Personally, I've got a lot invested in reaching my stunning current age, and I'm damned if I'm going to hang on to that youthful crap. (I liked the idea of being a sixty-year-old so much I started claiming that age before I turned fifty-nine.) Parts of it I don't like—the loss of energy that seems its inevitable accompaniment, for example—but when I consider how I used to boil that energy away as a younger man, and the things I boiled it away on, I am happy to accept a shorter tether and a more reflective way of going at things. What, after all, is wrong with age? See years, above, and the accumulation of as many as possible.

Furthermore I must confess to being a purveyor of the aging clichés myself. For a quarter of a century I've been in the dubious profession of writing about the physiology of athletics—which, strangely enough, is only the flip side of the physiology of aging. Aging, one might say, is athletics turned upside down: the physiology of decrease rather than increase.

A basic tenet of that field of thought is that aging *is* a disease, one of *hypokinesis:* literally, too little movement. It's an argument that's hard to refute. As arthritics eventually come to understand, we move to move. (The arthritic's motto: Use it or fuse it.) We hang on to function by functioning. Some of us find this physiological approach a great relief. What happens with the body is real and concrete and practical as all get-out—and therefore very unlike the mistier psychological regions of aging. Besides, age itself says, quite plainly, that it is through the physiology that it is going to come at you. There are ways to fight it, but that will be the battlefield.

(I learn from my son-in-law, as he attempts to deal with a two-year-old granddaughter's tantrum. Distraction fails, and he gives in. "I ask myself," he says as he hands her whatever it was she wanted in the first place, *"is this the hill I want to die on?"*)

Fighting age in the body, however, does unfortunately fuel the impulse to denial. Nobody likes to admit he's losing, but, courageous attitudes aside, it's not as if you're actually going to win. My brethren in denial who think aging is all in the head should spend time around aging pets. Ours have always been reasonably natural animals—non-Hamletian, disinclined as far as we can see to ponder their purpose on earth—who enjoy a vigorous existence for as long as it is pleasurable. But when they start to go, what specifically happens is that they stop moving around so much. And the moment they stop that, they become quite old. The cause is not in their heads, it's in their muscle mass, their nerve endings. It's in the cells.

Retain function, then, my current theory advises, and the rest is gravy—except perhaps for the dying part. To retain function, however, means accepting that you're in for the fight of your life. Holding it off is a rearguard action, and it is never going to get any easier. Retreat never is. At some point we have to let go—bit by bit, perhaps, but still let go. I assume that breakover point marks the change from a glorious old age to an unpleasant one. But the grace with which we conduct the fight and with which we accept the outcome must have a direct bearing on the quality of the time left: as we old codgers used to say in World War II, the duration.

Actually celebrating birthdays feels silly after a certain age; acknowledging them is enough. Forget the year, remember the day, says my seventy-plus stepmother. My sixty-fourth began with a drizzly drive to the pool and twelve hundred very slow yards, swimming so slowly I had trouble keeping water from running into my mouth. Then home to a well-earned breakfast, to my desk for a productive morning, lunch, a nap, an afternoon fire in the fireplace, Thoreau's journals and a cup of tea. A thoroughly satisfactory day. I'm a lucky bastard.

If a certain smug factor kicked in, it was because after only a few days of swimming I was feeling better than I had in months. The throttle on my metabolic engine had clearly been shoved forward a notch. Not that I'd felt so bad, I'd just forgotten what a reasonable level of strength and energy was like. I'd forgotten what it was like to respond positively—unthinkingly, automatically—to any requirement for initiative. It has made me realize I've already spent too many years, far too early, dismissing opportunities only because they seemed more suitable for a younger person.

Swimming also demonstrated again that I am a catastrophist, not a gradualist. On my first day back at the pool I asked where the pace clock was—the big sweeping-hand clockface, visible from the water, that allows swimmers to keep track of their progress. The new pool didn't have one installed yet. There was a faster swimmer in the next lane, and I had to fight the urge to try to keep up with her. I swam too much too soon, and was quickly thrown into despondency by sore shoulders; oh hell, *that* again. The soreness cleared up in a day or two. Despite having demonstrated the process to myself dozens of times over the past thirty years, I still haven't learned that physical improvement—or restoration—also takes place at the level of the cell. I always, stupidly, expect instantaneous change, a thunderclap, a bolt of lightning. It never comes. I somehow don't believe in wear. How can we use up a whole tube of toothpaste when we use it in such little dibs and dabs?

Sore shoulders set me brooding about how many more pain receptors we are given than the ones for pleasure. How hard it is to accept that. If you don't think mankind is fated for a life of suffering, says the physiologist, count the nerve endings devoted to pain (every square millimeter of skin, for starters) versus those devoted to pleasure (taste buds, a few of the smellers, a small patch here and there on the intimate anatomy). It is a gloomy truth, but the painful part of life (of hard work, of arthritis, of muggings) is the part that most often lets us know we're alive. Sybarites face empty lives simply because the nerve endings of pleasure dull so quickly. Comedy is transient, tragedy permanent. It is our suffering that authenticates us. Who could be authenticated by pleasure?

I tried a little of this philosophical maundering on Chris. There must be some evolutionary reason, she suggested, why too many pleasure sensors might keep you from surviving. On that score, she pointed out, New Englanders, being pure pain receptors from head to foot, should outlast everyone.

"In November," Thoreau wrote in his journal in 1852, "a man will eat his heart, if in any month." I doubt he'd ever have come up with the line about lives of quiet desperation if he hadn't lived through some New England winters.

What our media experiment amounted to was only letting go of the culture. Within a shockingly short time it virtually replaced itself. We no longer knew names, music, what the jokes meant. You let a Bosnia, an Internet, call-waiting and a few other developments go by, and suddenly you're in a very placid sea. Amazingly, it's the real world there, behind the wave. If this be geezerhood, I find myself thinking, so be it.

It also led to a kind of experiment in what might be called anti-stamina. After a certain age sitting still becomes a delicious enterprise. But how long do you dare do it, knowing how it's going to make you groan when you finally rise? Sitting still happens to be about the worst thing you can possibly do, and with age you suddenly discover a remarkable talent for it.

My theory, at that rather fuzzy outset, was that fully conscious acknowledgment of the fact of aging, and even of impending mortality, was a good idea, an appropriate area of inquiry for a sixty-five-year-old man. After all, I would become an authority on the sixty-fifth year simply by arriving at that age. No one in the history

of mankind has ever acquired more sixty-fifth years than I would—
if, that is, I survived it. I thought it only sensible to approach the
year as a kind of forced matriculation in Old Man's School. I would
agree to learn how to be one, but retain the right to define the term
for myself.

Besides, at some point mortality becomes an extremely interesting
subject—in some senses the only one, and not necessarily morbid
or depressing or gloomy, either. Mortality becomes the shady um-
brella from under which you view the world. Like a bill on your
cap: you see better, or think you see better, if in a narrower range.

This is in contrast to that previous, premortal state when you're
busy trying to get more. Of everything. This occurred to me the
other night as I was watching, with the sound off, some blurry succession of jittering images intended to sell me something. This much
data is not healthy, I found myself thinking, then realized what an
old-fogy perception that was. In youth we are ravenous for input,
we cannot get enough, we devote most of our energy to seeking it;
as we age we begin to find it necessary to shut more and more of it
out. Or at least we start reserving the right to choose, and from an
increasingly narrow selection. Chris, master of succinctness, suggests an old guy's bumper sticker: ONLY DISCONNECT.

Growing old in an age of technological eruption has its frightening aspects. I'm a long way past job-hunting—luckily, since my age
group is considered unemployable—but I recently flipped through
the want ads in the Sunday *New York Times,* which I hadn't done in
twenty years. It's not exactly the butcher, the baker, and the candle-
stick-maker out there anymore: I couldn't get a clue to what most
of the offered job titles even required. I now have good friends
whose job descriptions I do not understand. I understand less, tech-

nologically, every day—and so quit caring. I'm volunteering to be left behind, mostly because I really don't think I'm ever going to have much use for all this incomprehensible newness.

Every aging geek in every era has surely had the same complaint. My whine is just that the *rate* of expansion is also exploding, and the supply of nerve endings and brain cells is not; not for me, not for anyone. And my supply is necessarily declining.

Poor me. "Don't get old," my aging mother used to warn me in a quavering voice. It was her little joke. She said it so often that I eventually began to want to whack her with a pillow when she did.

To stop trying to get more is also an attempt to get off my own back, a vow I've been vowing with metronomic regularity, not just on birthdays, since my late forties. I swore a long time ago I would cut out the driving, whirling part, the career upward-striving, the pushing-shoving-urgent suit-and-tie-wearing part of modern life. To a certain extent I succeeded with the physical details, but never quite acquired the mind-set. I am always about to start a mindfulness program. Any day now.

I used to joke that I planned to retire when I turned fifty-five: I was going to pull back, live in the country, and just write books. The external joke was that that's what I'd been doing for the previous fifteen years; the internal joke, on myself, was that somehow attaching the word "retirement" to it would make it all work out, make it as idyllic in fact as I made it sound in my little joke.

I read up on Type A behavior, and rituals for modifying it: driving in the slow lane on freeways, choosing the longest checkout line. A few years back I began building stone walls on the place, in part as an attempt at just that sort of behavior modification. Sometimes it worked, a little—at those rare times when I could remember not to try to do the whole thing in a day.

It didn't last. I keep running past things. I've always done that, pushing past them, trying to shove my way in, over the edge, to increase, accelerate, keep the pressure on. It's the very characteristic I find most repellent in others. I keep myself so numbed out by urgency that I wouldn't know what to do with myself if it were relieved.

Urgency, *that's* the part I'm trying to give up. The weird thing is, I don't have that much time left in which to learn how. That makes it an urgent task.

"I feel ripe for something, yet do nothing, can't discover what that thing is," wrote Thoreau, during one of his Novembers. "I feel fertile merely. It is seedtime with me. I have lain fallow long enough.

"Notwithstanding a sense of unworthiness which possesses me, not without reason, notwithstanding that I regard myself as a good deal of a scamp, yet for the most part the spirit of the universe is unaccountably kind to me, and I enjoy perhaps an unusual share of happiness. Yet I question sometimes if there is not some settlement to come."

DECEMBER: *Demographing Out*

Lake swimming the previous summer did not allow swimming *hard,* with the outright physical abandon I'd enjoyed so in earlier years, but I had been able to go in and peck around the edges, gliding and lolling, appreciating the water. Cooling off. I can no longer swim hard, any more than I'd dare sprint on foot. It's a peculiar realization. I've always enjoyed doing things all out. A while back a young doctor asked me to squeeze a hand dynamometer as hard as I could. When you're my age, I told him, you don't do *anything* as hard as you can. He was not nearly as amused by this observation as I was.

Every attempt to study the physiology of aging eventually runs into this particular stump: is age the cause of this change, or the consequence of it? You don't do things as hard as you might like because your connective tissue isn't up to it. Overload it and it breaks down. (And injuries to it heal very slowly.) Is it age that deteriorates the connective tissue, or lack of activity? The textbooks quite clearly describe "age-related" changes in the mechanical structure of connective tissue, but fudge when it comes to cause. There's no way to be sure. Building up to full force on the hand dynamometer gradually, over weeks, would eventually make it possible to go all out. Put old guys on a treadmill, measure their fitness, then start them out on a training program, and in a few weeks they'll put up markedly better numbers. Good numbers require an effort to exhaustion, or as close to exhaustion as the subject dares come. Have the oldsters improved their actual physiological state, or just become more comfortable with the level of effort?

The textbooks don't mention it, but there's also the old man's secret weapon: efficiency. One of the great pleasures I got from swimming again was trying to inch out a little more speed without increasing the physical load on my arms and shoulders: going faster for the same energy input. You do that by smoothing out all the motions, streamlining the body, reducing drag, stretching out the glide between strokes. To do so lays a little mental challenge on top of what could otherwise turn into boring routine. It gives your mind something to do while you're cranking out the necessary work.

Recently I bought a small economy coupe, the least expensive car I could stomach. It turned out to get quite good gas mileage. This delighted me, and I soon found that with patience and a little judicious coasting on these rural back roads I could rack up some remarkable figures. Getting good gas mileage became my new hobby, amusing me endlessly. The goal often transcends the purpose of the trip. I bore my friends about it, crowing about new personal records.

Not only does getting old make you cranky, it also makes you cheap. So far I see no reason on earth not to go ahead and become a crotchety old man.

My father was a sometime map draftsman whose hands shook too severely, when sober, for the fine lettering his profession required. Or at least that was his excuse. I inherited the tremor, and my son inherited it from me. It occasionally embarrasses me, making me look as if I'm coming off a three-day drunk. More than once at parties I've spilled a drink, social uneasiness compounding the neurological twitch. It is humiliating. Okay, so I inherited the taste for alcohol too. I haven't yet experimented with the three-day drunk.

Usually, however, I don't notice the tremor. Recently I was repairing a small appliance held together with tiny screws. As I was putting it back together my hands were vibrating so badly I was reduced to blind stabs with the business end of the screwdriver as it swung back and forth past the slot. Chris looked on at some point, and afterward, when I'd finished, said it had looked impossible that I could ever get it done. I'd noticed the trouble with the screwdriver but had been almost oblivious to the shakiness that caused it.

I am writing a check to pay for new bifocals. "Are you making a carbon of that?" says the clerk. I don't understand her question. "You're pressing so hard you're shaking the counter," she says. Ah, penmanship, I say; you don't know how hard this is for me. The computer keyboard is no problem, but I almost never write anything by hand anymore. "Lucky for you there are computers," she says. When I get home I hand the checkbook to Chris. By the time I've dealt with our monthly bills my hand is in spasm. It's her turn.

In grade school I got Ds in penmanship, and knew that wasn't fair. Good handwriting was something you were given, like perfect pitch. (I also got Ds in music.) Practicing those drills forever—the overlapping loops like drawings of a Slinky toy, the endless line of Ws—wasn't going to help. I didn't get it; give me something I can *learn.* I got Ds in typing, too, but I did learn the touch system, and became a rapid if sloppy typist. That was essentially the end of my handwriting days.

But losing handwriting, like losing any other ability, was distressing. Would my signature go too? Would I sign my last will and testament, if I ever got around to making one, with an X? Signatures, like short putts in golf, get progressively harder as you age. Golfers call it the yips; physiologists call it *intention tremor.*

Handwriting is one of aging's dead giveaways. Once during the start-up period of a feisty new magazine, the editor told me that the publication's smart-aleck tone was causing some subscription cancellations, but not to worry, they were mostly from old folks, and geezers did not represent the plummy market advertisers wanted. But how, I asked, could they tell the age of the lost subscribers? Oh, the handwriting, he said.

Before our media-free year—and contributing to it—the mail brought a renewal notice for a magazine I'd read for years but had lost interest in. Recent issues had been positively offensive, and I decided not to renew, throwing out the envelope with a mean small pleasure. Take *that,* I said to myself. Then I realized I was doing them a favor. I was cleaning up their mailing list.

The alienation of magazine affections is mutual. I miss them. I grew up with them, wrote for them, edited them, believed in them, but they sort of ran off and left me a few years ago, about the time the infobit and the cocktail fact took over the editorial product (as so perfectly satirized, if unintentionally so, by *Harper's* "Index"). Having manufactured my share of cocktail facts, I can no longer read them with equanimity. Besides, magazines are only about products now, and I'm not much interested in products anymore.

It's not just magazines. The things the electronic media consider worth talking about seldom engage my attention. Few films will get me out of the house. Politics no longer seem to require my constant monitoring. Every big issue that comes along reminds me of some earlier fuss, usually one that stubbornly resisted the kind of solutions that made sense to me. The arguments become like prison jokes: just mutter the number, and everyone will get it.

The result is a detachment that, like the increasing stoop in my shoulders, I swore would never happen. I remember watching old folks let their interests dwindle away; not me, I said, I would not lose touch. How could one exist without knowing what's going on? Now my adult children keep me apprised, if I bother to ask. Part of me is shocked at letting someone else do my keeping up. The other part no longer cares.

But, then, caring is difficult when your demographic significance diminishes as your age increases. The weight of my opinions withers at a startling pace. With focus groups and overnight polling and galvanic response meters, the demographers know ahead of time what we are going to like, what we will buy. Tell them your zip code and they'll tell you what kind of cheese is in your refrigerator, whether you prefer stick shift or automatic. There's not much point in trying to figure out how one feels about a product—be it a snack food or a political candidate—if it's all predetermined anyway. They have the numbers, or they wouldn't have brought it to market.

This may keep the economy working better, but lately I haven't found the economy all that interesting either. Sorry, but if the demographics say I no longer matter, then not caring can hardly be socially irresponsible. I suppose this could be characterized as a loss of faith. Demography, after all, is purest information, and one thing that time teaches us geezers is that information doesn't work either—except perhaps for making more money. In order to buy more products.

There is, I admit, a certain desolation in being elbowed off the media map, at becoming a target of society's Dumpster project. No longer to fit the numbers is to be thrown into a curious kind of exile. That may not be a bad thing. It's instructive, finally, to learn that while demography may have captured the culture, the culture is not the country. What the media have lost interest in are the things that are the same now as they were before the demographers started measuring. Maybe those of us who demograph out can now concentrate on matters invulnerable to hype: beyond advertising; no spin-doctors allowed. Our focus begins to switch to the unde-mographable—for instance, the phenomenal world. Weather, land-forms, watersheds. Flora and fauna. How the geographic world, rather than the demographic one, actually works. It turns out to be much more interesting to think about.

Besides, once you disappear, you're *free.* That's the dirty little se-cret of demographing out. It gives me the same mean pleasure as defecting from that magazine's mailing list. As soon as the demog-raphers can no longer sell us anything, they stop watching. Good. Go away. The noise you hear is a sigh of relief.

Thoreau and me, we go way back. I fell for his rhetoric in college and wrote an ecstatic—if, literally, sophomoric—term paper on *Walden,* professorial reaction to which seduced me into majoring in American Lit. What I was responding to was not Thoreau's political thought or his appreciation of the natural world or even his own tendency toward ecstasy, which I also found seductive. What ap-pealed to me then was pure punk revolt: the young man so scathingly denouncing the hypocrisy of his elders. The mass of men indeed. I was cheering him on.

A few years later, when I taught high school in West Texas in the mid-fifties, a brief selection from *Walden* was included in the text-book we used, and I relished exposing those blinkered little minds to my hero. You could predict ahead of time the majority's scornful rejection (What were they supposed to do, go live like *that*? What if everyone did, *then* where'd we be?), and just as clearly predict who would find Thoreau appealing, and why. The ones who did were already teacher's pets, long before we got to Thoreau.

In later years I did a stint as an ad writer, and I'm ashamed to say I shoved *Walden* at an agency colleague or two, to little effect. Proselytizing is never a becoming characteristic, particularly in a profession that owes its very existence to a steadfast refusal to examine values. I thought my fellows might find clear writing from the previous century a refreshing change. They found him irritating. When I attempted to follow my own advice and reread him for myself I saw why. I was appalled by the ringing self-dramatization, never mind the larger messages. He kept getting off good lines, but mostly to point out how pure his own position was. He came off as a sloganeer, an adman himself.

Worse, he came off as someone I didn't want to know. Having spent some time as a practicing contrarian myself, I had finally begun to recognize that stance as a license for jerkhood. "Everything that boy says makes merry with society," said the still-doting Emerson, but he would later undergo a change of mind, as the merriment factor faded. In our own preposterous 1960s I would meet scads of Thoreau imitators, haranguing me out of my belt and shoes in revolt against the gratuitous murder of cows, proving every word I uttered was wrong on moral grounds. I got so I couldn't stand the little creep Thoreau. "I cannot turn on my heel in a carpeted room," he wrote, when he was a cocky stripling of twenty-two. If only carpet could have forestalled his entry in the first place.

I still have a copy of *Walden* from that era that I had taken on a long airplane flight, expecting Saint Contrarius to help me while away the empty hours. "While away," says the dictionary, means to cause to pass "in a pleasant manner"; this time Thoreau sent me into a wrath instead. The margins of the first twenty pages are now embarrassing, filled with semihysterical (and still sophomoric) rebuttal. The misanthropic arrogance, the sarcasm, the snot-nosed cheekiness. "What means?" I kept scrawling in the margins every time he shot his stylistic cuffs and launched another one of his riffs on how stupid his neighbors were. A lot of *Walden* read to me like an adolescent's rebellion against hard work.

Maybe I was already beginning to feel my age: "Practically," he says, "the old have no very important advice to give the young, their own experience has been so partial, and their lives have been such miserable failures. . . . I have lived some thirty years on this planet, and I have yet to hear the first syllable of valuable or even earnest advice from my seniors." Probably because he turned on his heel at the time.

I ran out of breath about page 22, expiring, as an annotator, in a rage: "snobbish, elitist, morally superior," I scrawled; "how could I ever have fallen for this sanctimonious, pontificating, ice-cold prig?"

But still I loved the good lines. "Write with fury," he once advised an aspiring young author, "and correct with flegm." I keep that notice posted above my computer screen.

I'd been reasonably athletic from childhood, but the shaky hands had always been there. I was terrible at pick-up-sticks—although I could build model airplanes and loved doing so. It wasn't strength I lacked but sure control—and some element of patience, since haste exacerbated the problem. So did trying to hide it, which, considering the embarrassment, was hard to resist.

You have to hit bottom before you look for help, right? The check-writing experience convinced me the problem was getting worse. I began to consider physiological causes. I needed a remedial program, some kind of neuromuscular training, or retraining: something to get me using those small muscles, and the nerves that fire them, easily and swiftly. I wanted to be sure-handed again. I needed a fine-motor fitness program.

Juggling, it occurred to me, ought to do the job. I had learned to juggle in high school, minimally, for no reason whatsoever; nothing fancy, just the simple three-ball stuff, and I was never very good at it. It was so obviously pointless. I never had the slightest desire to be a performer.

Juggling is catching and throwing, nothing else. Your hands have to learn a fairly simple routine and then repeat it endlessly, or until you miss. You must become quick and accurate, although not nearly so quick as you think you'll have to be when you start learning. You do work the upper-body musculature—and motor nerves, mustn't forget the nerves—in a gentle, unforceful way, an almost effortless little dance with the hands and arms (and eyes). It is relatively effortless when you get the hang of it. Smoothness is the ultimate goal. Smooth, quick, and accurate are just what I wanted my hands to be. It might not improve my penmanship—if handwriting weren't a mysterious commodity, one's signature would not be a synonym for one's most personal possession[1]—but I thought it might be a significant way of resisting the inevitable deterioration of disuse. He said, betraying an unfortunate weakness for, not to say delight in, nutball theories.

My assumption was that like riding a bicycle, juggling was something you'd never "forget"—even if the last time I'd tried I could never get beyond the fourth or fifth toss. As a matter of fact, after

---

1. Why, for example, should you have the same handwriting when standing at a blackboard, writing letters three inches tall, as when seated at a desk, forming letters an eighth of an inch high? Handwriting, it turns out, is lodged in the brain, not the muscles. Perhaps what I needed was a small-brain fitness program.

decades of nonpractice you can get back on a bicycle and ride it, but you can't hop curbs and whistle your way home, hands in pockets against the cold, the way you did when you used to ride every day. Juggling, it turns out, is like that: you can pick it up again fairly quickly—if a dozen or so passes and then a miss can be called juggling.

With a few days of practice, though, I moved beyond the dozen-toss barrier, occasionally getting to twenty or thirty. Then I'd notice I had quit breathing, or that my shoulders were starting to cramp, and concentration would run out on me like sand out of an hourglass. It did seem to require that one get "in shape" for it, which perhaps meant it was rehabilitating unused neuromuscular connections. Actually, not concentrating—thinking about something else entirely—would sometimes lead to a long string of successful passes, until a bad toss snatched concentration back again to the task at hand, forcing a small muscular awakening. The Zen of juggling.

It reminded me of those countless glazed-eyed hours I spent as a kid, playing with yo-yos, spinning tops, learning to skate. I hadn't done anything like that for years, but I remembered vividly the cocoon of focus, and its accompanying pleasure. Fortunately, I enjoy being glazed-eyed, as my daily stint at the computer attests (not to mention the evening's hooker of gin). I like paddling a canoe and swimming long distances. Juggling, like meditation, is fundamentally boring—what could be more boring than watching three little balls go up and down?—and yet the object is somehow to concentrate on this totally boring thing. In fact the object is to *keep* it boring and still be able to concentrate on it, which is impossible, which is the very definition of meditation. You end up doing it for the pure pleasure of movement: as with swimming, for the strokes.

Anyway, it was sufficiently challenging, and sufficiently silly. I'd once read one of those interviews with the little old lady who lived

to a hundred and five, and when she was asked if she had any re-
grets, she said only that she hadn't been sillier. Whether or not juggling would help my handwriting remained to be seen.

My sixty-fourth summer was also when I finally began to get some
perspective on my older brother's death, five years earlier. Jud died
of cancer at age sixty-four, a hard death for which he seemed aston-
ishingly unprepared. It had been the longest relationship in my
life—our mother had died six years before, our father when we
were in our teens—and the most demanding, the most perplexing.
We had been extremely close through childhood and young adulthood, but by our forties had withdrawn to a wary distance. I'd spent
the previous couple of decades essentially avoiding him, but in his
last months had had two warm, affectionate, healing visits.

Nevertheless, his death had come as a relief, not an uncommon
emotion in such circumstances but one that had disturbed me ever
since. I hadn't consciously mourned him, sadly or angrily or any
other way; I also hadn't admitted even to myself how badly his death
depressed and frightened me, with its implication of a limit to my
own future. Mostly, though, as I approached the age at which he
died, I was determined not to be caught as unprepared as he was.

My amusement at my friend's reaction to his first Social Security
check is obviously of a piece with this determination. I intended to
be ready to turn sixty-five; I even thought I was going to have myself "ready"—at least psychologically prepared—for the final bad
news about myself, whenever it comes. I don't consider myself a
morbid person, but perhaps there was more dark fluttering going
on in the wings at this juncture than I quite realized.

Speaking of which, Chris and I finally did sign our wills—which
had been "in preparation," i.e., ignored on the lawyer's desk, for

nearly a year, there being little profit in and, as far as anyone knew, little urgency behind that kind of paperwork. Getting it done did not, so far as I was able to determine, represent a particular trauma, only mild comfort. Another little chore taken care of. My signature was legible.

By my sixty-fourth birthday the work on my next book was essentially complete. A three-year labor, it was to be published in the coming June. Until then, as it proceeded at the usual tedious pace through the editorial process, my job was to try to think of ways to improve its chances of public notice.

Maybe, it occurred to me, I should spend December enjoying its possible coming success, or otherwise getting maximum pleasure out of its potential wide acceptance. This success/acceptance had not exactly happened with previous books and might well not happen with this one. But since I could die at any time and not get to enjoy that success—as happened with Jud, for example, and the matter of Social Security—why not get the pleasure out of it beforehand? Besides, when such success finally did happen, if ever, there would be additional responsibilities and distractions, unpleasant side effects. I figured I might as well do the celebrating before the botheration started.

Driving home from Northampton at three on a December afternoon (coasting where possible), I decide to give myself permission just to read for the rest of the "working" day. I am restless during daylight hours if I don't feel I'm accomplishing something. If not "working" (computer, basement, yard) I have to pony up some excuse. Could I successfully take the afternoon off?

This scurrying regimen is generated by my reluctance to stop and simply take in the day, my surroundings, the present tense. I try to get around our loop most days—a mile and a third of logging roads and trails on a wooded hillside, thirty minutes of lovely solitude—but am predictably unable to pay attention to what I see there when I do. It makes me nuts. Wandering off the path, I stumble across a NO HUNTING sign that I had nailed up sometime in the past ten years but could not remember. It is identical with the ones I'd posted elsewhere, but I don't remember this location. In fact, I don't even know where this location is: I'm lost, for a few minutes, until I find the path again. I've never had a clearer demonstration that the fellow who did the nailing no longer exists, didn't exist at the time, was only a momentary construct of the jibber in my head. Jibber then, jibber now: never the same jibber twice.

I sit for a moment on a trailside stone, taking a breather, and suddenly feel my skeleton, *become* my skeleton, a loosely assembled bag of bones held together by aging tendons, a rickety tower in need of having its guy wires tightened. I am strongly reminded that to the basic stages of metamorphosis—egg, larva, pupa, and adult—one might add bone. Bone, the permanent us.

"An old bone is knocked about till it becomes dust," wrote Thoreau in 1850. "Nature has no mercy on it. . . . With time all that was personal and offensive wears off. The tooth of envy may sometimes gnaw it and reduce it more rapidly, but it is much more a prey to forgetfulness. . . .

"Some circumstantial evidence is very strong, as when you find a trout in the milk."

Getting lost, even so briefly, gave me an amused turn. It happens to me in these woods often enough, even after eighteen years here. I take a wrong turn—or stop paying attention—and the comfortable familiarity evaporates; when I get my bearings back it's like running into an acquaintance in a large crowd or a distant city. What you see suddenly fits a template in your mind, even if you can't immediately place it. It always comes with a small rush of pleasure.

The direct opposite of that pleasure is the small pang when you wake and your dream fades; that little wrench of regret—of grief, really—when the story slips away before you learn how it comes out. The content goes so very quickly, and then teases you, dodging away just outside memory, sometimes for several minutes. Not quite remembering sits in the back of your mind like an itch.

Insert here a first *frisson* of Alzheimer's. Every morning when we wake and so quickly forget our dreams, we rehearse our eventual loss of memory. The terror of forgetfulness with age is thus reinforced every morning. Occasionally we reinforce even that sinking sense of loss with a dream—a familiar dream—of forgetfulness itself. Where *did* I park my car?

Every old person I've ever known, from childhood on, has been grumbling about faulty memory. I do the same. The word I want slips away, there are far too many names in the world, the retrieval function is increasingly in the hands of a bored civil servant who has more important things to do. The grumbling, the mock exasperation, masks a real fear. Forgetting is a vision of the abyss. We practice it every morning when we wake. Familiarity with it, however, doesn't help a bit.

Never again as hard as one can: there's a certain desolation in that loss, which a younger person may not be quite able to understand. The reason, simply enough, is in the connective tissue: it won't take it. Your muscles—the part that gives you the strength to plop your legs over the edge of the bed and, if you're lucky, stand up—are still okay, it's the bags they come in that will give you trouble. "Man is as old as his connective tissue," said the noted Ukrainian physician Alexander Bogomoletz.

As I understand the physiology (and every day is another seminar), age does two peculiar things to you. It saps elasticity from your connective tissue, drawing you tighter (age as *filoche*); and it causes, or perhaps just allows, nerve endings to go dead. The sensory palate begins to narrow right along with the range of motion. Make that three things: age also dries you up.

If aging is a kind of detraining, then part of what it takes away is the safety factor in your connective tissue. You may still be able to train your musculoskeletal system to a sufficient level of strength to accommodate a given load, but you have no protective resiliency for the next step beyond that; the next little bit of effort has you bouncing off the ends of your tendons.

There's a view that what happens to our connective tissue explains everything that happens to us—and, conversely, that everything that happens to us is eventually recorded, in some more or less cryptic fashion, in the connective tissue. We civilians tend to think of connective tissue as tendon and ligament, but it's a great deal more than that. It's the essential structural material of the body, the internal and external lining of muscle, organ, and bone (bone itself is also a form of it). From it are formed lungs, diaphragm, arterial and venous walls. Meanwhile movement itself is always the result of muscle pulling on bone, and connective tissue is the material that ties the two together: it thus makes movement possible.

It's all made of the same stuff, wherever it is located, whatever its function. It is composed of collagen, elastin, and a gel-like ground substance, a mucopolysaccharide. Collagen is the fiber that gives connective tissue its strength; elastin is the fiber that provides, not surprisingly, its elasticity. The ground substance is a kind of combination lubricant and glue. As lubricant it allows the fibers to slide over one another; as glue it holds the fibers in a comprehensive mass. Think of connective tissue as a kind of fiberglass that doesn't harden: collagen and elastin are the fiber, the ground substance is the glass.

As you age, the fiberglass begins to set. The elastin frays and loses its elasticity, the collagen increases in stiffness, the ground substance grows dense. When stretched, the fibers return to their original length more slowly. Their nutrition is diminished, so injuries heal reluctantly. Cartilage, which is also made of connective tissue, undergoes the same kind of changes—drying as it ages, losing elasticity, thinning out, particularly in weight-bearing areas. The increased fiber density provides more sites for the deposition of bone mineral: calcification begins to occur. Our ancestors, who lived closer to daily experience with what they ate, knew that older animals would be stringy and tough. Subtle transformations begin to take place in the flesh, in effect changing muscle in the direction of tendon and tendon in the direction of bone.[2]

The effects of these changes are not unfamiliar. We begin to shrink and fold in upon ourselves. Skin begins to sag and wrinkle; joints stiffen; lungs lose their elasticity; rib cartilage begins to become more rigid. It is the drying up of fluid in the vertebral disks that leads to loss of height. Even the heart—the chambers, valves, and the arteries—suffers these changes, losing elasticity and contractility. Happens to everyone: *it is not personal.*

Ah, but is it cause or consequence? Age or lack of use? Those of us who like to be active prefer to consider the change a result of hypokinesis. We choose to believe that connective tissue, like muscle,

2. In a larger sense the body might better be considered to be a continuum, from blood to bone. Thus aging becomes a kind of transmutation of elements. Only science has the chutzpah to drop in dividing lines, divvying us up so specialization is possible.

can be kept viable with use. Unfortunately, we eventually begin to
run into changes to the connective tissue that do not fall into that
category. They are the ones from which we can—literally—run but
can't hide.[3]

All that said, it should be added that any studies of sixty-five-
year-olds, particularly those that gather nonphysical data, must be
taken with a grain of salt. Most of them are done by thirty-five-
year-old Ph.D.s—if not by their twenty-something grad students.
They may have trouble understanding the results they are collecting, or collect the wrong results. They don't quite get it. They think
they're doing exit interviews.

One of the reassuring things about canoeing is that while it requires
a lot of effort, it is also, always, a matter of searching for the less ef-
fortful way: of going with the flow, or at least attempting to. That
gets interesting. I tried to make building stone walls a similar exercise. The object of that game is to move heavy stones, but by working out the physics so you never have to strain at it. Never to have to
do things as hard as you can. So long as you don't have to, it can be
entertaining.

One may notice here a certain contradiction between hating effort and liking it. Perhaps this is what is meant by "the human condition." With age you begin recognizing the necessity of making
effort as a means of holding off aging's effects. That's physical effort

---

3. I would be derelict if I didn't register here my own opinion that the health of connective tissue
is best maintained by a proper level of work, and that stretching is a big part of that proper
level. But then (a) I love to stretch, for the sheer pleasure of it, doing so programmatically
every night; and (b) unfortunately my own connective tissue hasn't proved all that resilient, despite this careful maintenance program. I proselytize nevertheless, without much success.
There are stretchers and nonstretchers, by nature and by appetite, and never the twain shall
meet. We ought to have a secret handshake.

for the act itself; it doesn't much matter what you're making effort at. The alternative, which gets perilously seductive, is sitting still: giving in; stepping into age, as Marshall McLuhan said about newspapers, as into a warm bath. This is entirely too Nietzschean a view for my tastes, but it is the politics of the physiology. It is a politics one must accept, if ruefully: the effort goes on, as the sparks fly upward.

Not so incidentally, however, bringing a certain programmatic approach to these matters—putting in a little specific effort, routinely, every day—gets easier as you get older. You don't mind because it's how you keep the things you want to do from slipping away from you. Age lets you see how much you may have lost in the past to disorganization and confusion, to romantic notions like spontaneity. You begin to pay a better quality of attention. In that sense duty becomes pleasant—not duty in the God-and-country sense but in simple chores, the rounds of dailiness that maintain a manageable life.

In mid-December our eldest cat astonished all by turning up dead. She simply crawled under a bed and didn't show up for the next meal, an unthinkable lapse for this particular cat. Shocked the pants off me, anyway. She was only eight, not that old for a domestic feline. Probably an aneurysm. We'd had some snow but the ground was still unfrozen, so I was able to bury her in the northeast field.

On the twentieth came spitting snow on top of rain and I skipped my swim, preferring to avoid the commute on icy roads. This was solstice thinking, affected by the light. As a solstice celebration, incidentally, we turned our clocks to the wall for a day and a night, a weird experiment with no clear resolution. I suspect we ate earlier, went to bed earlier, and slept longer, but there was no way of telling. Going timeless didn't seem to make a great deal of difference in our daily routine. I skipped swimming again on the twenty-third for orthopedic reasons, my neck acting up.

On Christmas Day Chris saw a bald eagle soaring over the frozen pond out back, a little Christmas gift from the wild. There's a nest about twenty miles away.

It's just as well I wasn't swimming: this time of year it's pitch-dark for the drive in, which means the Christmas lights are on. They always throw me into a depression. It's a deep-seated neurosis of mine; call it fear of decor. In a household with neither kids nor organized religion to apply pressure, I Scrooge my way through the season anyway, using it chiefly as a means of locating myself in the natural year. That seems to me the best moral starting point, to which periodic reconnection is almost mandatory, although I tend to be sloppy about such matters.

Watering the house plants, for example, is Chris's turf, but I fill in, in her occasional absence. For her it is a reaffirmation of the natural world; for me it's a nagging chore, eating up time. If I only stopped to consider, however, I'd realize I'm thinking about the task only in terms *of* time. If I thought instead about putting water into the plants, restoring the hydrostatic pressure in these lovely green things that we like to have around us, I'd realize what a benign and satisfying thing it is, or should be, to do. I can't figure out why we don't reexamine all our nagging, tedious chores in this light. Remove the time pressure and you remove the nagging. Look at any task from the standpoint of what might be called eternal rather than temporal values, and few tasks are annoying. This may not seem like the most profound realization in the history of Western man, but it offers a solid handle on the urgency that dogs my days. If I can only remember it.

Perhaps I should mention a certain difficulty I have with mood this time of year. I wouldn't go so far as to characterize it as Seasonal

Affective Disorder, which really screws some people up, but it does get better when the light comes back. Really, it does. Says I to myself.

Anyway, by Christmas I hadn't swum for a week, my neck still bothering me. It was a bad disk that irritated the nerves leading to my right shoulder, threatening to put those muscles into spasm, and sometimes succeeding. As the year drew to an end it seemed to be telling me not to swim, a large disappointment.

Five years before, during a flare-up, I'd had an MRI and a diagnosis, and there's little mystery involved. At that time a poisonously haughty neurosurgeon told me the damage was insufficient to warrant surgery—saying, in effect, Come back when it gets worse. I had no medical insurance at the time, so this prognosis carried with it a certain relief, although not of the actual pain. Now, however, I was only ten months away from Medicare. Real relief might just be in sight.

Drifting toward sleep once, thirty years ago—when I was still young enough to sleep on my stomach—I realized how much tension I was holding in the muscles at the back of my neck. I began concentrating on relaxing them, letting go, letting myself sag more deeply into the mattress. I slipped over the edge and began dreaming, and the first thing I dreamed was of a giant fist, coming down through the ceiling of my bedroom and smashing into the back of my neck. See old joke: clearly, if I relaxed those neck and shoulder muscles, my arse would fall off.

JANUARY: *The Silence of Old Men*

~❧ When I resumed swimming in January, it was in a surprisingly crowded pool. Earlier in the winter I'd had it virtually to myself, but traffic was picking up; perhaps movement deprivation was going around. My first time back I shared a lane with a short, rotund, quite elderly male. He wasn't swimming much, mostly hanging out in the shallow end, but obviously enjoying himself. Whenever I paused he'd try to get a conversation going. During one such break he looked me slyly in the eye and said, "So, *are you still working?*" "Kid" was implied; I learned later that he was eighty-four.

After that swim I went shopping for a new computer monitor, the old one having winked out in a stench of smoke. My equipment is ancient, and color is for my purposes beside the point, but I soon discovered you could no longer buy a black-and-white model, at least from the usual sources. The office supply store where I began my search had floor samples hooked up to a video camera, showing live scenes inside the store rather than computer data on a screen. I only realized this when I caught a glimpse in the monitor of the tiredest, most beat-to-shit-looking old guy I ever saw, which of course turned out to be me. I almost ran from the store.

I was toying with a new book idea, tentatively called *Our Town 2000.* Chris has been a resident fellow at the MacDowell Colony in Peterborough, New Hampshire, the town that served as model for Grover's Corners in Thornton Wilder's play. As a result we'd both spent time in Peterborough, and liked the town. It's only seventy miles away.

Our Town, the ultimate depiction of mythic small-town U.S.A., begins its action in 1901. Wilder wrote the play in 1937 while in residence at MacDowell. Although he sometimes disavowed the direct connection, Peterborough is proud of the association. There's an Our Town Realty, an Our Town Landscaping Company, a restaurant named Grover's Corners. The Peterborough Historical Society publishes the *Our Town Cookbook.*

The MacDowell Colony hasn't changed much since Wilder's day, but Peterborough now has two large corporate headquarters, eight publishers, two newspapers, a sizable bookstore, a ski resort. There's a gourmet take-out lunch counter that serves exquisite quiches and arugula salads, and if you don't get there before 11:30 you can't get a parking place. As a small New England town, Peterborough has successfully made the transition from the requirements of 1901 to those of 2001. It also has an Alcoholics Anonymous chapter and AIDS services, and its newspapers were recently aboil with controversy over mandatory drug-testing of local high school athletes.

My notion was to write a biography of the town, a factual portrait of the place at four distinct points in time: in 1901, but as the town actually was, rather than as Wilder's dreamy Everyplace; in 1937, in the Depression-ridden mid-thirties when Wilder was doing his research; in 1968, during the turmoil of that era; and at the turn into the next century. The dates were one generation apart; the real-life counterparts of the play's high school sweethearts would have children who became adults in the Depression years, and so on.

My plan was to trace the life of the town, using the play itself only as a guideline: a reminder of Wilder's (and anyone else's) absolutely fundamental concerns—courtship, marriage, childbirth, getting a living, death. It would not be a sociological treatise but, I hoped, a readable picture of how small-town U.S.A. has evolved since Wilder mythologized it. The book might also give some indication of where that kind of life is headed as we roll into the twenty-first century. Besides, it would get me out of the house.

So a week after the New Year I began what I hoped would become a regular commute, driving up to Peterborough on a bitterly cold day, hoping to accomplish a day's on-site research without staying overnight. I visited the Chamber of Commerce, the public library, the historical society. I dropped by Our Town Real Estate, using as an excuse that we were planning retirement—Peterborough gets a lot of retirees, and Chris and I had actually talked about it. I met a lot of nice people, but my aching neck drained away patience for the required leisurely small-town conversation. I took out subscriptions to both competing weeklies and headed home.

My agent expressed a good deal of enthusiasm for the proposal but thought it needed more reporting, a stronger background. Perhaps, he suggested, I could find an old diary in someone's attic, or a knowledgeable oldster in a nursing home. I agreed, and said I'd get right on it.

In mid-January, meanwhile, my swimming program dragged to a frustrating halt. The swimming itself was no problem—in fact, felt wonderful—but the next day my back and shoulder would feel like a sack of hot doorknobs. The disk in my neck was beginning to be a real problem, forcing me to learn some new management techniques for nonswimming activities. Typing in the approved upright position had become a torment, but I could continue if I put my feet up and held the keyboard on my lap. If I stood for long my right arm would go numb, or my fingers begin tingling. Driving began to get painful, a significant handicap in our rural lives. Even sitting upright in a chair, as at lunch with a friend, would have me squirming before the coffee arrived. I was becoming miserable company. It was time, perhaps, to give programmatic exercise a rest.

Besides, I was eager to get hopping on the Peterborough project. Chris and I began considering the possibility that I'd need to take a small apartment there, to get sufficiently into the life of the town: a year, perhaps, and thereafter the rather long commute should serve. Meanwhile one more trip would conceivably turn up sufficient material to get a formal proposal working. Then there'd be time to figure out the details.

So on a red-sky dawn in late January I headed north on Interstate 91, full of big plans. After about fifteen minutes of driving, however, my neck was in sufficient distress—every tar strip a jolt of pain—to make me bail out and scuttle home. The journalistic footwork for such a project—trying to concentrate during interviews, spending long hours in libraries digging out research, attending school-board and town-council meetings—was a frightening prospect. By the time I got back to the house I realized that there was no way, in my present condition, that I'd be able to write that book.

I lied to my agent. I love the idea of the book, I told him, and would like to read it myself, but I don't want to write it. To lock myself into two or three years of listening to old men yammer in barbershops was not my idea of a good time. I'll be writing only so

many more books, and don't want to blow a good bit of my remaining time on a project I don't enjoy. I didn't mention that my
neck went into spasm every time the nose of my car turned north
(or south). My agent's disappointment was not exactly palpable.

There is a familiar image in marathons, when someone goes out
too fast; then the pack, as they say, begins to reel him in. I'd begun
getting the feeling that was what was happening to me.

One of the ways you begin to feel better when you start an exercise program, or resume an old one, is that you get a sense of being
physically larger. It's not the bulking up that body builders seek,
but pure extension: your limbs feel longer; you inhabit more
space. Women may find this disturbing, since unwanted size is
often the very thing that starts them exercising in the first place,
but the feeling itself is extremely pleasurable. It's part of growing
stronger, which is more helpful in everyday life than we realize.
When you ask your body to perform some task—as simple as
climbing a flight of stairs, or getting groceries in from the car—it
responds more crisply, wholeheartedly. You don't have to brace
yourself so much. You now have access to your full dimensions.
Your reach is extended, in every metaphorical sense as well as the
actual one.

Aging makes you feel smaller. Exercise helps, but can't do everything. It doesn't matter how many miles a day you run, when you're
not exercising you're less active. You use fewer nerve endings, and
the neglected ones begin to shut down. (Some—the auditory ones,
for example—are simply lost, irrecoverable as far as I've been able
to find out.) All we are, in a sense, are nerve endings; their loss represents an outright physical diminishment, even if you manage to
hang on to other functions. This diminishment, incidentally, is part

of what makes aging so bittersweet: as working nerve endings get fewer, your appreciation of the ones that remain gets that much richer and stronger.

In an attempt at least to slow this tendency—with swimming on hold—I began a gingerly weight-lifting program. I had weights and a weight bench in the basement left over from competitive swimming days. I devised a routine involving low weights and not that many repetitions either—just sufficient to keep the larger muscle groups toned. I wanted them reminded, in effect, of what they might be called upon to do. The plan I devised was not progressive, not predicated on improvement, which is heretical in weight-lifting circles, but was a neat little routine that took less than fifteen minutes and hardly broke a sweat. In the beginning it had me trembling by the time I got to my desk; once I got used to it it had me humming. I longed for a mental equivalent.

What I was fighting was *sarcopenia:* muscle wasting, a common concomitant of aging. What wonderful names the scientists come up with for these afflictions: senile ptosis (drooping eyelids), nocturia (needing to pee at night), dyspnea (shortness of breath), postural hypotension (keeling over in a faint when you stand up too quickly, one of many causes of falls among the elderly). My shaky handwriting? Scrivener's palsy. In my freshman psych class we talked about "need strain," about "visceral tensions" as a source of human motivation. Nocturia: there's a visceral tension all right. And one mustn't forget the intention tremor. Intention tremors are caused by deterioration of muscle proprioceptor activity—the ability of the muscle to sense body position, movement, and the like—or damage to the comparator function in the brain. Or both. It is renewal of proprioceptor activity that makes you feel larger when you resume exercising. Your limbs begin to get a better sense of where they really are and what they're doing.

Gerontologists are coming to agree that there is no such thing as dementia, at least in the absence of Alzheimer's, but there is what one study calls "benign senescent forgetfulness." I told Chris about this, we had a few laughs on the subject; BSF, we called it, comparing symptoms. A couple of hours later something reminded us of it. "Benevolent," I said, ". . . no, benign." "Senescent," C. interrupted triumphantly. There was a long pause. Neither of us could quite remember that other word.

My weight-lifting regimen fell apart on the reef of compliance, as so many exercise programs eventually do. It's almost as if the word "program" is what kills them. We find it almost impossible to stay with a physical routine that isn't intrinsically rewarding—not for its results but for the experience itself, while it's happening. There are a rare (and lucky) few for whom making themselves tired is in itself sufficient, but not for most of us. The phys-ed folks say the usual curve is high enthusiasm for the new program, and genuine enjoyment of its results, for from six weeks to six months. Then participation gradually fades, or we get irritated with the program's demands and quit abruptly.

I ought to know, I've done it dozens of times. My weight-lifting program was of the six-week variety. It made me slightly sore, which I actually enjoyed—the right level of muscle tightness makes you feel more alive, simply from being better used—but in the end it became just enough of a nag and not quite enough of a kick, and I let it flicker and die.

It could well be that to stop trying to get more is a physiological change, and the mind—and the emotional life—follow along behind. Whatever else it may be, age is compensatory. Maybe what the aging man discovers, if he is lucky, is that it is possible to be happy and depressed at the same time. If you can just survive the transition.

Also in mid-January I arrived at the age Jud was when he received his death sentence—arriving, as it so often does, in a single word: "inoperable." When he was exactly as old as I had now become, he was beginning, on the basis of hard evidence, to wrestle with the problem. *The* problem.

He lived four more months; in four months I would thus outlive him, an utterly meaningless statistic that had been engraved inside my forehead since his death in 1991. I of course was still far too young and beautiful to be able to accept with equanimity my own end, which forced me into a little retroactive tolerance for his blustery denial.

It bothered me a great deal at the time. He was an intellectual, a poet, accustomed to dealing with the great themes, but death didn't seem to have been among them. I kept thinking he was too smart to be so unprepared. I'm not so sure now that he wasn't, either smart enough or unprepared, but then I'm not so sure now of a lot of things I thought I understood at the time. He may have simply been sparing the rest of us, and himself, the emotional scenery-chewing, that final fatigue. As Sherwin Nuland points out in his magnificent book *How We Die,* nobody dies with dignity, however much we think we want that. Dying is the definition of indignity. It's messy. The dignity we're really trying to hang on to is among the survivors. Jud may have been trying to preserve that for us. No scenes, please, we're WASPs. Well, white-breads, anyway.

And perhaps my determination to be better prepared was an attempt to defuse the scenery-chewing. I was not shy about mentioning my enormous age to my loved ones. I wanted it clear in their heads that I was as old as I was and therefore on a finite track. I made jokes quite deliberately about not being terribly concerned with matters more than about fifteen years in the future. Those jokes elicited embarrassment, usually, and a quick change of subject. I hated that. I was not embarrassed or emotionally distraught at considering that I wouldn't be here, and didn't want others being so either. I'd have been gratified rather than offended if family and friends spoke comfortably about the post-me era. And I'd particularly have liked to be able to talk to my elders with that kind of unembarrassed matter-of-factness. Unfortunately, they didn't seem to buy my approach. I wasn't having much luck getting my cohort to talk about their impending deaths. Perhaps that would get easier as I came to understand the subject better myself. Perhaps I wasn't old enough.

I picked up, for the title alone, a book on middle-age male depression entitled *I Don't Want to Talk About It,* but it wasn't much help.

"By a well-directed silence I have sometimes seen threatening and troublesome people routed," Thoreau says in an undated entry in his journal sometime between 1837 and 1847. ". . . They cannot stand it. Their position becomes more and more uncomfortable every moment. So much humanity over against one without any disguise,—not even the disguise of speech! They cannot stand it nor sit against it."

On the way to bed I bend over to turn down the wall thermostat, then have to reverse myself and bend backward, away from the wall, in order to see the tiny numbers through the bottom half of my bifocals. Something about the movement pulls me out of myself sufficiently to see my own body language. It makes me feel twenty years older.

Maybe the years go by faster as you get older because each year is a smaller percentage of your total life span. After sixty the effect is very like time-lapse photography.

In my earliest flirtations with Thoreau, when I wasn't being swept off my feet by his punk revolt I was envying him his free time: "Sometimes, in a summer morning, having taken my accustomed bath, I sat in my sunny doorway from sunrise till noon, rapt in a revery, amidst the pines and hickories and sumachs, in undisturbed solitude and stillness, while the birds sang around or flitted noiseless through the house. . . . It was morning, and lo, now it is evening, and nothing memorable is accomplished." *I could do that,* I always thought when I was reading *Walden*—overlooking a certain youthful fidgetiness of my own when I was not involved in some personal pursuit.

Thoreau did preserve his free time, jealously, because he knew himself to be embarked on a gigantic enterprise, although he wasn't always sure what that enterprise was. "The scale on which his studies proceeded," his sometime friend Emerson pointed out, "was so large as to require longevity." Longevity unfortunately was not in the cards.

He was a self-described loafer, an idler, and, since he was also a good Yankee, was tortured by that self-description. To read *Walden* is to make the acquaintance of a joyous young man in revolt against his contemporary culture, an impassioned defender of the wild and free, an idealistic evangelist of simplicity. To read the various biographies is to wonder whether he ever knew a happy moment. To read the journals is to see him washed alternately with sunny humor and black despair. He was lugubrious and self-pitying, he was ashamed of his reputation, and he was in most of his personal relations the bitterest of men. "I could tell a pitiful story respecting myself, with a sufficient list of failures, and flow as humble as the very gutters," he wrote in his journal in the fall after leaving Walden. "The world is a cow that is hard to milk, life does not come so easy."

He almost summarizes this internal conflict in a journal entry in October 1853: "When, after feeling dissatisfied with my life, I aspire to something better, am more scrupulous, more reserved and continent, as if expecting somewhat, suddenly I find myself full of life as a nut of meat,—am overflowing with a quiet, genial mirthfulness."

And it is that quiet, genial mirthfulness that saves him. It comes through even when he is being grumpy about surveying, which he considered a waste of his time but which for long periods was his only source of income. He lectured as often as he could, but seems not to have been a charmer at that, either, tending to blame his victims for his nonsuccess. This irascibility comes through in his writing much more clearly than the underlying mirthfulness it rode on. He bitched in his journal when things went poorly, but felt it was unseemly to mention mere happiness. Then he simply described where he went and what he saw, and puzzled over its meaning. That was his work. It was also, at least for him, how to live, and its unacceptability to his peers bothered him so much it almost, but not quite, got in the way of the doing of it.

After some discussion Chris and I agreed to change BSF to BSW: Benign Senescent Whatever.

In late January *The New York Times* reported that Trondheim, Norway, would see the sun again for the first time since November 11—an event called, transparently enough, *Sondag.* In Manhattan the sunrise would come at 7:09, sunset at 5:10, making a ten-hour-and-one-minute day. I could live with that. I made a doctor's appointment to consult about my neck.

It was still definitely winter, though. My friend Willy asked me to help bring his ailing German shepherd home from the vet's. We did it on a clear, bright, frigid day, the January sun finally picking up a bit of strength, but the dog, fatally lame, was coming home to die. She'd been to the vet's for one more heroic cortisone shot, her owners hoping to buy a little more time.

I was helping because Willy's father-in-law, Marion, could not. Marion, who is eighty-six, had flipped his four-wheel-drive sport utility on black ice a few weeks previously. He wasn't seriously injured, but he'd hung upside down in his seat belt for fifteen minutes before rescue, which left him with an array of aches and bruises that limited his mobility. The accident also made him leery of winter driving, so he sat icebound at home, taking care of *his* elderly dog, also one step away from the knackery.

Shortly before leaving to fetch the dog, Chris and I got word that our seventy-eight-year-old friend Fritz, over in the Adirondacks, had been diagnosed with cardiac myopathy, from deposits of amyloid, whatever that is. No treatment known. It may have been a side effect of chemotherapy, after surgery for colon cancer, but nobody really knew. The condition was rare; Fritz, a surgeon himself, had seen only one case in a lifetime of practice. That one proved fatal within two years.

We didn't yet know the prognosis, no time frame or any details. He went for diagnosis because of shortness of breath—he's an amazingly vigorous man, and I can only imagine how short it had to be for him to admit it—but his wife, Janet, reported that he'd since been out snow-blowing the driveway, so he wasn't quite an invalid yet. I wanted to talk to Fritz about his diagnosis but wouldn't have a chance for some months. Besides, I had, and have, a growing sense that oldsters are entitled to their silence. It may not be helpful to their loved ones, but by God they've earned the right to it. To expect otherwise is a violation of their privacy, and as the functions continue to slip away, privacy looms larger and larger.

I have to confess to a growing sense myself that talk is particularly useless. As my son used to complain about us grown-ups, one eventually begins to know where any conceivable conversation is going to go. After the first fifteen minutes of catching up on personal news—refilling the gossip pump—you're on a pointless mission. Old guys' reputation for garrulity notwithstanding, most have enough sense to let things drop. After a certain point, corks are called for.

I realize this stance is in direct revolt against all current psychological wisdom. I don't care. I've experienced the relief of talking things out. I also know it comes when it's ripe, and seeking it out ahead of time can be as discomfiting, for both seeker and source, as its timely occurrence is comforting.

I grew up with a silent stepfather, with whom I had a perfectly terrible relationship. His brooding silence seemed aimed personally at me. I'd see him in social situations and be amazed to hear him talk at all, astonished that he could fulfill the requirements of social interaction. Working with him at chores, I'd pester him with questions, try to get him talking about *anything,* for God's sake, just to get something going. I'd fail; he'd put me quickly in my place, each subject put terminally to rest. The only times he ever really talked to me were to chew me out—a series of lectures, confrontations, really, years apart, in which he tried to give me some wisdom. I was afraid of him, although he never laid a hand on me. When he lectured I would stand and silently weep while he explained to me my mistakes, character flaws, irresponsibilities. I was long gone before he grew old. All that stern adult bullshit I got from him was from a man considerably younger than I am now.

Although I couldn't comprehend that silence at the time, I sometimes feel it lowering over me now, in conversations I choose not to have. It's as if aging were a process of making lists of subjects not to talk about. Maybe what causes old men to go silent is simple impatience. Giving voice to all those dying yips of the dying self only makes the noise go on longer. Noise itself makes the noise go on longer. A certain checking out may be going on, another level of retirement, of divestiture. Maybe the idiocies of the human family just grow too boring to give further brain-room to. You spend a lifetime trying to get into that family, searching for intimacy, and fail so often. After however many years of failure, the hell with it does not seem an irrational response.

As a baby, Saint Augustine says, he learned to talk to express his *will:* to break the silence, "and so launch deeper into the stormy intercourse of human life." First step toward creation of a self. To have a self is to fight back at what he considered the great injustice, which, it turns out, was to be born.

Maybe that's the source of the silence of old men: a giving up of the self. Get over it, they may be implying. It's a pain in the ass. Having a self is crying for the teat; abandon the self, go find some milk.

And then of course there's beginning to hear yourself. If that doesn't shut an old guy up, nothing will.

Anyway, there seemed to be a lot of death going around. Very winter.

My plan was to seek better ways to manage my neck until the next November, when I would become eligible for Medicare, and then see if surgery was in order. To my surprise my doctor, whom I'll call

Dr. X, said why wait?[1] He'd schedule another MRI, the pictures would go to a neurologist, and we'd proceed as necessary. In the meantime, physical therapy. Perhaps a little traction. That turned out to feel good while it was going on, but, like most manipulatory therapies, resulted in no lasting improvement.

I'd never had major surgery, and was not inclined to take that step lightly. It was clear, however, that my neck was shutting me down, an orthopedic barrier to a level of activity sufficient to keep the other systems, orthopedic or otherwise, healthy. If it wasn't fixed I'd gradually lose more function. With my usual capacity for over-dramatization, I began to imagine a progression that left me an in-valid by my early seventies. "In-valid," an interesting locution. This didn't mean, curiously, that the surgery was not elective, at least from the viewpoint of technological medicine.

Not to be undertaken lightly. One of the striking things about approaching sixty-five is entertaining the idea that one might have a serious condition—illness, affliction, deterioration—but after a certain amount of accommodation to that depressing notion, you realize that it just happens to be the rest of the story. The other part: how it works out. It seemed important, at that point, to hold to that idea. It was not inconceivable to be ill, not inconceivable that it could happen to you. It's a change that comes with age. Eventually you're going to get that phone call. When the tests come in, when they've looked at the pictures. Everyone does.

I come out of the supermarket with a small armload of groceries—another list crossed off—and am for a moment bemused, not know-

---

1. Preserving Dr. X's anonymity may imply shocking revelations to come, but nothing could be further from the case. Some doctors are simply shyer than others, and to disguise one while exposing others would seem unfair to all. There are two more anonymous doctors to come; all three provided superb medical care, and I'll continue to see all three as need arises.

ing exactly what I want to do next: go straight home, or was there something else, not on the list, that I could perhaps take care of while I'm in town? From some utterly unknowable source comes the urge to go buy model-airplane materials—a kit, some balsa, glue. I find myself wondering, briefly, if it might be possible to cut expenses to the bone, live on Social Security, and just build model airplanes for the rest of my days. Model airplanes as art form, ephemeral sculptures. Maybe other, nonflying structures—it wouldn't matter much so long as they're built of balsa and tissue, paint and glue. Razor blades and pins. Structurally sound ephemera, butterfly sculpture. Me with the shaky hands.

In adolescence I was something of an expert at balsa gliders, designing my own, winning a trophy or two. They were the kind you throw to launch, no power source other than your arm. They were physically beautiful objects, and so was their flight. With a good design and a limber arm, substantial flights were possible. Occasionally you'd catch a thermal, and have the conflicted pleasure of watching your invention soar out of sight.

Actually that was the object, to make something beautiful and then throw it away—which could only be done if it *was,* in effect, beautiful, i.e., well designed enough. To throw it away you threw it as high as you could, as hard as you could. I enjoyed that. To accommodate the speed of launch as well as the wafting, gentle glide-stage that followed required some fairly fancy design tricks. To make a glider perform well required a lovely combination of physics and physiology. For a while my interest was obsessive, even glazed-eyed. Maybe it was the glue fumes.

My wave of juvenile nostalgia came after a week devoted to attempting to sell some writing, which I hate, rather than its manufacture, which I love. I loved both in building model airplanes. Building them is manufacturing, flying them is sales: trying to get your customer (the sky) to accept your product. How nice it was, building model airplanes, to have a sales method that required only grunting effort, instead of attempting to discern market trends and then fulfill them. I suspect this nostalgia is part of what reimmersed me in competitive sports in my late forties: the impulse, when the body begins to become undependable, to go back to what worked before. (I'd been a swim-racer as a kid.) Now I found myself fantasizing about living out my days on a guaranteed income, puttering away in domestic bliss. There seemed to be an impulse there toward Getting Out.

I got started in balsa gliders because I saw a couple of adults flying them. I wondered at the time what the heck they were doing, wasting important adult time at such a silly, if entertaining, enterprise. Okay for me, but these guys were old. They were probably in their early twenties.

The thing about aging is that what's interesting changes. Sometimes it changes back to what was interesting before.

Few people realize that Heath Bar Crunch ice cream is good for you. For some part of you. Not for the coronary arteries perhaps, or your waistline, but for the part that needs and deeply appreciates gooey sweet stuff. Good for your taste buds, your sense of self, your inner child, your relaxation quotient. You can't stay on your own back all the time, you know.

I'd give up the sensual pleasures, as age seems to be wanting me to do, if the body weren't still this attractive nuisance: attractive to me if not to you, attractive in places and at periodicities that give so much pleasure. As in Augustine's famous plea, God grant me celibacy but not just yet. If I've got these places and periodicities, I figure I have a duty to the organism, to the life principle or whatever it is, to get the most out of them. To obtain maximum use, on the growth principle? (That's why not trying to get more is hard to accommodate: it's kissing the growth principle good-bye.)

The argument against, as I get it, is that these pleasures are ephemeral, and therefore keep you chained to what the Buddhists call the wheel of desire. The wheel of time, same thing. You can opt out of time for a moment, here and there, through pleasure, but its fading—the little death that comes through satiety and adaptation—is a continuing reminder of mortality. This must be the connection between sex and death, which the experts have been pushing at me, in academic language, all my life. Just words. I never had a clue. Why do I suddenly have the feeling I'm in a Woody Allen movie?

"The one supreme advantage that Old Age possesses over Middle Age and Youth is its nearness to Death," says John Cowper Powys, in *The Art of Growing Old*. "The very thing that makes it seem pitiable to those less threatened and therefore less enlightened ages of man is the thing that deepens, heightens, and thickens out its felicity."

Aging, I begin to see, is in some senses a matter of hearing footsteps, as they say in football, which can lead to alligator arms as a way of life.[2] It's the source of the impulse toward Getting Out. How do you accommodate this impulse and continue to function? How *do* you continue to function anyway?

In January, in New England, it's easy to accept the view that mankind is actually a virus. You can't help meditating on winter's causes, the tilt of the planet and all. Once you draw back in your imagination and picture that lovely blue sphere, you can't help

---

2. For nonfans, the terms refer to a certain shyness, evinced primarily by wide receivers, about reaching up to catch high passes, particularly in the middle of the field. To reach up high opens one's rib cage to terrible assaults. Hearing footsteps—from an approaching defensive back, who is drawing a bead on your rib cage—causes one to grow little, short alligator arms. It really is a nasty game.

noticing that we've accumulated at all the best spots, and are busily spreading our poisons from there. One imagines the Great Physician-Scientist in the Sky, contemplating this globe He's launched, studying it, seeing the grayish-brown stain spread and wreak havoc on His beautiful little experiment. Tsk tsk. The worry and concern. Maybe what we are is sinners in the hands of a worried God.

FEBRUARY: *Why Old Men Walk That Way*

Is not January the hardest month to get through?
When you have weathered that, you get into
the gulfstream of winter, nearer the shores of spring.
—Thoreau's journal, February 2, 1854

February began with a perfectly still gray day: gray sky, gray woods, everything muted, damped down, as if there were cotton in your ears. As I walked our hillside I could hear chain saws and traffic in the valley below, but the woods were still, stiller than ever, with the utter patience of winter. Still and waiting, implacably, undisturbably waiting; not teetering-on-the-brink waiting, but waiting with a perfect resolve to wait forever, if need be, for spring. Slapping my congenital impatience in the face with a moral lesson: it's going to work out the way it's going to work out.

"In the practice of the Tao," as Stephen Mitchell translates it, "every day something is dropped. Less and less do you need to force things. . . ."

Everyone says an MRI is a piece of cake—if, as it was first characterized to me, you don't mind lying with your head in a garbage can while someone beats on it with a baseball bat for half an hour. Mine turned out to be one of the least pleasant medical procedures I've experienced, after, perhaps, a recent colonoscopy. The technicians insisted on cocking my head back into the precise position that put maximum pressure on the very area causing pain; then they told me not to move, not even to swallow if I could help it. My right arm instantly went to sleep and stayed that way, numb yet aching, for the required thirty-two minutes. I was afraid I'd start weeping. Three minutes after it was over I was pain-free and had gotten over the whole thing.

Holding still caused the pain, as so often happens, and movement erased it. Funny how that works. There's a minor-key version of it when you sit still too long, although then it isn't pain, just stiffness, an unwillingness of the joints to allow movement to resume. When I do rise I walk like an old man for the first few steps, until the joints again allow free movement.

Thus I am on a curious cusp. I can walk like a younger person if I think about it. It takes a little more effort—mental effort—but of course feels better, relaxed and flowing, long and loose. I can also consciously walk like an old man. I know the form perfectly well— hips stiffened and rotated forward, shoulder blades pinned together, elbows swinging backward at each step—and can put it on like a persona. Actors, I understand, sometimes invent a walk as a device for successfully getting into a new character.[1] By forgetting to walk like a young person I cross over a threshold. Not to be old seems dimly possible, but it would require a level of attention for which I seem to lack, or don't want to supply, the energy.

---

1. "Throw away your own walk and learn three new ones. Find what you need. Choose the most difficult ones. Live with them and make them your own. Walk with them—three different ways—in a room, on the street, and then on a frozen pond. Locate where the ice is solid, where it is thin." Acting exercise, from *Stella Adler on Ibsen, Strindberg, and Chekhov* (New York: Knopf, 1999).

It *is* a matter of attention. Our ninety-four-year-old friend Pierre had a lady friend propose a paddle around a nearby lake. "In order not to demean myself in her eyes on getting into and out of that canoe with my stiffening joints," he writes, "I had to practice the forethought and concentration of an Olympic athlete bent on breaking a record."

More and more, though, I find myself forgetfully stumbling along in the old man's gait. It has become the default position, so to speak. Studies show that gait to be the product of an exaggerated sway, from impairment of balance, which in turn is caused by a loss of input from the specific nerve endings that give you a sense of muscle position, plus cellular changes to both the brain and the inner ear. We walk more slowly, on a wider base, and we shuffle. Much of this is caused by stiffening of the joints and loss of muscle mass and leg strength: again, cause or consequence? On the other hand, as a kind of compensation, old persons do apparently deal with motion sickness better than the young.

But at bottom the old man's walk is a protective device, albeit misdirected, generated by a false assumption about pain. Moving those stiff joints doesn't actually hurt, except for the briefest minor twinge, but some deep part of us, perhaps our limbic system, thinks it is going to. We stiffen against predicted pain, much the way an injured joint splints itself by swelling. A step or two—a *conscious* step or two, or a pause to stretch—and it's gone. It's an idea combined with a posture, resulting in an attitude, although not in the in-your-face sense of the term: a kind of attentional omission that takes a physical form. If we think about it before we start to move we can overpower this impulse, or habit. But who wants to have to think about how he walks?

Where's the exercise program that restores one's habitual, youthful looseness? How much of physical aging is simply growing weary of having to devote attention to such matters as simple movement? How much longer will one's style of gait be volitional? On the cusp: more and more often circumstances remove the element of choice from that decision.

"Do you know why you walk slowly when you're old?" wrote Mark Helprin, in *A Soldier of the Great War*. "Because with age you receive the gift of friction."

Waiting for the MRI results to get to the doctors, I indulged myself in a spate of glitz reading, the hard candy of the publishing industry. I even dipped into a magazine or two, knowing the risk. I worked on magazines long enough to understand their ins and outs, a knowledge usually fatal to happy magazine consumption, but I'm still not immune to the disease.

I first realized this a couple of Februarys before, on a brief winter vacation in a borrowed house in ski country. There were skiing magazines lying about, and car magazines, gun, tennis, and golf magazines, naked-woman magazines, a very masculine selection. Back in the sixties I'd been on staff at one of the car magazines, and then on one of the skiing magazines, so I began leafing through those, just to see what they were up to these days. Before I knew it I was devouring the stack, riveted. We'd go out for the day's activities and all I secretly wanted was to be back at the house, plundering those magazines. My nose was buried every indoor moment. I grew surly and uncommunicative when I couldn't get at them.

Their subject matter was, exclusively, things to want; they were collections of objects of desire, brilliantly machined metal and fully fleshed flesh, exotic plastics wrapped around sophisticated electronics. Ownership would obviously fulfill any unresolved needs in one's life. As a magazine staffer I'd driven the exotic cars and skied the distant mountains, and thought I had long since been cured of suckering for such transient pleasures. What I seemed to miss— what pulled me back indoors at the expense of real-world plea- sures—was the wanting itself.

Modern magazines are virtually all advertising, of course, even the parts disguised as "editorial," the product itself thus being about products. A few years ago a minor war of self-regard broke out in the media about the alleged wall between the business side and the editorial, or content, side. (The writers and photographers who produce the editorial part are now described as "content providers.") The wall is, in editorial parlance, between Church and State, the editorial side allegedly defending the wall, the business side trying to breach it.

That wall was breached years ago. We tried to fake it for a long time, going to great lengths to preserve the appearance of what we haughtily referred to as editorial integrity, but pretense has now just about been abandoned. Thus with magazines, as with the Internet, the customer is paying to be advertised to. This can't work: never mind the money, there's not enough *time* to absorb all the advertis- ing. Even if you wanted it.

I bought a lottery ticket once, when the prize had mutated to so many million dollars that I could no longer withstand the promo- tional frenzy. Then I went out for lunch, and amused myself, on the drive to the restaurant, dreaming of winning, of what I'd spend it on. The fantasy was so soothing that on the drive home I repeated it. When I got home nothing had happened—no phone messages, no mail, no business transacted. The lottery drawing was a week away, I hadn't expected any news on that front, but where was the *rest* of the action? Nothing in my life had changed, except that my stomach had been filled. I was supremely dissatisfied. Hope, it then occurred to me, is the engine of despair. How's that for an old man's thought?

In the woods Pawnee, our geriatric dog, stops, absolutely riveted, to smell a pile of droppings in the snow. Her hearing and sight are mostly gone, smelling one of her few remaining pleasures. The tracks are too messy to reveal much, but the disturbance looks as if it might be from a large canine, which would explain Pawnee's particular fascination. Could be coyote, we have them around.

"Big medicine, eh?" I say to Pawnee, and am struck by the term. Native American cultures, according to my assuredly imperfect understanding, used the term "medicine" shamanistically, to mean power. Medicine in that sense might be something very like a potent smell. The pre-Encounter Indians, who must have had very sharp senses themselves, lived all their lives among creatures with senses sharper than their own, creatures that got better information than the Indians themselves could sometimes obtain. This forced the Indians, in a sense, to a "mystical" interpretation of some events. Their own version of science, medical or otherwise, demanded that they conceive of realms of information available to other creatures that weren't available to them.

I've gone the route with nontraditional therapies for orthopedic ailments, in part because I find the theories interesting (or at least amusing) and in part because I've been so regularly and quickly dismissed by conventional orthopedists. I've gone to chiropractors and osteopaths, been Rolfed and had several other kinds of massage, experimented with Yoga. Most of these approaches made me feel better for a while—the laying on of hands is a powerful thing—but none lasted. Often the practitioners, or their theories, seemed to imply that the failure was mine. If I just held my mouth right and believed the right things my problem would go away. The orthopedists may well have thought the same thing—that it was all in my head—but they were subtler about implying it. What they implied is that if there wasn't an engineering approach to the problem, something to cut out or stitch up, the problem didn't exist.

Mysticism gets most irritating when mystics claim to be finer creatures than the rest of us, possessed of more sensitivity. If you accept that possibility, you have to believe anything anyone tells you.

The MRI—*big* medicine—showed a bulging disk between vertebra C5 (C for cervical) and C6, and a lesser one at C6-C7, with an appreciable loss of space for the spinal cord. The neurosurgeon, Dr. Y, pointed out that the white outline along the length of the spine, indicating spinal fluid, stopped when it came to those vertebrae and resumed when it got past them. It was a fairly graphic depiction of the source of the trouble.

The appropriate solution was cervical fusion: removal of the disk between C5 and C6, the resulting space propped open with a chip of bone from the hip. Dr. Y was of the opinion that surgery should give me considerable relief. I had resisted the idea in the past because of the implied loss of movement in the neck, but flexibility had become a luxury I could no longer afford. Actually, Dr. Y said, I'd probably have more range of motion in my neck after the surgery than before.

Dr. Y would remove the disk, working in concert with orthopedic surgeon Dr. Z, who would do the bone work. Dr. Y characterized Dr. Z as the best cervical man in New England and one of the most conservative. He assured me they discussed every step as they performed it, sometimes one of them talking the other out of a next step as things developed. I'd need to see Dr. Z first, but if everything went as predicted, we'd schedule the surgery.

My sense was that the operation was more routine than I'd presumed and the odds for a favorable outcome better than I'd heard. Two to five days in hospital, said Dr. Y, then two to three months wearing a hard collar. At that point if someone had handed me a collar and said if I wore it for three months my neck pain would let up, I'd have strapped it on in a minute.

I drove home, in pain and facing the likelihood of major surgery, in a cloud of euphoria: I wasn't nuts. It was structural. Relief was at hand.

We have a greenhouse window on the south side of our kitchen. Every year on the tenth of November, the ridge of our garage roof cuts off the afternoon sun to that window. On February 11, though, the sun again clears the ridgeline, an occasion significant enough in our light-starved state to have its own entry on the kitchen calendar. In my sixty-fifth year that week also marked what would have been Jud's seventieth birthday, and our mother's ninetieth.

One theory of aging lays the whole business to a decreasing ability to withstand stress. The old are simply no longer as good at adapting as the young are. This shows up commonly in adjustment to temperature extremes, which is why we geezers drop like flies in heat waves as well as cold snaps. Both sensory sensitivity and central information-processing get out of whack. One study showed that while the young can detect a difference in body temperature of a degree and a half, the old need a change of over four degrees to notice the difference. Heat tolerance, incidentally, is dramatically improved by good physical condition.

Our capacity to read feedback is also diminished, both externally (we fail to turn up the air conditioner or the furnace, or to dress appropriately) and internally (our systems lose the ability to increase metabolism and minimize heat loss when we're cold, and vice versa when we're hot). A consistent and reliable internal environment is *homeostasis;* making corrections to maintain it is the job of various homeostatic mechanisms. These mechanisms are a complicated system of feedback loops, the functional speed and effectiveness of which deteriorate with age. They gradually slow down and lose precision—again, because of changes that take place at the level of the cell. When you lose homeostasis you die. Even if trauma and disease were totally eliminated we'd still die; comparatively minor stresses would eventually disrupt homeostasis sufficiently to carry us off.

"Stress" is about as vague a term as medical science can accommodate, standing for a virtual encyclopedia of influences within and without the body. It was coined—from a German engineering term—by Hans Selye, of McGill University, in 1950. As a medical student, observing diagnoses by his professors, Selye noticed one specific thing that these more experienced teaching physicians never mentioned. Whatever the patients' ailments, all shared an apparent common state: "They all looked *sick*," as Selye later described his moment of illumination. There was something common in their response to illness that was not being identified.

Selye went on, brilliantly, to explicate that common response, or set of responses: it starts with the pituitary-adrenal system, which floods the body with steroid hormones, causing a host of changes: increased heart rate, elevated blood sugar, dilated pupils, slowed digestion, increased muscle blood flow, and faster breathing, among other adjustments. They are changes in state and revised internal timings that are caused not by a specific illness but by the fact of being ill—or under stress.

He went on to posit the time-honored fight-or-flight response, and demonstrated the physical cost to us moderns of failing to resolve, or inappropriately to resolve, its products—which are mostly hormonal. When the tiger pokes its nose into your cave, you get a flush of adrenaline. That flush is useful if you can either kill the tiger or run away from it. Nowadays you can seldom kill the tiger.

When you can't, the unprocessed adrenaline starts eating holes in your gut. Adrenaline is only one of the chemicals in that flush, and eroding your gut lining is only one of its effects.

Selye's theory of stress led him to propose the General Adaptation Syndrome, which has three steps: alarm, resistance, and exhaustion. Stress the organism and it responds with alarm, preparing for action. Maintain the stress past the alarm stage and the organism begins to fight back, dealing with stress's ravages and repairing its damage. Perpetuate the stress too long and the organism begins breaking down, unable to keep up with the task. That's where aging comes in: with age our homeostatic mechanisms slow down anyway, which means we reach the exhaustion stage more quickly, and recover more slowly.

Selye cannot exactly be credited with the discovery of what athletes call the training effect, but he was the one who codified it. Its discoverer, legendarily, was Milo of Crotona, patron saint of weight lifters, who began picking up a calf every day, until he supposedly was able to carry the full-grown bull around on his shoulders. The training effect is the everyday biological miracle that says that if you require more of the living organism, it will (until exhaustion sets in) respond. The training effect not only causes muscle to grow larger but also improves energy supplies and waste removal. It streamlines and sharpens neural and biochemical pathways. It causes the organism to make internal changes to prepare for a more demanding future. It is a way of deliberately tapping into the cell's capacity for growth, in efficiency and endurance as well as size. In the case of aging, it postpones loss of function.

Selye's stages one and three, alarm and exhaustion, have to do with illness; stage two, resistance, has to do with health. Athletic coaches and trainers (and Milo of Crotona) had no need of theory to develop almost infinite applications of it. All athletic training has always been based on deliberate *progressive* overload of the systems in question, to provoke resistance in them. It's the progressive part that requires skill and judgment—where good coaching comes in. You can overload any part, any function, and improve it, so long as the organism is given sufficient rest to avoid stage three.

In fact, creatively applied rest is the most powerful training tool available. For example, aerobic training is aimed at improving heart function, specifically its stroke volume: more blood pumped for every beat means more gain from less work—and therefore more time for the heart to rest between beats. Working the heart—stressing it—gradually improves stroke volume. But the interesting thing is that more gains are made by the heart muscle during the period immediately after the workload is reduced, when the heart rate is still elevated, trying to catch up with the muscle cells' demands, than during the work itself.

From that simple fact has grown the concept of interval training, which breaks training into periods of intense work interspersed with carefully planned rest periods. It has become the dominant training method among serious athletes, and most of the world records in athletic events in the latter half of the twentieth century are its result.

Coaches, incidentally, prefer the term "recovery" to "rest." To a coach "rest" implies laziness. In a sense this attitude is the athletic equivalent of physicians' well-documented reluctance to prescribe sufficient pain relievers. Both doctors and coaches would like to build our character while they are improving our physical state.

I sometimes make the mistake—see silence, above—of expressing aloud my interest in, if not exactly enthusiasm for, Thoreau. When I do, people take great delight in pointing out to me that he was a fraud. He didn't live all alone in the woods for two years, they always say. He came into Concord all the time—a brief stroll for such a walker as himself. He ate most of his meals at his mother's table, or at the Emersons', and his relatives took food to him. People seemed to enjoy visiting his cabin, and he had a good deal of company. People dropped in, especially young people. They reported that he seemed to be able to charm random birds and small animals to come to him, to clamber over him. He probably trained them beforehand, my fraudians would most likely say. Maybe these anti-Thoreauvians are related to the ones who didn't get it when I force-fed the subject in high school.

Yes, I say, yes, I'd heard that. To say otherwise would put me in the uncomfortable position of defending Thoreau, which is hard to do when the margins of my copy of *Walden* are so full of snotty comments of my own. He wasn't all he was cracked up to be, I tell his detractors.

He was a lot more, and the Walden Pond experiment was one of the smaller parts, although I don't attempt to make the point. A lot more interesting, at least to someone turning sixty-five and no longer swayed by punk rhetoric, was the fact that he retired, essentially, at twenty-three. He tried teaching school in Concord immediately after graduating from Harvard, but the trustees expected him to use corporal punishment, which he found repugnant; after two weeks of teaching—and a somewhat overdramatic caning of several students, picked virtually at random, to satisfy a trustee's request—he resigned the job. A year later he opened a private school with his older brother John, which lasted three years; John's ill health forced its close. That was about it for employment. In addition to surveying and lecturing, he helped in the family pencil business, and wrote a great deal but published little. He picked up the odd dollar along the way, sometimes at common labor—once selling cranberries—but mostly he tried to figure out how to live. I don't wonder.

Theories of aging abound, although an AMA committee on the subject once conducted a ten-year study only to report that they'd been unable to find "a single physical or mental condition that could directly be attributed to the passage of time." Lab rats live longer if they're fed less in the first half of their lives, fish live longer if their watery environment is kept colder in the second half of *their* lives. It must seem a lot longer to the rats and fishes. There are theories having to do with cell damage from radiation or the ravages from the breaking down of oxygen, which prevents proper repair or replication. Thus the antioxidant craze, which products are now available virtually on your breakfast cereal. It is unclear whether they have any effect.

One line of research approaches aging as an autoimmune disease. Immunity is regulated by the thymus, which is the first of the body organs to begin to atrophy, and shrinks so predictably over time that its size is the best single measure of physical, as opposed to chronological, age.[2] As the thymus shrinks, so does the system's ability to fight off infections. Fortunately, it has sufficient overcapacity built in to hang on to its immune function well into normal old age.

Unscientifically, aging is easy enough to recognize by the visual signals alone—thinning hair, sagging skin, stooped posture, tentative movement—but no theory yet attributes these signals to a single cause. By careful selection of breed pairs, researchers have succeeded in doubling the life spans of nematodes and fruit flies,

---

2. Actually, an even better measure is by counting gray armpit hairs—a research finding that is hardly likely to enhance science's reputation for seriousness.

implying that longevity is genetic. Finding what is bred into, or out of, these extremely long-lived creatures would seem to be a useful approach to solving the aging problem. (Note that to science, age is a "problem" to be "solved.") Another currently hot approach involves the telomere, a structure that in effect counts the number of divisions certain cells have undergone, and eventually puts a stop to the dividing. It may be telomeres, rather than radiation or oxygen damage, that make cells lose the capability of repairing themselves. Cancer cells, which are in effect immortal, seem to have found a way of turning off the regulating function of the telomeres. Research is now aimed at finding how to turn it on again, which might effectively destroy the cancer cell's immortality, and at how cancer turns it off in the first place, which might lead to breakthroughs against aging. There turns out to be an "immortalizing enzyme," dubbed telomerase, for which there is a gene. Science has now succeeded in transplanting it. The implications are stunning, although applications are still years away.

Any new theories in this area of research are immediately swept up by the life-extension people, the all-time champions of denial, who want to live forever, hang the cost. Perhaps if I were thirty or forty I'd join them, but from the point of view of sixty-five they're working on the wrong end of the problem. Statistics say that if I went immediately onto a diet of roots and berries—a Pritikin or Ornish or some other fat-free, all-roughage, perfectly balanced and otherwise nonflavored regimen—I could add something like three years to my life expectancy. As there's a strong likelihood that that would be thirty-six more months in a nursing home having drool wiped off my chin, its appeal is minimal. The problem is maintaining what demographers call active life—fully engaged, independent, participatory life—as opposed to the inactive version. As opposed to being kept alive. At the moment I can't imagine wanting

to be eighty. Ask me again when I am seventy-nine. But I know
eighty-year-olds who aren't particularly enthusiastic about being
eighty-one.

There's another, unexpressed dilemma implied in life-extension research. Michael Rose, the researcher who has doubled the life span
of fruit flies, points out that the long-lived version doesn't breed
with anything like the fecundity and urgency of the normal, short-
lived version. Organisms with brief lives must produce offspring
much more rapidly and frequently than species with long lives. In
this sense sex, in effect, shortens life. It's true of drosophila and it's
true of trees. Maples will casually wait two or three years between
seed crops, if conditions for survival of the seeds aren't favorable.
With a three-hundred-year life span there's not exactly a sense of
urgency. As Rose told Malcolm Gladwell, who profiled his work in
The New Yorker, if we materially increase human life expectancy, "I'll
tell you what the trade-off will be. Randy teen-agers will be a thing
of the past. James Dean, Kurt Cobain. All those people. We'll lose
that. We'll lose the high-testosterone surge of insanity that so much
of American culture is based on."

Maybe I don't want out of this culture as badly as I thought I did.

Telomeres to the contrary notwithstanding, and all that, and all
that: they represent another one of those interesting medical stories
the outcome of which is not likely to be determined within my lifetime. Along with the arrival of an infinite assortment of future geniuses and great athletes and magnificent scoundrels.

Curiously, this is the most mortal thought I've had yet, hitting me
with surprising force. I was watching a slick young college athlete

perform on television, and thought about how interesting it was going to be to follow his pro career. Then I realized I might well not get to. There are an infinitude of spectacular human beings to come, none of whom I'll know about. One only gets to enjoy the little package of people that comes along in one's own life span. Of course that's the appeal of history, allowing you to enjoy the geniuses who've gone before. Perhaps you can enjoy, in imagination, the ones to come, if you can accomplish the mind-set. But even if I expected an afterlife, I wouldn't expect it to provide a box seat on the living.

"My conviction hasn't changed," says Wilfrid Sheed, "that the best of all outcomes would be to expect an afterlife and not get one." Here's a toast to the ones to come, about whom I will never know a thing. . . .

Chris comes home from a three-day trip, and we spend a pleasant evening debriefing each other, assembling little narratives to describe what happened in each other's absence. "Ours is a long marriage," says Carolyn Heilbrun of her own, "and we have found solitude together."

What we are doing would nowadays be called downloading, I suppose, rather than debriefing, a thought that sends me to the dictionary to look up "brief," the noun: a summary. It comes from the same root that means "short" but has almost the opposite import: a brief may be a summary but it is a detailed one, specific, spelled out. The connotation is that in briefing and debriefing there is some editing going on, some judgment. Downloading implies only that a dump is taking place. Sheer information. Take it all in, don't bother to think about it. Maybe *that's* what's wrong with the computer age. Talk about your yadda-yadda.

The Journal of Henry D. Thoreau still lies on the reading pile, mocking me. It's the Dover edition, the fourteen original volumes bound as two, a total of 1,800 pages in large format, each book too heavy to be held comfortably on your lap. You almost have to lay it on a desk and sit upright to read it, which militates against a leisurely approach. How ludicrous its author would find it that a reader might be foiled by sheer lack of stamina. It would confirm all his suspicions about readers, mostly generated by their reluctance to purchase his books.

I regularly resolve to persevere, get started again, and enjoy these mighty tomes—and then fail, distracted by something else to read. Spencer Tracy, among others, is alleged to have read them all, for goodness' sake. Surely actors don't have more free time than I do.

I bought the set a few years ago, for an intriguing project that also failed. I got thinking what kind of old man Thoreau might have been if he had lived longer. He died two months short of his forty-fifth birthday, in 1862, of tuberculosis (as did, startlingly, one fourth of the population of that era). I began speculating about how his contrarian nature might have mellowed after the Civil War, particularly as we began to take up the wilder western half of the nation. Chris was researching the year 1883 at the time, for a book about the Adirondacks. Dinner-table conversations necessarily reflected the period, and I began getting ideas. In 1883 Thoreau would have been sixty-seven.

I'd written no fiction since college days, but a novel began emerging in my head: *Thoreau's Journal, 1883*. Plotting a way to keep him alive was easy. His last trip outside Concord took him through North Elba, former home of the abolitionist John Brown, one of the few Thoreauvian heroes. North Elba is only a few miles from

Saranac Lake, already, in 1883, a TB convalescence center. Twelve years later, Dr. E. L. Trudeau would establish his famous sanatorium there.

I saw Thoreau stepping off the train in North Elba and deliberately disappearing, presumed dead. His Concord life and his books were failures anyway. I'd have him seek out the Widow Brown for a prolonged convalescence. He'd recover, change his name, and set out on another life. He'd travel widely, despite his earlier rebukes to travelers, and attempt finally to establish a successful human relationship or two. There might even be a romance. Finally, in 1883, I'd have him return to the Adirondacks, intending to build a new cabin and resume the Walden experience, this time abetted by the wisdom of his years.

I particularly intended to have him sign on—under his new name—with John Muir's party surveying glaciers in Alaska. I envisioned the scene where Muir, our second secular saint of conservation, would be quoting someone named Thoreau to the man himself, who, under another name, would of course be seething with the customary Thoreauvian wrath at the experience.

The homeostasis metaphor in aging lies at the base of one of Sherwin Nuland's stronger points. "Of hundreds of known diseases and their predisposing characteristics," he says, in *How We Die,* "some 85 percent of our aging population will succumb to the complications of one of only seven major entities: atherosclerosis, hypertension, adult-onset diabetes, obesity, mental depressing states such as Alzheimer's and other dementias, cancer, and decreased resistance to infection."

If the right one don't get you, then the left one will. After a certain age, heroic medicine aimed at one or another of the dreadful seven is almost pointless. Heroic attacks on disease are stressful for the host as well as the disease. Stress destroys homeostasis. Attack one disease and open the door for the other six or some other virulent affliction. See, for example, Nathan Pritikin, the maverick nutritionist whose strict dietary regimen has attracted thousands of converts. Pritikin himself died, in his sixties, by his own hand. He successfully cleaned out his coronary arteries but couldn't deal with his own depression. Similarly, Nuland points out, attempting to determine a cause of death is an empty exercise. We have this bureaucratic need to inscribe words on the death certificate, but whatever it says there is for the bereaved—or for the authorities—and is a convenience: a fact, perhaps, but not a truth.

If loss of homeostasis is such a threat, then to age comfortably must require damping out the amplitudes. Seek stimuli, one might say, but don't let them grow into stressors. Take an even strain, as they say in Texas. The unaccustomed is stressful, change is stressful. Polish your routine and stick to it. Let go of the unessential. Take deep breaths and consciously relax your muscles. Even things out, don't go whole hog. Forget—forever—doing something as hard as you can; dance with the girl who brung you.

(During our intended media-free year we would occasionally backslide, and feel guilty. Not to backslide would have required a more rigid ideology. One large point of the exercise was to reduce stress, by removing noise. Holding to a rigid ideology is also stressful. So is feeling guilty.)

This is more of the stop-trying-to-get-more business, which sounds like a death sentence to the young but is one more small parcel of wisdom to the elderly. The oscilloscope comes to mind, with those waving green lines, electronically interpreting the forces at play. Or the heart monitor in the intensive care unit, the steady beep that says, yes, life is continuing. One does not want to let the line become flat, goodness knows, but avoid also spiking. Spike and die.

This strikes me as a kind of androgenizing effect, which perhaps shows a sexism I didn't know I had—the notion that greed and ambition are masculine attributes. Gender issues notwithstanding, it's a product of age, I think: enough becomes in fact enough.

Or maybe it's that anything becomes plenty. Maybe we geezers can discover that below the line that used to indicate "enough" lie infinite riches. Such a realization would come, finally, from giving the body its due. Attending to its nurturance—its sensory nurturance—first, without getting sidetracked by intellectual and even emotional demands. Since feeling *is* first, as the poet e. e. cummings pointed out.

At the time of Jud's death I spent a good deal of social time with more or less distant relatives. I don't ordinarily think of my blood relations as frozen-faced WASPs, but I was struck then by how carefully we all avoided the expression of any emotion but a kind of gentle, caring amusement. The jokes were about anything other than the actual subject at hand, but joke we did (and I was certainly the worst offender). Mild affection and amusement were, are, the apogee and perigee of our social and emotional lives. I found myself thinking what a relief it would be just to let go and be a little more, I don't know, other-cultural for five minutes. Third-worldly. Some part of me wanted to shriek and rend my garments. And now, the older I get, the harder would be that kind of letting go. The harder I hang on to my watchamacallit dignity. Silence improves the grip.

The wobble of the earth, we must understand, plays hob with our brain chemicals. (My ills are chemical, yours are psychological, his are genetic.) For us New Englanders—even transplants like myself—October is a lump in the throat, November is steel-gray anger (if not black depression), and December thus sets up for bawling your eyes out. Smoke if you got 'em: those of you with working tear glands flush them out, get that lump processed before it metastasizes. That way you'll be all cleaned out and in shape for January, and the dogged dead trot that the New Year requires.

Thank God for February, when the light comes back. Begins to come back.

Surgery was scheduled for March 24 in Hartford Hospital, giving me a month to brood about it if I chose to brood. I didn't, really. My son, Marty, wittily pointed out that a first surgery for a degenerative ailment was a rather more startling shot across one's bow than a mere Social Security check. Okay, was my reaction, so let's get on with it.

Marty also wondered if I was frightened at the prospect. So did Willy, actually using the word "courage." It didn't feel that way to me. I wasn't frightened, I think because I had a clear mental picture of the structural nature of the operation. It came from a modicum of wood carving and a lifetime of bad carpentry, not to mention model airplanes. I thought I understood which piece was going to go where.

On the other hand, the disabling nature of this particular degenerative ailment was definitely increasing. My neck hurt more, more often, more continuously. It was setting me up, I thought at the time, turning the screws tighter to keep me convinced that surgery was a good idea. I had no idea whether the increased pain was a result of further degeneration or from the prospect of relief. Clearly, my body had a mind of its own.

"My second fixed idea is the uselessness of men beyond sixty years of age, and the incalculable benefit it would be in commercial, political, and in professional life, if as a matter of course, men stopped work at this age," said Sir William Osler, in a speech at Johns Hopkins University in 1905. OSLER RECOMMENDS CHLOROFORM AT SIXTY, said the headlines; to be "Oslerized" made a brief appearance in the language.

MARCH: *The Sock Zone*

꧁ Spotted a robin on March 1, a good ten days earlier than we'd ever seen one around here. An anomaly, though; we wouldn't see another until well into April.

When I was twelve and too old to be playing with matches, I made a mistake with them that momentarily welded together, in sulfurous fire, the tips of two fingers on one hand to two fingers on the other. No permanent damage, but that was pain, and I remember it well. Compared to it, compared I'm sure to what others suffer with chronic pain, my degenerating neck was little more than a headache. Well, some days, maybe a toothache.

I was a little surprised therefore at my own willingness to undergo the disruption and invasion of surgery—not to mention the likelihood that there would be a serving or two of real pain somewhere in the process. It was the sitting-still business, I think, that got to me. I was sick of it, but movement itself had become un-pleasant.

It's a condition that creeps up on you insidiously, like nearsight-edness. What happens isn't denial but accommodation. It's not so much the constant firing of nerve endings but their giving up—or shutting down. My neck didn't hurt *that* much; nothing made me wince or say ouch. What pain was there just never quite stopped, laying a leaden blanket over my response to things, over energy and ambition: a depression not of the mind but of the musculoskeletal system. What I needed was Prozac for the bones. There was no *brightness,* in movement, in mood, even in fundamental appetites. Pain ages you. I was being made older faster than necessary. That was happening plenty fast enough without assistance from a bum neck.

Below the fingers-on-fire level, pain is a subject that quickly gets murky—and never mind the psychosexual component, a perfectly fishy and disturbing consideration all by itself. The human animal does seem to have a predilection for experimentation with pain at other levels, in other enterprises. This has always disturbed me, even when I was a willing participant. As a middle-aged competitive swimmer I learned to spend long periods of time, both in training and in actual competition, playing around the lower edges of levels of discomfort that I would ordinarily have gone to considerable lengths to avoid. It seemed highly inappropriate behavior at the time. That was the kind of thing you did when you were young, I thought, but then grew out of. (Yet I'd generally rejected such dis-ciplines when I was young.) I often jokingly wondered what it was I had against myself. But it led to something I enjoyed very much, and I counted it worth the unpleasantness.

The discomfort that athletes experiment with is also not in the burned-fingers category. The most common form results when you exhaust your superficial energy supplies but choose to continue. Lactic acid and other waste products begin to build up in muscle tissue, trying to drag your efforts to a halt. To continue is to work muscles that are simultaneously running out of fuel and choking on their own exhaust. Lactic acid itself does not hurt, but using a muscle that's loaded with it does. It comes on as an unpleasant tiredness, at first in specific muscles, then overall, as the sagging ache of whole-body fatigue. "Feel the burn," say its merchandisers. The burn is a signal the muscle is about to "tie up," as the athletes say, and drag you to a halt. That part in fact is fairly painful, specifically so (but still well below the burned-finger level).

Athletes learn, however, that if you spend your energy judiciously you can continue to perform for a long time at a level just short of tying up, and that's where a good part of athletic training, and almost all of competition, takes place. By regularly taking the muscle near the point of failure, then letting it recover, you not only make it grow stronger, you also improve its efficiency at storing supplies of energy ahead of time, and at grabbing and using them when required. That part is all Hans Selye's Stage Two.

To work there, just short of failure, is to begin tapping into a larger, deeper well of energy. These are reserves the body is reluctant to utilize, but it can be trained to do so. You are also training your ability to judge your rate of energy expenditure, in order to last longer before athletic rigor mortis sets in. You are learning that the early levels of fatigue (of which there seem to be several, hence the boyhood myth of second wind) need not stop you. You can in fact ignore that pain and continue to perform effectively.

Continuing in those circumstances is not pleasant duty. I never *liked* it. I whimpered to myself every moment while it was going on, in my mind tossing back and forth excuses to quit, continuing only by promising myself hugely self-indulgent rewards. But I really loved having done it. I loved the way it felt after I'd used myself hard for a couple of hours. I loved dragging my tired body home from an evening workout and plonking it into bed. You lie there then in a fog of generalized, nonspecific pain, sometimes wondering if this time you might have actually done yourself harm. After a while you begin to relax, though—sometimes muscle group by muscle group, consciously—and the pain turns into a humming glow, your entire body buzzing, discomfort replaced by a deep pleasure. I came to think of that as the buzz of the metabolism itself, repairing damage, restoring supplies, setting me up for a harder workout next time. It is a glorious way to let go of consciousness—which usually happens within about ninety seconds.

The bedtime fatigue isn't really pain either, in the irate-nerve-ending sense. Some of us have a rather romantic tendency to regard such bone-weariness as the pain of life itself, but it's hardly a pain at all, just the general underlying churn of systems at work, being used to good effect, for, presumably, a good purpose. Fatigue is only identifiable as pain when it zeroes in on a specific part of the anatomy. Yes, you then clearly perceive, you've overused *that* one.

Fatigue is inescapable anyway in a useful life, and infinitely preferable to the pain of boredom, of non-use, of stasis. It made me believe, fervently, in *rest,* which is a very different commodity from stasis. It teaches us, brilliantly, how to make rest sweeter than we've ever found it before.

Chronic pain is entirely another matter. What I hadn't realized was that I was losing functional nerve endings at a rate that now alarmed me. I had accommodated too well for too long, which is what one does with chronic pain, but which is truly exhausting. It is not an optimistic way to live.

What pain does is force you to splint yourself, braced against stimulus, input, disturbance of any sort. Against change. It makes you sit still.

On March 10 the Hale-Bopp comet became visible for the first time, which was certainly exhilarating, but otherwise March was mostly waiting—for the birds to come back (and the light, and warm air). Waiting for surgery. The birds demurred, March marking the beginning of what would turn out to be a maddeningly long, cold spring. In a pathetic demonstration of hope Chris restored to its place under the kitchen sink the plastic container in which we save vegetable scraps for compost. It was possible then to deliver those scraps to the compost pile out back, but you needed boots, mackinaw, and gloves to do it, and it seemed rather doubtful that in that pile any composting was actually going on.

On the other hand, Mike, who owns one of those global positioning gizmos and with it keeps track of such things, reported on March 19 that in Nova Scotia, at least, daylight clocked in at a perfectly respectable twelve hours plus fifty-one precious seconds, the equinox right on schedule. That was news we could make use of.

I wasn't working much. I spent a lot of time cannibalizing old files, storing clippings, writing irritating letters to people who probably didn't want to hear what I was talking about anyway (age and death). We got a good bit of snow. The week before surgery had at least four extra days in it.

Our friend Pierre, a lifelong student of French literature, writes: "There are days when I feel like a character in Cesbron's *La Ville couronnée d'épines,* a collection of *romans de poche* about an assortment of lives in the suburbs. One concerns an aging retiree who, in his suburban cottage, no longer has the strength to garden all day and is losing his taste for reading at all hours. Carried over from his thirty years of teaching at the lycée is his habit of keeping a memo pad, filled up during the day, about what he has to do on the following day: grease the lock on the gate; water the rosebush by the back porch; write to Ernest. But when on this Wednesday he puts on his glasses to read, his memo pad is blank! Nothing to do! He envies the postman. When that one returns to the post office, his bag empty, his day will have been full."

I'd about run through my lists. Perhaps that's what began giving me mortal thoughts—not premonitions of doom but a certain weary impatience with life's nagging uncertainties. I had been riding a wave of energetic optimism virtually since the possibility of surgical relief was raised; now, gut turgid with apprehension and pre-op codeine, I seemed to be taking a look at the other side of the equation. I think this was part of aging's natural editing capacity, its tendency to help you recognize when you're wasting mental time and just let a particular subject go. Letting go, letting go, so much of aging is about letting go. You're going to die anyway; you're either going to spend a long painful time with some kind of disability, or get lucky and wink out. As far as the latter is concerned, devoutly to be wished ain't in it.

On the other hand, I'd done what I could do to ensure a successful outcome, and had complete confidence the medical people would do the same. It helped to remind myself that however it turned out would just be what happened next.

Perhaps my fanciful imagining of Thoreau as an old man was unnecessary. His best biographer, Robert D. Richardson, Jr., points out that although Thoreau died before his forty-fifth birthday, and did the work by which we know him before he was thirty-seven, he was in many ways always an old man.

"Though he was not yet thirty-five, he felt himself aging," Richardson says, analyzing Thoreau's journal. "He found it 'ominous' that as he grew older he had more to say about evening, less about morning." "I am older than last year," Thoreau wrote. "The mornings are further between; the days are fewer." Surely he took on early the protective coloration of the old—cranky, cantankerous, determinedly contrarian—by the time he graduated from Harvard, at twenty. In *Walden* he is youthfully contemptuous of the elderly, perhaps from fear—of nothing less than one of those lives of quiet desperation for himself.[1]

Two deaths had sharply affected his thinking, those of his beloved brother John, of tetanus, when John was twenty-seven and Henry was twenty-five; and of Margaret Fuller, by shipwreck, when he was thirty-three. John was the star of the family, light to Henry's darkness. Henry was so affected by his sudden death that he developed the symptoms of lockjaw himself and was not expected to live, and was an invalid for months thereafter. Margaret Fuller was the female star of the Transcendentalist movement, editor of *The Dial*, which published some of Henry's earliest work. When she was shipwrecked off Fire Island with her husband and infant son, Emerson dispatched Henry to rescue what he could of her personal effects, including a book-length manuscript. The mission failed, Thoreau returning with little more than a button off her husband's coat, and a grisly report of a shark-mauled skeleton, unidentifiable even to sex. According to Richardson, death, particularly by shipwreck, thereafter became a major theme in Thoreau's work.

When his final illness came he didn't seem to mind all that much. The autumn leaves, he said, teach us how to die. "Henry accepts this dispensation with such childlike trust and is so happy," his sister Sophia wrote to a friend, "that I feel as if he were being translated

---

1. Maybe that's where Abbie Hoffman got the idea about never trusting anyone over thirty—an idea I found attractive well past the cutoff age, then hilarious for a decade or two, and now curiously charming. How sweet, how innocent, how blindingly self-confident. No, you shouldn't trust us. We know too much, and are weary. Don't listen to us; we will only tell you how you will fail.

rather than dying in the ordinary way of most mortals." "When I was a very little boy I learned that I must die," he said himself, "and I set that down, so of course I am not disappointed now."

But then he was an accomplished dissembler. He proudly characterized himself as a loafer, a view that for many years his townspeople shared, but he was clearly as driven by the need to work, to accomplish, as anyone. He just preferred to hide away the need, the insecurity, the gnawing ambition. Hence the ringing confidence, or false confidence, of *Walden*.

Surgery was scheduled early on the twenty-fourth, requiring that we leave the house at 4:30 A.M. It might be noted that the drive down to Hartford, three days after the vernal equinox, was brightly lit by a predawn full moon on the right side of the car, nicely balanced by the glories of Hale-Bopp on the left. If, that is, one were inclined to look for signs. *Big* medicine.

I can't report on the surgery itself, not being present at the time, but I awoke feeling about four inches thick, as if I'd been put through a thousand-pound olive press. It was abundantly clear that I had been heavily done to, but clarity extended to little else. That day and the next were a blur; on the third I began ambulating the hallways, attempting to persuade my bladder to release a little urine, key to both avoiding catheterization and getting discharged. Didn't succeed; came to look forward to catheterization, which I had deeply and sincerely dreaded, as one of life's sweeter rewards. The ancients credited the major organs with various emotional states; I nominate the bladder as the seat of urgency.

I broke the seal that evening, tricklingly, but was clearly losing ground on the problem. In the predawn hours I went to the john again, a not uncommon occurrence at my age with or without surgery. This time I figured I'd wait it out, and thereby ensure release the next day. Standing for God knows how long to pee into the required bottle (the output had to be quantified), I noticed my heart had begun to race rather extravagantly. I crawled back in bed and called the nurse. In quick succession I was recatheterized, visited by various doctors, injected with various drugs, and slapped into intensive care. I felt fine; tachycardia seemed to alarm them a lot more than it did me.

They quickly had me stabilized, and released me from the ICU in midmorning. I was convinced the heart response was almost pure fatigue, from standing so long, sample bottle in hand, so soon after surgery. One haughty young intern suggested it was withdrawal from alcohol, which rather hurt my feelings. Just because I'd ingested a few ounces of the stuff daily for the previous thirty years was no reason to go getting accusatory, I thought. My surgeons decided it was only a stress reaction to the surgery, nothing to get alarmed about, and released me the next day. But I could now say I'd been in intensive care, another small campaign ribbon of the aging process. Caught a nice nap while I was in there.

The difficulty peeing was in large part from the battery of drugs, which had effectively shut down various internal systems, and in small part because I have the traditional middle-aged enlarged prostate gland, so far (knock wood) benign. Okay, late middle-aged. Peeing freely is another of aging's little losses. Along with the ability to scratch between your shoulder blades and to turn your head sufficiently to back safely out of the garage, one also loses the ability to sleep through the night without getting up to go to the bathroom. Subhead 1a in this category is the ability to go back to sleep after getting up to go to the bathroom. Make that Subhead 1b;

1a is the ability to go to the bathroom when you get up to go to the bathroom.

This is—again, so far—a minor bother. It is an ancient custom that aging males have to pee all the time. Call it the pregnant woman's revenge. It is not nearly so frustrating as attempting to sort out the information surrounding the problem and the gland that causes it. We are currently awash in good-hearted attempts to turn the prostate into a glamour gland. Frank Zappa (deceased), Norman Schwarzkopf, Arnold Palmer, Bob Dole (the last three at this writing still surviving), and others have attempted to bring prostate cancer out of the closet, so to speak, or at least into public awareness. It is now second only to lung cancer as a cause of death from cancer in males.

Aging males are implored to seek regular screening in pursuit of early detection. It's a perfectly reasonable thing to encourage us to do, except that there are no tests that reliably detect the disease, and the remedies upon detection are both harsh and of debatable effectiveness. So far the significant choices are surgery and/or radiation, which sometimes result in incontinence and/or impotence—and do not improve survival rates all that much. "There's no way to know whether testing and treatment change the outcome or improve the health of patients," one doctor told *The New York Times*. In other words, it's a bit of a roll of the dice. Everything we can do about prostate cancer sounds unacceptable to me. Ask me again when I get it.

I almost surely will. Discussing an elderly mutual acquaintance, my surgeon friend Fritz once said to me, "He'll die in his nineties of prostate cancer, as a gentleman should." I asked what that meant. It's a disease of the elderly, he explained—80 percent of those who get it are over sixty-five, and 90 percent of the deaths from it are in that age group. Incidental prostate cancer cells are detectable in 40 percent of us past the age of fifty, in one out of two after sixty. In fact, it's statistically unlikely for a male to die at seventy-five or older *without* at least a trace of cancerous cells in the prostate—and yet not terribly likely that prostate cancer will be what kills him. Most prostate cancers are of the slow-growing variety, and at that age one isn't going to live long enough for it to become a problem. In fact, if your life expectancy is ten years or less anyway, early detection and treatment isn't going to make that much difference—and aggressive treatment can make those remaining years less than pleasant.

My life expectancy is fifteen to twenty years. These numbers will necessarily inform any future decisions about medical treatment. (As I understand it, at sixty-five I become ineligible for a heart transplant. This strikes me as just and appropriate, since I do not yet need one.) Death from prostate cancer is not from what happens to the prostate itself but from the disease's spread into lungs and bone. Bone cancer is an extremely painful way to go, as I understand it. It was in Jud's case. (It had metastasized from the lungs—he smoked until the end.) I've known one man who did indeed die a painful death from prostate cancer. I have two other friends for whom it is an irritating difficulty, but at this writing one is eighty-six and the other is ninety-four, and they grumble, but continue to survive.

I grumble myself at the indignity, but dutifully go in for the checkups, doing as I'm told. I accept an aching bladder as a fact of life. Actually, I think that particular pressure has always been there, in just about the same degree, but when we're young we're just too busy, or perhaps too numb, to notice. When we get old and cranky we start noticing the little ongoing pressures and pains that we could once ignore. Maybe that's what makes us cranky.

In 1980 writer Malcolm Cowley published *The View from Eighty,* a charming piece of only occasionally rueful reflection mixed with good-humored advice. He asked his aging friends for their own experiences. "I stagger when I walk," one of them wrote him, "and small boys follow me making bets on which way I'll go next. This upsets me; children shouldn't gamble."

Six years later Cowley published a brief follow-up essay, "The View from Eighty-Six," a good deal of which was given over to a description of the method he'd worked out for putting on his pants—leaning in a doorway, making sure he was balanced and secure before he started, and so on. I found this disappointing at the time; didn't this wise old man have something more important to tell us about great age? Chris then pointed out to me how important it must be, when you are eighty-six, to be able to put your pants on by yourself. First things first.

When Tracy Kidder was working on his book *Old Friends,* he spent many months observing and interviewing in a nursing home. Tracy lives not far away, and I talked to him about that experience. I advanced Chris's theory about the donning of pants. "Oh yes," he said, "but the big problem is socks. Socks are terrible. None of those old guys can manage socks." When I repeated this to Jud's widow, she howled with laughter. Jud hadn't bothered with socks the last six months of his life, she said. Too damn much trouble.

Bard Lindeman, author of *Be an Outrageous Old Man,* is a former editor of *Today's Health,* the magazine published by the American Medical Association. He once suggested that the AMA might improve its public image by opening a free clinic for the elderly in its headquarters building. The idea was vetoed as impractical. "Do you know how long it takes those people to take off their clothes," an AMA executive said to him, "and then put them back on?"

Chris suggests a Velcro solution. Perhaps we could come up with a mail-order line of walk-in clothing. Tap the geezer market.

Chris checked me out of the hospital on March 28 and had me home before lunch; recovery from the really debilitating part of surgery was extremely rapid. I was back at my desk on the twenty-ninth, dealing with correspondence but not much else. Irritating letter to another aging friend: "If one can in fact ignore the aging process, one probably should. There'll be some rude shocks along the way, but they're coming anyway; the difference will not be in kind but in scale. My current stance is to figure out ways to get a kick out of it. So far the pleasure is limited to not being expected to do any heavy lifting. Or to stay up late: we have the occasional whippersnappers over for dinner, and are trying to figure out how to tell them they're not allowed to stay past nine. Makes me cranky about five the next morning, when my best working hours come along."

My mind seemed particularly empty, a result I'm sure of all the drugs. It was a pretty boring time, frankly—until Easter Sunday, March 30, rolled in with a vicious surprise blizzard, with two feet of snow and sixty-mile-per-hour winds. What a chuckle *that* was.

Never mind the tree in the forest, a symphony orchestra doesn't exist—or might as well not exist—unless there's a cochlea to transmit the vibrations on toward the receptor nerves in the brain. Or at least that's my prejudice: that it is at the interface of physics and physiology that pleasure comes, where the sensory life takes place. By sensory I don't mean sensual, necessarily, but sense-able, right there at the nerve ends. It is at the secondary tier of receptivity, with its overtones of interpretation, that emotional life begins. Barbra Streisand territory. See e.e. cummings.

Most of us have seen somewhere, perhaps in a high school science text, the drawing of a motor homunculus, a little man with the body shape distorted to represent the supply of nerve endings for the various parts, a schematic representation of what we feel with. The cartoon figure has a tiny, almost inconsequential body, surmounted by a huge head and hands, the lips and tongue grossly exaggerated yet almost matched in size by the thumb itself. (If the sex organs were represented they might run off the page.)

It is a peculiarity of aging that these areas of relative neural sensitivity seem to shift, if not actually to change places. Mostly they just dwindle on us. "Put cotton in your ears and pebbles in your shoes, and pull on rubber gloves," a gerontologist tells Cowley, "smear Vaseline over your glasses, and there you have it: instant aging." With age we undergo a decided loss in hearing, taste, smell, and sight, and the fine motor control implied by the oversized thumb and hands begins to abandon us. Remember that spidery handwriting.

The losses in this case are in the details. The Vaseline on the glasses comes from a host of structural changes. Our arms get too short to read fine print because of loss of flexibility in the lens of the eye; near-point focus distance increases by a factor of ten between ages twenty and seventy. The world begins to conspire to take advantage of our new weakness: for example the dosage warnings on patent medicines, printed in two-point type in gray ink against a blue background. (One suspects the makers are afraid we'll be able to read them.) But distance vision sometimes actually improves. The eyeglass restriction has been removed from my driver's license, twenty years after it was first put on.

We need brighter light to read because the pupil becomes smaller and doesn't dilate as well: by age sixty, one-third less light arrives at the retina. The pupil constricts more slowly, too, so sudden bright lights dazzle us. Central cells in the lens begin to crystallize, putting a layer of dust on our windshields. No wonder Dad quit driving at night. "Floaters," those vague brown swimming shapes that don't actually hamper vision but do distract us, multiply like rabbits. We lose enough receptors to shrink the size of our visual field. This effect is exacerbated by deeper eye sockets, from loss of surrounding fat and drooping eyelids. Chemical changes also slow our adaptation to dark conditions, and add a yellow tint to the lens, giving us trouble distinguishing blues and greens. Again, nothing personal.

Then there are the taste buds. Sigh. Up to 70 percent of them atrophy between childhood and age eighty. Meanwhile the taste threshold—the point at which those nerve endings that remain are stimulated sufficiently to start sending signals—declines linearly, leaving us with as little as a fifth of our childhood sensitivity. Most of us notice that food gets a lot drier, and begin slathering on lubricants: reduced flow of saliva and changes in its chemical content reduce the flavor of foods. (I grew up in the Southwest, where Tabasco sauce is regarded almost as holy water. It's a wonder I have enough taste buds left to tell sugar from salt.) The sense of smell, on the other hand, is not much affected, at least in scientifically measurable ways, although some of us begin picking up fragrances—make that odors—we never noticed before. This is not always a blessing. Because we can't smell as well, we sometimes don't smell as good. Old people smell funny, I remember that. I probably smell funny now too, but can't know it. Maybe I'll never know it. What do I do, ask my grandkids?

The cotton in our ears comes from changes both in structure and response. We lose elasticity in the eardrum itself, and flexibility in the joints between the three tiny bones that turn sound waves into waves of hydraulic pressure on the inner ear. These are changes in connective tissue, as are so many of the other effects of age. Our auditory mechanism loses some of the hair cells that, waving in the current from those pressure waves, send signals on to the brain. We lose nerve cells from the hearing portion of the brain itself. We hear best at about age ten—at the high end of the register, for example, up to 20 kHz. By sixty we've lost most of what lies above 5 kHz. We lose a good deal of acuity, the ability to make sharp distinctions. We don't lose a great deal in the ranges of normal human speech, but people seem to be mumbling at us anyway, mostly because we're having trouble processing what they say. We simply hear more *slowly*—and also begin having trouble locating where sounds are coming from.

The miracle of the training effect abandons us here—exercising one's hearing muscles won't help, although improving listening techniques may. If we abused our ears in our youth, we now pay a direct price. Rock and roll and motor racing come immediately to mind. That's one reason ear-protection devices have become so ubiquitous, even when using lawn mowers and other small-engine devices. I thought the earmuffs were a bit self-indulgent at first, but now discover they actually make the work easier.

(Eye exercises, i.e., the training effect, can help to restore some aspects of fading vision, at least in my own experience. I suspect that the lifting of my eyeglass restriction from my driver's license has to do with canoeing. After a summer's outings my prescription always seemed to need changing—and the measurable change, if any, was always in the direction of less rather than more correction of distance vision. Spending long hours staring at distant horizons seems restorative. I've been able to abandon my bifocals entirely for everything but reading and close work, and expect to switch soon to reading glasses alone. The eye-care industry, however, seems little inclined to promote the exercise approach. Said he, paranoiacally.)

Unfairly, this encroaching general sensory fuzziness is occasionally matched by a sometimes painful—and totally undependable—increase in nerve-ending sensitivity. Loud noises, for example, can become actually painful. And what sensitivities you lose in the conventional five senses you seem to pick up again in the aforementioned bladder, the digestive tract, the musculature: pain thresholds are lower, and response times slower. Sensitivity to light touch—caresses and related pleasant sensations—decreases from loss of nerve endings, but the nicks and dings of an active life seem to hurt more, for no detectable reason. Perhaps thinner, drier skin—caused by loss of subcutaneous fat as well as of the sweat and fat glands that once kept it lubricated—has something to do with it. Not all of us are stoic about this. Some of us whine. Drives the young folks crazy.

Along with loss of flavors, the changes in the digestive tract are particularly irritating—and not just to the individuals undergoing the changes. My childhood kitchen memories are of middle-aged aunts complaining of their husbands' pickiness about garlic, green peppers, onions, a host of specific individual food quirks. My aunts always implied this was just stubbornness. I didn't understand what was meant by the word "indigestion" until I was in my fifties, and cheerfully devoured anything edible on God's earth except snails and eggplant. My own list of avoidances now begins to grow, shaming me. My palate shrinks from marinades; some sauces have begun to seem intrusive. This is a small-scale tragedy, as Chris is an adventurous and inventive cook who enjoys exploring the world's cuisines, just as I've started to become a culinary stay-at-home. There's no discernible pattern to these changes: my fondness for Tabasco sauce is unchanged, even as my tolerance for the exotic shrinks. I used to have a cast-iron stomach and an insatiable appetite. Now I'm losing the cast-iron stomach. If life were fair the appetite would diminish too, wouldn't it?

That the digestive tract—taken all in all, that is—becomes the central topic of geezer discourse is the oldest cliché in all of aging. It is its *uncertainty* that is the problem, considered from either end. Matters that in younger days could be blithely ignored now require a good bit of planning ahead. You don't start out the door without a certain application of foresight, which is guaranteed to sap the romance right out of an otherwise adventuresome day.

It is well in these matters to remember writer Tim Cahill's utterly sound advice to "adventure travelers," that new category of tourist that is the fastest growing segment of the industry. People who go to unusual places just for the experience (or terror), in groups or alone, should keep in mind what I like to think of as Cahill's First Rule: Nobody, ever, is interested in your bowel movement.

A new, more fact-based offshoot of the age-denial industry has begun to warn us that we'd damned well better get used to old age, simply because we're living a lot longer. Gail Sheehy points out, in *New Passages,* that these days a sixty-year-old woman has, in effect, a third of a life span ahead of her, and men who reach sixty without dying of heart disease "can expect to be stronger and less bothered by chronic ailments than women." We face the real possibility of being old for a very long time.

Most of this advice is by way of urging us to find a healthy lifestyle as the best-known means of staying self-sufficient and viable as long as possible—not to mention saving a bundle on medical expenses. To make such changes, or even to assess whether changes are needed, requires a level of self-regard that many of us, particularly the males, seem to consider unseemly.

Fortunately, I've never suffered from that, um, virtue. I don't *think* I'm a hypochondriac, but I'm surely some kind of neurasthenic, paying far too much attention to nerve endings and their messages. As a child I sought ever bigger sensations—I loved roller-coasters unnaturally—and as I grew older I was drawn, it seemed unavoidably, to high diving, motor-racing, skiing. I'm sure I survived to my present ripeness only because they didn't invent hang gliding until I'd quit that kind of thrill-seeking. I was as sex-crazed as anyone I ever knew, choosing to become a Lit major only after, and in large part because, I discovered sex in fiction. (But not in Thoreau. Never in Thoreau.) I would romanticize this pursuit of sensory fireworks as some kind of attempt to hang on to or recapture childhood's unspoiled freshness, except that I always went about it by piling more sensation—more Tabasco—on top. It never occurred to me then that the restoration of sensory sensitivity might be better achieved by cutting back, by the ascetic approach.

Now it has occurred to me, not altogether by choice. So far I'm not much good at it. I still think it's damned unfair for the pleasure receptors to start winking out while those for pain seem to be multiplying, or at least increasing in sensitivity. Crankiness has many sources. One of them is sex—but then it already was, before we started getting old, wasn't it?

A few years back there was a Buick advertising campaign that talked about reaching that stage in life when we begin turning the thermostat up and the volume down. I thought this was an extremely acute encapsulation of the effects of aging. It was also a perfectly dumbfounding advertising strategy, since everyone knows you don't market to geezers. Not even Buicks.

"Having occasion to-day to put up a long ladder against the house," wrote Thoreau in March of 1852, "I found, from the trembling of my nerves with the exertion, that I had not exercised that part of my system this winter. How much I may have lost! It would do me good to go forth and work hard and sweat. Though the frost is nearly out of the ground, the winter has not broken up in me. It is a backward season with me. Perhaps we grow older and older till we no longer sympathize with the revolution of the seasons, and our winters never break up."

APRIL: *The Chronological Imperative*

The April Fool's snowstorm blew itself out quickly enough, but, not surprisingly, took our electric power with it; April 2 was bright and beautiful, warm enough to melt the local roads down to blacktop, allowing me a gingerly walk down our hill, in restorative sunshine, to look for downed power lines. The problem did not appear to be local. Walking downhill was weird, with my head balanced in its new hard plastic collar like an egg in an eggcup. Uphill was a challenge; the bone chip in my neck had come from the crest of my right pelvis, leaving me with what felt like a groin pull in a rather strange place. I was not taking large strides.

That hip was my only muscle damage, however, the only thing needing rehabilitation. As promised, it gave more initial discomfort than my neck. My plan was to walk the rather long hill daily, inching along at first, going to twice a day as strength returned. Warm weather held, and for the next day's trip—after electric power had been restored—Chris came with me, along the way sighting the first redwing blackbirds of the season. The sun was warm enough to allow sitting outdoors afterward, in a sheltered spot, for an extended period, contemplating my good fortune. In the afternoon I attempted a second trip down the hill. Pawnee had come along on the first, but refused to repeat herself; a third of the way down I realized her doggy judgment had been better than mine: two-a-days could wait a while. But at sundown, finally off codeine and able to tolerate the taste of alcohol, I made myself a small martini. Daylight saving time was a week away, promising another hour of light. Things were working out just fine. Recovery might yet prove unpleasant, but, unlike the condition that led to it in the first place, it at least promised to be an upward curve.

I'd come away from the hospital with only some new sore places, a little residual shakiness, and (I hoped) a newfound patience (which I'd need a great deal more of). There was nothing scary, emotional, or mystical about the experience. Well, maybe one small moment, an entirely satisfactory one. In pre-op everyone in the room—five or six other surgery patients and a dozen attendants—was required to wear a little paper hat. As I was wheeled out I jokingly asked Chris for a mirror to see how stupid I looked. Cut to recovery room, drifting in and out of consciousness: I dreamed I found a hand mirror and looked at myself in it, checking out the hat. Sure enough, there it was, as silly-looking as I'd expected—and over my right shoulder, watching me in the mirror with a big grin on her face and wearing an identical silly paper hat, was my deceased mother. I woke up laughing.

It was a delicious combination, to get outdoors and take in the melting early springtime, and feel strength returning as I did. To be outdoors was ravishing—a pleasure too long denied. Make that avoided: I could have gotten out before the surgery if I'd cared to, but hadn't much felt like exposing myself to the cold. Didn't go well with pain.

The next snowstorm—it was a busy April, meteorologically—was probably also beautiful, if I'd stopped to take it in: watch the flakes fall, enjoy the cozy house and animals, just sit and watch the snow. Instead I fretted, too pumped up with recovery, wanting so badly to get going again. It made me crazy not to be able to get to town, get the mail, the papers. Me, the media-refusenik. How else was I going to occupy my head?

What a gift aging would be if it ever cured me of that. Fear of boredom steals so much of my time. It's as if whatever it is I'm doing, I prefer to be thinking about something else. Anything but the present tense. I check in for a second or two now and then—flicking my eyes at the present, warily—if I think of it, but I'm usually far too busy for nonsense like that. I'll be bitching about this on my deathbed: *that's* where my life went, this life that went by so swiftly. I will so regret having missed it. Sorry, but I was thinking of something else at the time.

So they slit my throat, pushed my windpipe aside, sliced out the pulpy little cervical spacer that was no longer doing its job, and cleaned things up in there, scraping open as much as possible of the stenosis—the "idiopathic loss of space"—that had sent me there in the first place. "Idiopathic" means from no known cause. In this case the cause was aging. Whatever that is. Then they clipped a wedge of bone from my hip about the size and shape of what you have left after you bite an Oreo in half, popped it in—literally drove it home, Dr. Y told me later, with only friction to hold it in place—and closed me up.

Apologies to people who have to have real surgery for real problems, compared to which this little adventure of mine was almost
cosmetic in nature. I was left with small incisions on pelvis and
neck, a sore hip, and a certain small difficulty swallowing: otherwise pain-free, although not what you would call full strength. I was
to wear a soft collar for sleeping, the hard collar for everything else,
for ten weeks. My body's only responsibility was to lay down new
bone to secure the wedge: rather like healing a broken leg. I began
collecting reports of golfers and other professional athletes—the
only media figures about whom we regularly get medical reports—
who had similar procedures done. They would quietly disappear for
a few weeks but soon enough were back at work. Piece of cake, obviously.

The hard collar also shoved my chin up. (Until I got used to it I
thought I was going to need the line on my bifocals lowered.) Upon
full recovery I could expect to be taller, as I'd been folding in on myself for years, and the procedure would slow if not quite reverse
that. I was not to do anything that required bending, lifting, or
straining, and not to drive, the last an intolerable hardship in rural
life, at least for me. I'm afraid I honored that instruction only in the
breach. Once off narcotics I was mentally alert and physically sound
except for a semi-rigid neck. I experimented first with a twenty-
mile errand for Chris, on back country roads, careful to avoid situations that required backing up. It went okay. A few days later I
drove to Hartford to see Dr. Y, which also went well.

The orthopedist, Dr. Z, couldn't see me that day, so I called to
schedule a later visit. By then a couple of more weeks would have
passed, so I asked if driving was okay yet. No, said his secretary, and
pointed out that driving with a cervical collar was illegal in Connecticut. I may have giggled. Dr. Z, she told me, considered it a
moral issue as well—a responsibility to others in addition to one's

self. I quietly went to the soft collar for driving in Connecticut, fig-
uring I could pull it off and stash it if I saw cops. I did not feel im-
moral, just sneaky. I did not inquire whether Massachusetts had a
similar law.

Otherwise I was a model patient. I discovered that, as Chris had
long maintained, lying down is underrated.

Most of the aging men I know refuse to see themselves as old, and
go on as before. This seems to me unrealistic. My own planned
strategy is to know I am old—there's plenty of evidence—but to go
on as before anyway. My claim is that I will be able to do that selec-
tively, choosing which things to continue with and which to let slip
away. This is arrogant, I realize; God, or Father Time, or the idio-
syncrasies of certain cellular mechanisms, will do the selecting for
me. I'm just trying to maintain the illusion of choice—okay, delu-
sion—as long as possible. I suppose this means I'm every bit as
much in denial as the guys who won't admit their age. I'm just applying the denial in a different place.

All of which is aimed at taking the sting out of that point at which
denial finally crumbles—a strategy driven, I now realize, by my
brother's example. Never mind unexpected Social Security checks,
Jud was the one who was truly blindsided. He got the bad news, in
no uncertain terms, less than four months before he died, and spent
his remaining time in the traditional combination of rage and panic.
Our mother, on the other hand, received the same news—inoperable lung cancer—and was given the same grace period. She accepted it as such, dealt with it in good spirits, and seemed to slip
away fairly easily, leaving us all filled with wonder and gratitude
rather than shock and horror. She was seventy-eight when she got
the news, however—fourteen years wiser than Jud at sixty-four.

Maybe this kind of thinking is what they mean by postsurgical depression.

The soft collar is an elongated, contoured foam pillow in a cotton sleeve with a Velcro closing; it is firm, placing a resilient wedge between chin and shoulders, resisting but not prohibiting movement. It was quite comfortable to sleep in, and by the end of the day I looked forward to its softness, after the harsher support of the hard collar.

The hard one, called the Philadelphia model, is a kind of bustier for the neck, made of fairly stiff plastic, contoured to fit chin, back of the head, breastbone, and shoulders. It has a small moleskin cup at the point of the chin but otherwise puts plastic against flesh, which felt tacky. I circumvented that sensation with a bandanna. The collar's two clamshell halves also fasten with Velcro—quite powerful Velcro, almost fierce in its grip strength. Chris never got used to the sound of Velcro ripping open at regular intervals, as I fiddled with the fit.

I expected to hate the hard collar but secretly liked it. It was very reassuring, and restful, to have my head supported, to take the load off my neck muscles. It was like always having an elbow to lean on—along with a good place to prop it. I'd be heartily sick of it by bedtime, but I didn't mind putting it back on in the morning. I showered without any support, which gave me a good reading on how unstable I felt without it. The hard collar was a security blanket.

Of course my neck muscles were atrophying as I was wearing it, contributing to the instability. I've always been a pencil-necked geek, and that got worse, my neck becoming increasingly scrawny. The collar also affected my balance. We use the weight of the head to maintain balance and stability, abetted by a kind of inner gyro-scope that attempts to keep the eyes level. Accommodating to that made me realize the head might actually be thought of as another limb. We use it as a counterbalance, a coordinator, a pry-bar—much the way cats use their tails. This is what made the collar disorient-ing: I *did* have a limb in a cast. I floated the revolutionary concept of head-as-limb by Dr. Y, but he wouldn't buy it.

One of my hard-collar jokes was that when I removed it I felt as if my head might topple off and roll across the floor. The other, when friends inquired about it, was that, just as the vet had promised, it kept me from chewing the fur off my rump.

I did not fall down while I was still in my collar—surprising, perhaps, given its effect on balance.[1] The young don't realize the epidemic na-ture of falls among the elderly. (A third of community-based elders suffer falls in any given year.) They're caused, physiologically, by a diminished sense of balance, slowed reaction time, and muscular weakness—and mentally, at least in my experience, by daydream-ing. Oldsters who remain vigorously active do less damage to them-selves when they do fall—but by their very activity they put themselves more at risk, and so probably fall as frequently as the ones who just sit still.

Reaction times are especially slowed if the required response is part of a complex task or requires making generalizations or select-ing from competing signals. Fitness pays off here, too: aerobic exer-cise improves balance and reaction time—but strength training and

---

1. Dr. Y did not quite recall the head-as-limb conversation when I checked with him later—prob-ably because I had garbled its presentation at the time—but agreed that the head did have a kind of limblike function. It's a matter of *tonic neck reflexes,* he said, important in balance, gait, and body alignment.

flexibility exercises do not, at least in measurable ways, which is surprising. Among previously sedentary seniors who begin exercising, cerebral function, measured by mental test scores, rises right along with maximal oxygen uptake.[2] Again, whether this is cause or consequence nobody quite knows. Work physiology, a.k.a. exercise science, still awaits its Newton, who can devise experiments that tease out the difference.

Getting oldsters moving also improves walking speed, stride length, and postural sway, all of which likely lessen the incidence of falling. More than a little of the improvement comes from improved nerve transmission, particularly from the proprioceptors in the ankle joints. Proprioception—literally, self-sensing—is the unacknowledged sixth sense that makes the other five so-called special senses available. It does so through *change,* a.k.a. movement. (Sensory information diminishes rapidly when it comes in a steady state.) Age diminishes sensitivity to movement, affecting one's capacity to detect small displacements of the limbs. That's part of where the intention tremor comes from.

"At eighty-nine I fell, unaccountably, on a smooth sidewalk," Pierre writes. "The cause seemed to be faulty balance, the nerve center of which is in the inner ear—where in my case hearing impairment had also taken place. This time I suffered a blackout, multiple bruises, and a broken wrist. It was time for drastic measures. I rummaged in the attic for a cane I had bought in Paris in my and the century's twenties. Then Frenchmen of all ages were sporting walking sticks. After all, for a creature short in the number of legs, it is only sensible to supplement them. But seventy years later in my vil-

2. Maximal oxygen uptake, or VO_2 max in jock parlance, is the maximum rate at which the body can use oxygen. It is the single best measure of general physical fitness—so definitive that it is sometimes referred to as "athletic capacity." It's also the specific index most improved by aerobic exercise.

lage . . . just two old ladies use canes. The men refuse to follow my lead. I am the conspicuous exception. At street corners cars, suddenly courteous, wait for me to pass. So that cane has become a daily *memento mori* in the last five years."

Pawnee accompanied my early trips down the hill but soon decided that programmatic rehabilitation was not for her. Her forequarters were still willing but her hindquarters were becoming reluctant. When she arose after sleeping for very long she'd stagger, trying to get her rear end functioning again. (I often did the same.) It was not football season, but Chris pointed out that it was as if her rear end had missed the snap count. Chris always spots these manifestations of age in our pets before I do, which annoys me. I'm supposed to be in charge of physiological matters around here.

Pets—companion animals, to be politically correct—also age in a kind of time-lapse photography. Puppies and kittens mature so fast, the obvious changes occurring weekly, even daily, and we enjoy them so. Then they settle into a kind of anatomical stasis for several years, unchanging. Near the end, though, the fast-forward button is punched again, and the animal quickly goes geriatric. It's the seven-years-in-one thing, and an excruciatingly exact demonstration of what to resist, physiologically, in ourselves. The form it takes, always, is loss of movement.

Straining to put dishes on a top shelf, I think perhaps we should rearrange things, put our everyday items within easy reach. But that's exactly wrong. We should arrange our kitchen to make things more difficult rather than less. Reach more, strain more, move more. This is kitchen as metaphor for our daily lives, the workshops of our quotidian days; daily is exactly how the losses accumulate.

If we're going to resist those losses, that is. Some of us are not so inclined. It takes a kind of hormonal, hard-nosed refusal to give in, and these are hormones I'm not sure I still have a sufficient supply of. According to the experts, the moxie for successful aging usually comes from the need to accomplish some larger purpose. Crumbling old gaffers such as myself need a project, something outside of—more important than—ourselves. This is morally and socially profound, I guess, but somehow it reminds me of that strategy which, applied to two-year-olds, is called constructive redirection.

Unfortunately for the moral argument, that kind of motivation has also always brought with it, at least for me, a kind of restless urgency that I'd now like very much to put behind me. Relief from that is a good part of what I've had in mind for my golden years. Before surgery—before the prospect of relief—I'd been guilty of thinking I probably wouldn't bother to mount much of an anti-aging campaign, unless I was specifically challenged in ways I didn't foresee. The surgery was among the things I didn't foresee.

Surgery aside, the difficult part is finding out where to draw the line between fighting and accepting. How do we achieve a graceful acceptance of aging's inevitability, the chronological imperative? How do we even recognize where we are on that curve?

At mealtimes a two-person household, unless it is a lot cleverer than ours, is continually forced into a kind of vegetable triage. We make salads with what needs using up before it goes bad, which means it's the stalest stuff in the fridge. We buy vegetables for their crispness and then don't get around to eating them until they threaten to wilt. It's really stupid.

With guests for dinner I found myself delivering a lecture on this subject—and then, as I wound down, began to hear myself. Gaffering. Droning on after I'd lost interest in the subject myself, never mind my poor listeners. I might as well have been on a park bench, spitting and whittling. Next thing I knew I'd be starting sentences, "These young folks today . . ."

Lectures about vegetables, however, spring from aging's relentless rearrangement of values. What's important changes on you. Simpler and simpler things become interesting. Maybe it's fatigue. With more and more of our daily lives controlled by black boxes and automatic feedback systems, it is very reassuring to identify areas in which one can understand how things work. Paying attention to them becomes rewarding. I find myself increasingly seduced by hardware, by practicalities. That's "hardware" in the hammer-and-nail sense, not the opposite-of-software sense. I make my living with words, ephemeral things. Personal relationships are frighteningly vague, subtle, indeterminate. This leads to a kind of nostalgia for the concrete. It is such a relief to deal with what works. I suppose that's where the model-airplane daydreams come from. Maybe some kind of loony Eiffel-Tower-out-of-toothpicks looms in my future.

Gaffering away again, I claim it's a process of shifting from the particular to the universal. When you're young you assume you ought to be able to manage everything at once; with age you realize there's too much for that. No need to add anything more to the pile; there's plenty of stuff already there. You haven't begun to exhaust its riches. More? Whatever for? Here, *you* take it. Where's that Dumpster?

The change is not only inevitable, it seems to me also honorable, even moral—in fact the most one can possibly wish for oneself. What you have to do is learn the importance of the simple. The misanthropy of aging comes in large part from looking about and seeing what all those other idiots still think is important.

Simplify, simplify, eh? Look, I don't mean to imply here that my connection to Thoreau is anything more than a deep but puzzled interest. He is not my hero; I am not a wannabe, a Thoreau *manqué*. Not in my life, my work, or the quality of my thought do I hope to achieve a Thoreauvian life, and most certainly not in the size of my ambition. I'm just trying to figure out why, for nearly fifty years, he has kept getting my attention. Besides, a collar around my neck gave me plenty of time to dig back into his journals.

The size of his ambition adds another unfortunate element to the somewhat cartoonish figure we tend to hold in our minds, the T-shirt Thoreau. The thing is, nobody has ever given us a clear picture of the fellow. He is so humanly self-contradictory, so willfully so. The rest of us are too, but we at least attempt to filter out, or hide, our contradictions; Thoreau chose not to, another reason why he's so irritating.

He is definitely lodged in our minds—and we probably have him wrong. As the late Walter Harding, dean of Thoreauvian scholars, put it, "The man in the street knows that Thoreau went to Walden Pond to live and went to jail, but has a vague notion that he spent one half of his life doing the one and the other half the other." He was a stubborn little man who spent one night in jail. After it, and surely during it, he thought about his assumed illegality long enough and hard enough to write one brief essay, "Civil Disobedience," on which were constructed, among other things, the liberation of India and the American civil rights movement. In those struggles he was sort of an outside agitator, albeit long deceased.

But that wasn't his ambition. The other thing he did with his life, which consumed the bulk of it, he never quite got around to writing down. This was the ambition for which, in Emerson's words, he was not granted sufficient longevity. He was gathering the Natural

History of Everything. I probably should say "writing" it, but that's the part he didn't get around to. "I think I could write a poem to be called Concord," he wrote in his journal in September of 1841, when he was only twenty-four.[3] Over time that "poem"—he surely meant the term metaphorically even at the outset—grew into a larger work. He was going to catalog Concord: to determine when and how everything occurred in the natural world there, in what order and what effect each part had on the others.

He was a natural scientist in the nineteenth-century sense, what they used to call a "curious man": a serious biologist, meteorologist, ornithologist. He seemed to like birds more for their colors and their sounds—he loved and could imitate many of their calls—than for their habits. He was an obsessive botanist. He constructed a small shelf in the top of his hat for bringing back specimens of everything, for dissection and analysis but also just for pleasure. He was always bringing back wildflowers in bud stage, which he kept in vases in his room so he could watch them open. He loved smells, and tried to catalog them, too. He was a hands-and-knees field scientist, wading streams nude with his clothes piled on his head (under his specimen hat), digging wild things from their burrows with his bare hands (speculating as he did on his chances of being bitten or stung), measuring snow depths for miles across the countryside. Some claim he contracted the ague that finally killed him from kneeling in the snow to count the rings of a stump.

He was a natural scientist because that's the way you did it in the nineteenth century: if it was natural, you studied it, as hard as you could with the limited means at hand. He got a lot of things wrong, some by nineteenth-century standards, some by twentieth. Some were wrong for a while but then became right again. What some

---

3. It seems strange that for a man who had so many quarrels with his fellow townspeople, who lived in Concord so discordantly, and who was an incorrigible punster, Thoreau never seems to have made any jokes about the name of the place—none, at least, that I've run across.

consider to be the big idea in *Walden* was almost silly to the science of the times: "a living earth; compared with whose great central life all animal and vegetable life is merely parasitic." "There is nothing inorganic," he says, in the famous sand-foliage passage. Animal, vegetable, and mineral are almost false distinctions. That can still seem silly to us, even knowing as we now do, or think we do, that if the analysis becomes fine-grained enough, at bottom nothing exists but charged particles. Wherever the bottom is.

He wrote all his observations down in detail, but they are field notes, tough going for even the most besotted Thoreauvian. He also charted these things extensively, dates of blooming and hatchings and frosts, livings and dyings, and always seeds, the production of seeds, although there is no evidence he sowed any of his own.

That effort was what Thoreau's life was all about, and what fastened him in the minds of his Concord fellows. *They* knew who Henry was. That was the real Henry, real as a nail. The night in jail and the two years in the cabin were just youthful high jinks, showbiz. The cabin, in the minds of the American consciousness, was the most contrarian aspect of all. And what was contrarian about it, what lodged it in our minds, was the solitude. That, to the American mind, was the truly shocking part.

I take it back, there is one area in which I am deeply and at times almost unwillingly connected to Thoreau. I am hopelessly jealous of how well he said things. Some things.

I read them as conscientiously as I can, but about two million of the two and a half million words in his journals go fluttering by me like autumn leaves, unobserved.

People with prior experience had warned me that recovery from surgery would be discouragingly slow. ("At your age" was gently

implied. Note the block letters over the portal to aging: IT'S GOING
TO HEAL MORE SLOWLY THAN YOU THINK.) They were correct, although I couldn't judge how much of the disappointment was the
product of unrealistic expectations. I got tired easily, early, often. I
was spending a lot of time in Selye's alarm stage, the severity of
which I'd forgotten. I also felt extremely heavy. The world had become a heavier place, as if it had suddenly acquired a kind of hyper-
gravity. When my mother lived with us a few years before her
death, she complained about the weight of one of our frying pans,
which at the time I couldn't quite understand. I now noticed I'd
begun to avoid using it.

"Man's slow decline in stature is a sign of the unequal contest between our bodily powers and the unchanging force of gravity," says
biologist D'Arcy Thompson, "which draws us down when we
would fain rise up. We strive against it all our days, in every movement of our limbs, in every beat of our hearts. Gravity makes a difference to a man's height, and no slight one, between the morning
and the evening; it leaves its mark in sagging wrinkles, drooping
mouth and hanging breasts, it is the indomitable force which de-
feats us in the end, which lays us on our death bed and lowers us to
the grave." Gravity, now, there's something even Unitarians can believe in.

At the same time, though, I could feel myself healing, improving
daily. What a miracle that seemed, what an absolute gift. It gave me
a virulent case of what early German psychologists called *Funktion-
lust*.

In mid-April I hobbled around our mile-plus loop for the first
time since the previous November—a minor triumph. Totally
wiped me out, however, bringing on a wave of depression that was
almost chemical in nature. While I was out I'd gotten a good look
around the house and its exterior, and begun to brood on the

amount of sheer physical labor needed to get things back into shape around the place. Chores awaited that I'd been putting off for years. In that state I could not imagine a favorable outcome for anything on the horizon.

The fact that it was income-tax day may have had something to do with my frame of mind; by the next morning I was ready for another loop. Chris came along, and we spent nearly an hour at what was ordinarily a half-hour walk, not for my gimpiness but because we were enjoying the springtime woods so much we didn't want to come in. My face got sunburned; how good *that* felt.

"I have been out every afternoon this past winter, as usual, in sun and wind, snow and rain, without being particularly tanned," Thoreau wrote in his journal on April 14, 1852. "This *forenoon* I walked in the woods and felt the heat reflected from the snow so sensibly in some parts of the cut on the railroad that I was reminded of those oppressive days two or three summers ago, when the laborers were obliged to work by night. Well, since I have come home, this afternoon and evening, I find that I am suddenly tanned, even to making the skin of my nose sore. The sun, reflected thus from snow in April, perhaps especially in the forenoon, possesses a tanning power."

By late April the ice was out of the pond, open water bringing lovely movement—continual, restless, wind-dappled movement—to our view, after the long stasis of winter. The peepers returned, their first evening chorus nailing in place the arrival of spring with dead-set certainty. The open pond immediately fetched a couple of migrating mergansers, some mallards, and another goddamned beaver.

We'd had one a few years earlier. It would dam up the pond outlet every night with a gloppy assortment of mud and sticks, which I would disassemble again the next morning, a psychological war that went on for weeks. That beaver had proved thoroughly undiscourageable. Finally it toppled a lovely birch into the pond, and began girdling an ornamental weeping cherry that we'd nursed along for twelve years. With deep regret we called the Environmental Police—yes, that's what they're called—about having it "removed"— i.e., shot. (Trapping and releasing elsewhere just hands the problem on to someone else.) This required locating a licensed trapper and applying for a formal permit. We are not of the hunter-fisher persuasion and disliked the violence, but less than we disliked the violence to trees and pond.

I found it truly discouraging to be facing the same problem all over again. With the warmer weather I was logging serious deck time, working on a laptop, and every time I looked up I'd see this new interloper motoring up and down the length of the pond, dragging alder trash behind him. Or rather her; we decided she was female, in order to name her Simone de Beavoir. Simone began getting seriously on my nerves. Maybe, I thought, if the discouragement was applied early enough and often enough it would let us avoid mayhem. I strolled down to the pond—about fifty yards from the deck—and tried lobbing rocks at her, a physical act I immediately discovered was inadvisable while wearing a hard collar. Well, if I couldn't throw, perhaps a slingshot? . . .

I whipped into Northampton to a gun-and-tackle shop, where I was advised that slingshots are illegal in Massachusetts. After several tries I located some surgical tubing (lacking the requisite bicycle tire from which to swipe an inner tube). I came home and cut an appropriately Y-shaped branch from an apple tree near the house, made a sling from a worn-out leather garden glove, and had myself a launch mechanism, or illegal weapon. If the authorities dropped by, I figured I'd hide it under my laptop.

Beneath the deck was a bed of large-caliber ammunition—loose stone, laid down to discourage weed growth, ranging in size from pinto bean to cherry. The slingshot had terrific range, easily plopping stones into the woods on the other side of the pond seventy-five yards away, but no accuracy whatsoever. The projectiles were lumpy, irregular in shape, and upon release fell immediate prey to aerodynamics, every shot turning into an unpredictable curveball or slider. Furthermore, Simone did not deign to notice unless I plunked one within about eighteen inches of her nose. Then she'd slap tail and dive satisfyingly, only to reverse direction immediately and surface again within a few seconds, seemingly unconcerned. That first afternoon I must have spent an hour and a half, and fifty or sixty shots, attempting to discourage her. The next morning, merely from drawing back the sling, I was as sore as if I'd gone horseback riding, except that the soreness was in arms and chest instead of buttocks and legs. The exercise-free winter had turned me into a wet noodle.

The adventure, however, had fully occupied one more hard-collar day, of the total of seventy the doctors had sentenced me to. I was beginning to understand what the AAs are talking about with their one-day-at-a-time approach. One day closer to freedom. Besides which, after another couple of days of harassment, Simone, amazingly, abandoned us. I'm quite positive it was my daily presence on the deck and not my marksmanship that did the job.

By way of celebration, and in anticipation of the summer to come, we ordered a new tent, which I set up on the deck so I could apply sealer to the seams. Unpacking it put me in a snit: it came with L. L. Bean's large, garish logo plastered front and back on the rain-fly. Taking advertising into the wild seems to me hideously dissonant, particularly in the form of in-your-face four-inch-lettering. Said the grumpy old fart, covering the offending trade-marks with duct tape. But the tent was large, airy, and comfortable, replacing one that was cramped and worn. An old-folks tent, which now seemed appropriate. We spent the evening making plans for its use.

Then we changed them. From a mechanistic point of view I may have needed only to knit some bone, but I'd spent years banging away on the nerves that moved my arms, and letting them recover meant not using those arms, at least not that hard, for another little while. We'd been talking about a canoe trip in mid-May, but that now was out of the question. So seemed the rapidly accelerating schedule of yard work that springtime presented. Some postpone-ments were easier to take than others.

On my next visit, one month postsurgery, Dr. Z reinforced my patience. I was whining my way through the list of things he wouldn't let me do, complaining. When *could* I swim, or run, or do anything else vigorous? Didn't he realize I was going a little nuts? I think he lost patience. "It's time," he said, "to hunker down and *heal*." I accepted that.

Acceptance, however, was not sufficient to make me sit still. I was getting up early, putting in an hour or two at my desk before breakfast, running errands, pursuing leads, driven by a frenetic if short-lived nervous energy. Most days I hauled myself around the loop before lunch, which dropped me like a stone into an afternoon snooze. I'd be exhausted again by bedtime but also exhilarated, bouncing back a little further each time, the next day's energy last-ing a little longer. I slept every night as if I'd run a marathon. Heal-ing. It was glorious.

Bone and the healing thereof is a subject whose implications are more philosophical than physiological; age does bring changes to bone, but, osteoporosis aside, they aren't that significant. The stuff of bones is yet more connective tissue, in bone's case a soft organic matrix made hard by the deposition of mineral salts. It is well supplied with nerve fibers and blood vessels: bone cells, like any other living cell, must be nourished and relieved of waste. The organic framework is mostly collagen; boil it and you get gelatin.

Overstress bone abruptly and it snaps; do the same slowly, over time, and it develops the osseous equivalent of metal fatigue, known as a stress fracture. Stop using it and it atrophies, just like muscle, although in bone's case the loss isn't in dimension but in strength, from loss of substance. We think of it as a virtual mineral, hard and permanent, but it's surprisingly plastic stuff. Use it properly— stress it—and it gets bigger and stronger, changing size and shape in response to either compression or tension. It will lay down new cells to make reinforcing bars and braces, building arches and flying buttresses and vaulted roofs of itself, structures that are aped by the great cathedrals. It would not be surprising if those medieval architects, yearning to build ever more upward, had studied bone to learn how.

In a child's bones the ratio of hard to soft material—inorganic to organic—is roughly 1:1; by young adulthood it's 4:1, in the aged 7:1, which increasing brittleness results in more fractures. A woman of eighty has one chance in five of fracturing a hip. There is speculation that the hip may snap in normal use—a "spontaneous fracture"—which is then blamed on the resulting fall. With age and reduced activity the bone begins to erode from within. Part of this loss may be from reduced calcium in the diet, or reduced uptake of the calcium we do get. The hucksters certainly try to sell it that way.

But more of the loss is from our growing fondness for sitting still. The bone's favorite stress is gravity itself, which is why astronauts exercise in gravity-free orbit: they lose bone rapidly if they don't.

Exercise in this case is nothing more than a way of generating load, or artificial gravity. The gravity that pulls us ever downward at the same time keeps us strong.

We ignore our bones most of the time, until we miss a step and feel the jar, demonstrating their irreducibility. Bone is the non-squishy part of our otherwise squishy selves, protecting the more vulnerable soft parts. When it fractures it heals better than many of the parts that don't. Orthopedists prefer dealing with fractures to dealing with tears; maybe that thinking is behind "Break a leg," the upside-down blessing traditional among superstitious stage actors.

Because immobilization speeds healing, when one does break we strap on artificial bone, in the form of a cast (or hard collar). As healing begins, a blood clot forms, which is then replaced with immature connective tissue. (Remove the blood clot and debris and other irritation from the site of the fracture and it won't heal at all.) Eventually the immature connective tissue converts into a denser form, making a kind of cuff around the site, which fills in gaps between the fragments and seals off the marrow cavity. Young people, naturally, produce more new bone and thus heal more quickly than the old.

Excess bone is formed around the fracture site, but it'll be resorbed when healing is complete. No longer stressed, it isn't needed: the bone will be the size it needs to be. In other words, bone isn't permanent at all—until it's dead. That's when it turns into a kind of stone, the part the anthropologists dig up when they're trying to understand our origins. Maybe we ought to give bone more respect. It's the part that endures when "we"—whatever that is—are outta here.

Besides which, say Per-Olof Åstrand and Karre Rodahl, in their excellent *Textbook of Work Physiology,* it's the stuff that "prevents the entire body from collapsing into a heap of soft tissue."

A friend to whom I'd been going on about the four stages of life sends me a copy of Colin Turnbull's *The Human Cycle,* a sort of memoir disguised as cultural analysis. Turnbull is the anthropologist who brought the Ik to our attention, that peculiar tribe in Africa so devoid of human sympathy that adults make fun of babies who stumble into the campfire. I gather that Turnbull's anthropology has occasionally been challenged, but he's an entertaining writer—and of an age to begin thinking about life's stages.

In *The Human Cycle* he addresses among other things the Hindu version of the four stages. They are *brahmacharya* (youth, devoted to celibate education, preferably in a religious school away from home), *grhastha* (family life and worldly duties), *vanaprastha* (after the kids are gone; withdrawal from worldly life and material attachments), and *sannyas* (a completely nonmaterialist life as a religious mendicant). With the details filled in, this turns out to be a little harsher scheme than I had in mind.

Turnbull is amused at our hurry to reach adulthood so we can start bemoaning our lost youth. He points out that we regard "work," as in supporting ourselves, as one of adulthood's unpleasanter adjuncts, a loss of the very freedom that adulthood was supposed to bring. In an ideal society, we seem to feel, there should be a way of getting through life without working.

"In other cultures there *is* such a way," says Turnbull. "It is really quite simple. In such cultures 'work' is seen merely as doing whatever you are doing at that particular moment in your life." As play is a child's "work," so adolescent daydreaming—and sexual experimentation—are the adolescent's work. (And stealing is a thief's work.) Making love to one's wife is part of one's work (and, one supposes, making love to the wives of others is a philanderer's work), "for in such cultures making love is a very real part of the 'work' that is expected of adults."

Maybe I won't go on to stage four after all, I'll just stick it out here in stage three.

In youth the traveling I did and the experiences I sought out— motor races, ski resorts, events and spectacles—were in large part so I could tell about them later. I couldn't say I always enjoyed them while they were going on; in fact, I squirmed uncomfortably through a good many of them, putting up with them to acquire material, so I could tell good stories about great places—which I then tended to tell in Guinness Book style, exaggerating everything. I seemed to be hoping that some recognition, maybe even respect or admiration, would cling to me for the telling. I suppose this is part of what makes a writer.

The experiences I seek now, or the ones I'm trying to learn to seek, I have little inclination to tell anyone about. It's as if I've stopped wanting to see the new and started wanting to see the old, the familiar, in order to understand it better. Life as it goes on day to day is becoming richer and richer.

This is an old guy's attitude, much frowned upon by the people who are always telling old folks how to live. We're supposed to keep ourselves fresh by seeking new experiences, not letting ourselves get into ruts. "Men, much more than women, find it easy to put themselves into a comfort-box as they age," says Bard Lindeman. "Over time, the box gets smaller and smaller. Then creativity is precluded, and becomes beyond reach." Or as John Cowper Powys put it, in *The Art of Growing Old*, ". . . we poor dullards of habit and custom, we besotted and befuddled takers of life for granted, require the hell of a flaming thunderbolt to rouse us to the fact that every single second of conscious life is a miracle past reckoning, a marvel past all computation."

"As Sartre said, not to choose is to have already chosen," says Carolyn G. Heilbrun, in *The Last Gift of Time: Life Beyond Sixty*. "The major danger in one's sixties—so I came to feel—is to be trapped in one's body and one's habits, not to recognize those supposedly sedate years as the time to discover new choices and to act upon them. To continue doing what one had been doing—which was Dante's idea of hell—is, I came to see, and the vision frightened me, easy in one's sixties."

Well, maybe.

MAY: *Fool on Board*

One of the great joys of springtime in New England has to do with winter garments, specifically the flinging off thereof: more or less ceremonially, whether the garments are of repentance, polyester, or linsey-woolsey. The folklore abounds with backwoodsmen who have themselves sewn into their long johns in October, and in spring—after the blackflies—simply cut their way out and burn the result. Repentance in that case is not at issue.

The turn of the season thus initiates a series of replacements, of thick clothing with thin, and then of thin with as little as possible. In May I moved as soon as temperatures made it bearable to T-shirt, shorts, and sandals, the shirt only to keep the plastic collar off bare skin. Felt like I'd tunneled out of a dungeon.

But then age is a force in that direction anyway, as in the matter of socks. Carolyn Heilbrun describes her change, postseventy, in a lifetime of dressing habits, rhapsodizing about how Victorian matrons must have felt on those rare occasions when they doffed "the stays and dresses that inhibited motion, and flexed their bodies, moved their unbound muscles." Exactly: movement again, unfettered. Delicious. I have little enough to complain about on that score, however. Once I escaped from office work I moved into jeans and T-shirts, and never went back. As Moritz Thomsen points out in *The Saddest Pleasure,* when an old man chooses to wear working-class clothing he becomes invisible. This is useful.

"There is some advantage in being the humblest, cheapest, least dignified man in the village, so that the very stable boys damn you," wrote Thoreau in 1851. "Methinks I enjoy that advantage to an unusual extent."

Comfortable clothing aside, however, May proved more maddening than not. It did include that lovely but sobering morning on which I awoke with the realization I had lived longer than Jud had—a moment of no outward significance whatsoever but of powerful internal resonance. He never knew what it was like to be this old, I found myself thinking. So what, my cynical side immediately responded: neither did Aristotle (sixty-two), Beethoven (fifty-seven), or Hitler (fifty-six). I looked them up. Not to mention, of course, Thoreau.

Among other nonmaddening May events was the arrival of a new granddaughter, joining two others and a grandson in that generation, making me a grandfather in spades. On the other, anxiety-producing side, however, was the approaching publication of my next book, which would mean casting aside three years of privacy for a certain amount of exposure, welcome or not. There seemed to be a certain amount of psychic tension. I made a note to look up "displacement behavior" but couldn't find a good source.

Spring is an itchy time even without your neck in a brace: buds popping, birds returning, blessed color reemerging, finally, in the landscape. (And winter, in New England, anyway, is something of a

near-death experience.) Makes you restless. I did not have the traditional impulse to buy a new car—well, only a small one, I did eyeball the floor models while having some service done—but the
seasonal mood had me by the throat. Or would have if it could have
gotten past my collar.

A rural residence requires a certain predictable amount of physical labor when the snow finally goes; with a collar to hide behind I
didn't have to do any of the actual work, and my ambitions began to
soar. Time to get cracking on the Dumpster project, postponed
since fall. The dock that serves our swimming pond was rotten and
needed replacing, and I began putting myself to sleep at night designing its repair. And why *not* turn the area below the pond—currently an infestation of alder trash and blackberry vines—into,
well, parkland? All it would require is sweat—if, that is, one has regained use of one's musculoskeletal system, precisely what my
surgery was designed to do. Not to worry, I told the mother of my
new granddaughter, when she questioned some of these ambitious
plans for the coming summer; by then I'll be twenty-five again.

Meanwhile, some days it was still a struggle to walk around our
woodland loop. I was getting a valuable peek at the very future I
most wanted to avoid—at what it's like, for example, to face a flight
of stairs with reluctance. Ten years before, I'd been competing for
national championships in an endurance sport; five years before, I'd
begun making wilderness canoe trips, paddling six or seven hours a
day. Now a woodsy mile and a third was giving me trouble. I'd been
put on the bubble—between activity and inactivity—a little earlier
than seemed quite fair. Puffing at a flight of stairs wasn't the way I
wanted to go out. I didn't know how I did want to go, but that
wasn't it.

What if, I couldn't help occasionally thinking, the neck repairs
had not worked? What if the previous winter's level of decrepitude
persisted? What if my current level of physical capacity—with,

okay, a little added mobility and strength when the collar comes off—was *it*? All there was, the limit of my future? The motivation for the surgery, after pain reduction, was resumption of an active life; what if that did not obtain? Never mind never being twenty-five again, what if this tottering semi-invalidity was my permanent fate? It was an eventuality as hard to look at as that other outcome, the mortal one. What if this aging body, which I had enjoyed so much in the past, turned out now to be a lemon? How *does* one, in that situation, make lemonade? Why did this possibility never occur to me while I was considering surgery?

To calm myself I took inventory. I was climbing back from something like five months of almost total inactivity, preceded by three or four years of dwindling vigor. God only knew how much I'd actually lost. Thirty days still to go. Simple removal of the collar would probably not significantly restore what I'd lost, which was when real patience would be called for. If I overdid things and crashed—as I had consistently done in the past—the stakes were considerably higher. I had no idea what might go wrong, but the prospect of asking the surgeons to repair a repair was not attractive, never mind however much additional recovery time *that* might entail. (Dear HMO, If we don't repeat this horrendously expensive procedure I will die sooner and stop paying your premiums. Plus the cause will be cardiac disease, treatment of which will be more costly than neurosurgery.) Some kind of physiological wisdom *must* set in, must come with age, I kept telling myself. Otherwise I was in for a terrible fall.

Welcome to the world of self-mourning, before the fact. In a way it is liberating. It frees you up to mourn everyone else, how you'll miss them. And life, and yourself. So: mood swings. Activity would get me out of them, when activity was permitted, or even possible, but my mental state was as erratic as the spring weather.

I began taking the collar off now and then, for brief spells, when seated. It was quickly tiring. The neck is a subtle batch of musculature. You don't lift things or twist wrenches with it, but you do use it, extremely actively, in keeping the world oriented, and to have it get so tired so quickly was dismaying. What was most disconcerting was the return of the familiar old dull ache in neck and shoulder, from irritated nerves. It wasn't nearly as severe as it had been—ibuprofen handled it—but I hadn't yet started really using my arms. It was almost too depressing to think about. I of course decided—about every other day for the next couple of weeks—that the next disk would also have to be done. But did I want to go through the surgery again? How badly did I need relief? And how soon? And other questions, as I trembled on the lip of despair.

Besides which shorts and sandals were short-lived, as May seemed determined to remain gray, gloomy, windy, and cold. Dr. Z opined that my neck pain could be a result of "fighting" the collar, which made a certain amount of sense. I resolved to learn new habits of movement, and otherwise to be a good patient (that oh so appropriate term) for the remaining weeks. I had a weak, stiff, relatively unfunctional neck, and until I got the collar off and some movement restored I wouldn't know where I was at. I tried to keep reminding myself that there was little point in making myself crazy ahead of time.

Dear Mike [I wrote to my brother-in-law],

I've been commiserating, however silently, with your complaints about stamina and energy levels, as the spring has broken and concomitant physical demands have escalated. I suffer ditto. My theory is a metabolic one: there's a hump to get over, I know it, but I just can't seem to get there this year. I suppose the hump grows higher, or the slope steepens. Problem is I am so tottery on my feet that I'll break my neck if I ever start down the other side. Besides which, it'll be October and time to come indoors again, right?

I'm sure this is what the tradition of a springtime tonic of sulfur-and-molasses was about. Or bleeding. My imagination, or maybe it's my limbic system, envisions some kind of system-wringing hyper-emetic para-acidulous super-tonic, to cure all in one shuddering gulp. Maybe get vomitous drunk, then find a sauna and an icy stream? I don't *think* so.

Walking the loop on a blustery day, I turn to look back up the trail and suddenly see myself doing it, the stiff way I turned, almost as if on film footage: an old man in the trail. I know that guy—he's the anxious fool. He's usually at my desk, doing the writing. He thinks he's trying to be the other me, the person I want to be all the time, but he hasn't a clue. He can't pay attention.

It was through building stone walls—attending to the risky business of stacking heavy stones—that I first made his acquaintance. The anxious fool was not allowed to do stone work. Since then I've tried at least to restrict him to sitting at the computer—twitching in his seat, trying to get sentences to work out right. When he does he hands them to me, and I get the pleasure.

Perhaps I'll organize a Society of Anxious Fools. You must be at least twenty-six years old to join. You have to have realized that if you're twenty-six, you're aging. Not very fast, perhaps, but aging nonetheless. Deal with it: the curve has taken a new direction.

Actually, I do a little better at physical tasks if I pretend I'm Japanese. I can imagine wisdom better in the Japanese—they've had the reputation for it. Imagining myself to be Japanese, I can work in reasonably intelligent and judicious fashion for upwards of five minutes at a time, but eventually the world comes pressing in and I start hurrying again. I am not able to sustain the game. The anxious fool regains possession of my frame, my musculature. He is trying to get this over with, in order to . . . what? I've never figured that out. The anxious fool can't tell me.

There are surely a lot more important things to do with your life than worry about how your body is holding up. Unfortunately, you can't go do any of those other things if your body won't take you there. Pierre had to give up his wilderness adventures in his eighties. He developed an arthritic condition in his feet—"a nuisance rather than a handicap"—and found that his endurance had declined: "Outings became fewer, shorter, and less exploratory, a five-mile hike being as tiring as a twenty-mile one had formerly been." (That history of high mileage probably explains why he broke only his wrist and not his hip when he fell.)

"Now, in my tenth decade," he goes on, "I take almost daily half-hour walks in the village . . . or in bad weather pedal an exercise bike. Once or twice a year I go into the woods for a short hike or paddle. Even reading sometimes palls; it is harder to find the captivating book. The appetite for living drains away bit by bit in a psycho-physical complex that helps to reconcile one to death. Shaw, longest lived of literary men, experienced this in his nineties, as I am beginning to do. Perhaps this is what Edgar meant, in *Lear,* by 'ripeness is all.' "

Objectively, my continuing old-fart's whine about media is pretty pathetic. After all, it was the media that got me off tobacco, got me started exercising, got me in shape, opened up that whole fascinating world of physiology to me: gave me a thirty-year career in that field; gave me my living. What an ingrate I am, biting the hand that fed me.

On the other hand, it was that experience—working in the fitness business, writing magazine columns composed almost entirely of cocktail facts—that convinced me of the media-advertising world's crazy-making emptiness. I suppose the real problem has to do with media as boss. I've never gotten along well with bosses. Maybe what I'm trying to do is fire the media.

Going without for a year rather *felt* like retiring, and that's the way I tried to play it. I'd tried in the past to retire but just couldn't accommodate it mentally. The one thing I had to do, I said, was get out of the swirl, the buzz. Funny thing was, once you're out of it, who needs to retire?

What retirement seems to require most is giving up urgency. I don't understand why we are so enamored of it when it turns out to be such a bad idea. I'm always amused at the strident urgency in the music with which they kick off the news every night on TV. Or I was, back when I watched news.

Now at dawn, putting away the previous night's dishes so I can get on with my breakfast, I stop, take a long breath, and begin putting things away one at a time, slowly and deliberately. Something about my haste has brought to my attention the fluttering pressure I am putting on myself just to get through this mindless little task more quickly. In order to get on to my breakfast, in order to get through that more quickly, in order to get on to whatever else I am going to hurry at all day long. To get to my computer so I can type as fast as my fingers will fly. Computer engineers redesign chips to reduce the distances between circuits by zillionths of a micron, just to pick up speed. They pour millions into research into reducing the width of a chip the size of a pinhead, so the electrons won't have to journey all that way across the width. We are all, always, pushing the river. Pushing the river is feeding the monkey, pass it on. Shouldn't retiring mean you stop feeding the monkey?

At the end of the day, as I change into softer clothes, I obsessively review. Have I done enough today? I know full well there is no satisfactory day on this score, that whatever I have accomplished would not be enough. I even realize that if I accomplished nothing I would not actually go to hell for that particular day's failings. Actually, I have it backward: if I do go to hell, and I may, it will likely be pushing the river that sends me there. I vaguely recall a line in an old book by a western psychologist named Jack Huber, who spent time in a Zen monastery, and look it up: ". . . I realized that no matter what thought or feeling I had, it passed on. It either never recurred or never recurred in quite the same way. I realized that nothing will ever come again as it comes to me at any one moment. Nothing exists but what exists now."

A green wave of envy washes over me, imagining that state of mind.

Willy, who readily admits to a good deal of anger but wouldn't hurt a flea, had a blood-pressure rise sufficient to get the notice of what is now known as his health-care provider. (However did we let the language so get away from us?) He was put on drugs, which he rather resented, and modified his diet. Exercise was also recommended, but he has always been a runner. He also began making a concentrated effort at learning stress-management techniques, including meditation, which he found rewarding enough to continue regardless of what happened with his blood pressure.

For the aging the hypertension problem can be very nearly as frustrating as the prostate. It affects one third of today's elderly, and ignoring it can lead to kidney failure, congestive heart failure, and stroke—and stroke, with its threat of severe functional loss but continued survival, is, after Alzheimer's, one of the most frightening specters the aging have to face. Control of hypertension, we are told, significantly lowers "risk of death," a somewhat misleading piece of advice since the risk of death for the elderly, to say nothing of everyone else, is always and exactly 100 percent. Perhaps the authorities mean it delays death, all else being equal—which of course all else never is.

For most of us it's unavoidable, blood pressure rising progressively with age, largely as a consequence of changes in the arterial walls—which stiffen, predictably, since they, too, are made up of connective tissue. Inelastic blood vessels resist distension, driving the pressure up for a given cardiac output. In effect the vessel walls lose their shock absorbers. The rise is especially marked in systole—the first, higher of the two numbers muttered by the nurse—and even modest increases in systolic pressure are an important risk factor for stroke.

Hypertension is popularly referred to as the silent killer, because you don't feel it: no overt symptoms until the damage is done. No symptoms mean no reminders, no stimulus to persist in its management, whether by drugs or so-called lifestyle strategies. Your doctor is reduced to trying to scare you into compliance. The dividing line beyond which hypertension is formally recognized is usually considered to be 140 over 90, but that's a somewhat arbitrary figure. "Nature is continuous, not dichotomous," the MacArthur study points out.[1]

---

1. In 1984 the John D. and Catherine T. MacArthur Foundation—the genius-grant people—commissioned a Study of Successful Aging, gathering for that purpose a group of distinguished scientists. Ten million foundation dollars later, a popularized version of the result was published as *Successful Aging* (by John W. Rowe, M.D., and Robert L. Kahn, Ph.D. [New York: Pantheon, 1998], a careful interpretation of the latest gerontological research. It says, essentially, that more lost function can be regained than we realize, and that successful aging requires staying active, productive, and connected to society.
   They'll get no argument from me, and it's their money, but somehow this reminds me of a similar foundation-backed study of international-conflict resolution. After a comparable expenditure of years and dollars, the study announced, to considerable fanfare, that future conflicts could be expected to arise from ethnic, geographical, and economic differences.

You don't suddenly contract high blood pressure as you would an infection, you develop it gradually—your arteries lose elasticity over time. At some point the numbers get high enough for your doctor to get on your case. We'd all do better if we monitored our blood pressure regularly, and took appropriate measures in diet and exercise before the red flags go up. A certain amount of higher blood pressure used to be regarded as "appropriate for your age," but the more epidemiological stance of modern medicine now regards almost any rise as worth treating.

It's the "almost any" part that brings frustration. If 140/90 is the upper limit, do we start treatment at 141/91? (Even with digitized equipment, the readings are never that exact.) The numbers vary throughout the day, depending on the circumstances. Chris, for example, has a virulent case of "white-coat" high blood pressure, fairly common: it shoots off scale the moment she walks through the doctor's office door, and returns to a comfortable low-normal range when she leaves. By careful monitoring Willy has discovered his own pressure spikes at the sight of a blood-pressure cuff—or the mention of the words "blood pressure." If it spikes at all there's probably reason for concern, since the damage is done over time and in small doses. But aggressive treatment for high blood pressure, when most of one's waking hours are spent in the "safe" or "normal" range, is a hard sell. Drugs may reduce the risk of stroke by a third and of heart attack by a quarter, but side effects include feelings of weakness and fatigue, drowsiness, dizziness, impotence, depression—and are likely to reduce physical-activity levels already inadequate for health.

Hypertension, in short, is age-related but not age-determined, and normal but not harmless. There is a hereditary component to it, but genes are not as significant a factor as lifestyle. Diet and exercise are most important, but not failproof. Stress management, on the other hand, at least feels more immediately rewarding. And yet, as one medical professional pointed out to Willy, high blood pressure can be *fun*.

For that matter, so is caffeine, the hot new drug of the nineties. Or was it the eighties, and it slipped by when I wasn't paying attention?

By mid-month Mount Washington, New England's maximum weather magnet, had broken its all-time record for May snowfall, and would go on to add another two or three feet before June rolled around. Spring refused to break, which I took personally. I did, however, take advantage of a relatively benign day—warm enough to handle tools with bare hands—to begin prepping the tractor for the mowing season.

It's an awkward job even without your neck in a brace, requiring, in addition to a tune-up of the engine, unhitching the mower that hangs beneath, dragging it out, sharpening its blades, lubricating it and everything else, and reinstalling it. It's a dirty, greasy task, bending over and crawling under, reaching deep within, usually with insufficient light: not exactly heavy lifting, but the first substantial physical task of the year. An hour into it I was being swarmed by the first blackflies of the season, even on a cool gray day in the shelter of the garage. That meant that along with the usual barked knuckles and aching back I ended up with the diluted, unclotted blood from their bites trickling down into my neck brace.[2] But I got the job done, and felt I'd accomplished something considerably realer than anything I'd put my hand to in several months.

2. Like mosquitoes and other bloodsucking insects, blackflies first inject saliva into the wound, which contains an anticlotting factor that keeps the blood flowing until they've finished their meal. Unlike mosquitoes, but like deer- and horseflies, blackflies do not insert a siphon into the flesh, but instead bite out a little hunk of it, then drink the blood that accumulates in the resulting hole. The mean little bastards.

I am not by nature a maintainer, despite a good deal of training in that regard. I've been advised plenty of times, for example, to drain the water heater regularly to prevent the accumulation of sediment, but have never done it; as a consequence I've replaced at least one water heater in every house I've lived in over the past forty-five years. I'll oil a squeaky door, though, and sharpen knives—dull knives make me crazy. I follow the automobile-maintenance schedules. I *believe* in maintenance, I just don't get around to it. The tractor demands it, though, and part of me relishes the task. It's one of the last things around here that electronics haven't corrupted. It isn't a sealed black box, something you just replace. You don't unplug the old one and throw it away when it's on the fritz. Fixing up the tractor is a way of trying to hang on to a small piece of the Machine Age.

I always forget, over the winter, how I did the tractor maintenance last time. I really ought to review the procedure and come up with a less taxing future scheme, instead of just blundering and bludgeoning my way through it. Bludgeon I did, though, even if at about one quarter my habitual pace. This time, actually, I took a perverse pleasure in slowing down. Aging *is* a matter of pace, I kept reminding myself: pace versus duration. You spend your energy more slowly in order to make it last longer. You also notice more clearly when you have come to the end of it—and you will come to the end of it, no matter how slowly you pay it out.

Anthropologist Turnbull's fantasy about work as whatever one happens to be doing at the time seems worth trying to achieve. There is another sense of the word that is similarly cheerful. Work, says the dictionary, is the transference of energy produced by the motion of the point of application of a force. I can't quite get my mind around

that—the language ought to be able to do better with such a subject—but I think I get the idea. Push on something—or pull—and
if it moves, that was work. If it doesn't budge, it was merely effort.

In this sense—call it Turnbullian—lifting a champagne glass to
your lips is work. So is stepping into a hot bath. Movement in response to force. Add time to the measurement and the result is
"power." These quantifications are in no way moral.

I find such definitions deeply comforting. Somehow in my bringing up I was taught quite another definition: work was to be got out
of. Work was our punishment for being born, being alive, and only
suckers even attempted to expiate that sin. Work was to be kept to
a minimum, done as little of as possible, dodged, shifted off onto
others. And, if all else failed, done in the quickest, easiest, least
energy-taxing way possible.

It wasn't entirely my parents who were responsible for this per-
version. They set chores and expected them to be accomplished,
but that was work as duty, not punishment. Perhaps it was the
school system, which persisted in laying on empty drills and exercises long after we'd gotten the concept, when the willing part of
our attention had gone on to other matters. Teachers demanded the
copying down of things, the making of lists, the filling of pages. It
was the same in anything else that adults organized for kids. It was
not a scam we could ever have articulated, but we recognized it
clearly enough, in our not-so-innocent little hearts: *they were keeping
us busy.* If left to our own devices, whatever we would busy ourselves with would obviously be wasteful, destructive, violent, or
sinful. We were being kept in line.

On the other hand, work was, always, to be taken full credit for.
Verisimilitude—the appearance of working—was therefore desir-
able. I can still remember the embarrassment I felt at seeing work-
ers spring to their feet and try to appear busy when the boss showed
up. Furthermore, work's *result,* in actual product—acres plowed,

bushels harvested, cords stacked—was the ultimate value, worth far more than the money it might bring. I suppose my attitude toward wealth got twisted at the same time as it did toward work.

As a result of all this training, inappropriate or not, I guess I'd come to think of retirement as the end of work: the final reward. With such an attitude it was silly of me not to arrange its possibility, but I could never stand the kind of jobs that would earn it; failed miserably at becoming what the Japanese call a salaryman. However, since in both the Turnbullian and the physiological senses there will never be an end to work, retirement is impossible anyway. It's as foolish a dream as "security," or that other well-known oxymoron, enough money.

Here is another aspect of the sitting-still problem. Chris and I regularly swear we will adopt as a firm routine the practice of stopping "work" once an hour to, oh, walk around the house three times, or some other such silly ritual. Whatever gets us up and moving. She suggests I hang a sign on my computer: MOVE, STUPID. By "work" we mean sitting at our desks, concentrating hard at solving some problem or other with words. Which, in the physical, or Turnbullian, sense is hardly work at all, words being fairly light objects that we never have to move very far.

To be faced now with the sitting-still problem is something of a parody on my adolescent determination to escape manual labor. I tried scut work and didn't like it one bit, so I always chose a course, or courses, aimed at avoiding it. Those courses—journalism, editing, ad-writing—naturally made me more or less crazy. And then, another parody, in near dotage I began athletic competition. What that parodies is manual labor itself, being an exploration of how hard, exactly, you can use yourself and escape injury.

The greatest pleasure in grandparenthood so far is watching toddlers solve the physical problems of the world: walking, moving heavy objects, putting things where they want them to be. They go at it so seriously, so intently, with such burning concentration. They are learning to work the world. It's very reassuring to watch. It is confirming. One might as well get one's pleasure from making things work, the other forms of gratification—making money, wielding power, seeking acclaim—having by a certain age revealed their painful components. Working the world also has a pain component or two, but with care it is entirely self-referential, a closed circle, so minimal harm is done. Minimal harm, maximum gratification, that's the ticket. (Sounds a bit like victimless crime, but let us not distract ourselves.) The curious thing is the satisfaction in working the world, getting a result. It is a satisfaction that doesn't wear out. The nerve endings, as you get older, just get rubbed raw a little earlier. The trick is to learn to quit early, or earlier. It is very hard. But then it always was, wasn't it, learning when to quit?

How badly I was introduced to the concept of work doesn't hold a candle to how badly I was introduced to religion.

By May the birds were definitely back, the young of the year emerging, parents and young everywhere you looked, teaching, learning: bluebirds, tree swallows, bobolinks. A lot of dazed-looking juveniles and their rather distracted forebears, who appeared to want to get on with things. Do *what*? the young seemed to be asking their parents. Are you *crazy*?

A few years ago we quit haying our fields in early summer, in order to protect the bobolinks that nest there, so in May we are surrounded by a lot of tall grass, early seed heads bobbing, greenness everywhere. Grapes were now visible on the deck trellis, in tight little bunches about the size of poppy seeds. Everything was fully leafed out, many of the blossoms gone by: full green fecundity. Birds had incubated, hatched, fledged, the sky now full of baby fliers. The cats were mere transients, wandering home an hour after dawn to scarf down a couple of cans of cat food and sleep, poleaxed, until late afternoon and time for the next expedition. The dog just slept. The first act of the evening's entertainment was usually tree swallows over the pond, followed by thunderstorms for a second act, and a long, slow, rapturous descent into evening silence for the third. From the pond on one such evening came the sound of a frog croaking piteously in the twilight; "Green veiner," said C.

The thing about Thoreau is what for lack of a better word one has to call wisdom. There is a great deal of it in his writing, however silly, or grumpy, he is around its edges. Or at least it's always struck me as wisdom, at whatever age I've read it. Despite my always wavering loyalty, I've ended up taking his advice, or rather trying to take his advice, all my life.

I suppose that as you age your thirst for wisdom grows. No matter how well things go, enough bad is happening to you that you need some wisdom to salt it with, to make it more palatable. I certainly hunger for it. There's no evidence that age is going to make me wise, but it certainly increases my appetite, my need for wisdom.

Thoreau never shrank from giving advice, even if it was secretly for himself. "Do a little more of that work which you have sometime confessed to be good, which you feel that society and your justest judge rightly demands of you," he wrote to his friend Blake:

> Do what you reprove yourself for not doing. Know that you
> are neither satisfied nor dissatisfied with yourself without rea-
> son. Let me say to you and to myself in one breath, Cultivate
> the tree which you have found to bear fruit in your soil. Re-

gard not your past failures nor successes. All the past is equally a failure and a success; it is a success in as much as it offers you the present opportunity. . . . If you can drive a nail and have any nails to drive, drive them. If you have any experiments you would like to try, try them; now's your chance. . . . Do not eat unless you are hungry; there's no need of it. Do not read the newspapers. . . . As for health, consider yourself well, and mind your business. Who knows but you are dead already? Do not stop to be scared yet; there are more terrible things to come, and ever to come. Men die of fright and live of confidence. . . . Do not engage to find things as you think they are. Do what nobody can do for you. Omit to do everything else.

The winter's snowplowing had removed most of the gravel from our driveway and deposited it in a pair of parallel eskers, thirty yards long and a foot high, sinuously tracing the driveway's borders. They had been making me crazy all spring, needing to be knocked down, their gravel contents spread back on the driveway proper. On the next decent day, blackflies notwithstanding, I got out shovel and rake and attacked them.

I couldn't find work gloves, and my winter-softened hands wouldn't get a grip on either tool. Feeling a weird nostalgia—probably from old movies—I spat on my hands. That worked just fine, although it produced blisters within about fifteen minutes. I got the job done with no other ill effects. With it came a truly strange realization: it was the first time in memory I'd actually spat on my hands. In sixty-four years. How bizarre. Push up your sleeves, spit on your hands, get to work. The feeling was almost folkloric.

Then I walked the loop, drove to Greenfield for lunch with Willy, and came home and mowed the lawn: no nap, full-strength all day long, not a murmur of protest from any physical systems (except for blisters). Stayed up past 9:30, slept seven hours, awoke raring to go again the next morning. It occurred to me then that I might be okay after all. I'd be allowed to start swimming again in eleven more days.

Psychologist Mihaly Csikszentmihalyi points out, in *Flow:The Psychology of Optimal Experience,* that people are happier working than at leisure, happier with friends than with family, happier sometimes even in discomfort than in comfort.There's a clue here somewhere.

Anyway, a certain smugness factor seemed to be setting in. Spring had a lot to do with it.That night Chris suggested a new message for the answering machine: "Sorry, but we're being actively happy right now, and your call might interrupt that. If you want to leave a message, push *OFF.*"

Thoreau's journal, May 29, 1853: "Bathing has begun."

JUNE: *A Little Song, a Little Dance,*
a Little Seltzer down Your Pants

"I hear the note of a bobolink concealed in the top of an apple-tree behind me," Thoreau wrote on June 1, 1857. "He is just touching the strings of his theorbo, his glassichord, his water organ, and one or two notes globe themselves and fall in liquid bubbles from his tuning throat. It is as if he touched his harp within a vase of liquid melody, and when he lifted it out the notes fell like bubbles from the trembling strings. Methinks they are the most liquidly sweet and melodious sounds I ever heard."

Which is the reason we stopped haying our fields in early summer.

"That ought to be very good for you," said Dr. Z, when I asked permission to resume swimming. I considered kissing his hand.

It was my ten-week checkup, the end of the hard-collar regime. I saw my X rays for the first time: less bone in the implant than I'd pictured, not quite where I expected to see it. I was still having a bit of trouble swallowing, which Dr. Z assured me would clear up. (It did.) I had no pain to speak of, although I was still cautious about movement of my head. He seemed pleased with my range of motion to right and left, and told me that craning my neck backward, to look up, would be slowest to come. The visit was reassuring but somehow disappointing. I wanted more guidance, how to get better quicker. He seemed to feel things were coming along just fine.

Freedom day would be June 4, seventy days postsurgery. The thermometer dropped to 35 degrees the night before, the miserable raw, cold, wet gray spring refusing to let up, but I rose at dawn, ritualistically packed my kit, and drove to the pool for the first time since January for a re-inaugural swim. I was early, and sat quietly in my car, meditating on what had had to transpire for me to resume this practice, anticipating the pleasure to come. No one else showed up. After a while I tried the pool door, which had a small sign on it, CLOSED FOR REPAIRS, COME BACK TOMORROW. I went home and walked the loop.

The next day, however, I would swim a very slow five hundred yards, my crawl stroke so sluggish that I was being lapped by fat ladies with kickboards. It felt wonderful. That evening, after an immoderate dinner, I was overtaken by a great, euphoric rush of well-being, of reinhabiting my body. It was as if my head were now suddenly, finally, back in place on my neck. That this purely subjective surge came approximately twelve hours after I'd resumed swimming was almost spooky.

It was not a mystical experience but a physiological one, I thought at the time, and swimming probably had little to do with it. There is a concept in work physiology that improvement runs on an approximate twenty-one-day cycle. You are always in shape for the life you're living, say the physiologists; if you want to do a little more, more is exactly what you have to do. You have to enlist the training effect. Bump up your level of activity a notch and you'll begin to gain capacity; you'll continue to do so for twenty-one days, at which point you're trained up to the new level of effort, and the rate of gain slacks off to zero. If you want to continue to improve, says this principle, you have to bump up the workload another notch.

In a peculiar way, what that means is that you're actually in shape not so much for what you're doing as for what you did ten and a half days before. Rounding this off for convenience, I looked back in my journal to see what I'd done eleven days before. That was the day I spat on my hands and grabbed tools. I loved that piece of information. I was exaggerating the effect, of course. I had not maintained that level of workload in the intervening time. I'd done nothing programmatic, had carried out no sustained push. I had, however, become generally more active day by day. The euphoria of healing seemed to demand it. I contemplated with pleasure what I might be ready for in eleven more days.

Writing and editing, as Chris and I do, is a painstaking business. We are both meticulous, if about different things. Chris has more capacity for meticulousness than I. She concentrates better. Meticulousness is a synonym for concentration. You concentrate on something, usually, to do it as well as you can. As well as you can is only a different, gentler version of as hard as you can. It's a worthwhile substitution to make as you get older. There are few greater pleasures than doing something as well as you can.

But therein lies one of aging's sadnesses: the things that you're still able to do as well as you can begin to be circumscribed by pure physical limitations. Physiology again. That the legs go first is one of the

older athletic clichés. It is specifically true for athletes, and metaphorically true for the rest of us, substituting whatever function you
need most for the word "legs." No, "need" isn't quite true either—
you need to breathe more than you need to walk—but that's the way
it feels. This may be the origin of the saying "God'll getcha."

One psychological reason for being meticulous is that trying to
do something exactly right holds off demons. This also is not mystical. You have to think hard about what you're doing to do it exactly
right, or as nearly right as possible. Thinking hard gives you a vacation from the demons—the distracting thoughts and worries—that
would otherwise be plaguing you.

Maybe that's where the lust for control comes from: to be able to
do something with real precision every once in a while. Anything:
sing, hit golf shots, whatever. The controlling itself gives as much
pleasure as the result. Control is a lust that grows with age, as it
tries to slip away. You allow yourself a little sloppiness when you're
younger, perhaps assuming you have time to learn to do things better. You'll be more careful later. When precision begins to fade—
from failures of hand or eye—a small panic sets in. The urge to get
it back is overwhelming. This leads to a certain amount of perseveration. Throwing up your hands and walking away in exasperation is
easier when you're young. As you get older you don't abandon any
skill lightly. Just as you begin to feel you've earned the right, by seniority, to say the hell with things, you start also feeling a stab of loss
at each thing you say the hell with.

In June we hit bottom in one of our periodic bouts with insol-
vency. We were owed for work done, but the checks kept not arriving, not arriving. It's one of the freelance's occupational hazards, or
as we Wobblies like to say, how big business likes to balance its
books on the backs of the peasantry. Pieces of paper keep arriving in
the wrong order. Chris says it's all a matter of tense.

When this inconvenience gets particularly maddening, we like to remind ourselves that we are wealthy almost half the time. Every evening, as we talk our way through cocktails, dinner prep, and the meal itself, we generate big ideas. A notion for another book, invention of a badly needed kitchen gadget, a line of bumper stickers. Foot glue, for example, that was a recent one: a product that would let you glue a light, flexible, protective shoe sole directly to the bottom of the foot, as the ultimate sandal. Lightweight, cool, and, look, pebbles then wouldn't get caught between the footware and the bottom of your feet! You'd never get a rock in your shoe!

Sometimes these are, clearly, million-dollar ideas. Those are very enjoyable. We are rich from the moment one presents itself until the next morning, when we have to return to the real world of five-dollar ideas. Thus we are given an evening of rolling in wealth, worries about the future banished, and a good night's sleep. This adds up. It's almost half a day, almost every day, of comfortable wealth, for at least a few hours of which we are even conscious. And while we never get to spend the money, we also never have to do any of the work to make the idea pay off. All conception, no execution: what more could anyone want?

Cool weather had not stopped the greenery from sprouting, and as warming gradually set in it positively exploded. I began hacking away at it. Halfway through June's first lawn mowing, on a muggy afternoon, the tractor chose to die stone-dead a hundred yards from my tools, not to mention from shade or shelter from the blackflies. Couldn't be pushed; I either had to go borrow Willy's four-wheel-drive pickup to haul it back to the house, or had to fix it where it stalled. Fixing it required more disassembly than I liked to contemplate, but there wasn't much choice.

There ensued an hour's steady cursing, as I fetched tools and applied them nervously to hot metal parts, pursuing an obvious electrical failure deeper and deeper into the machine's entrails. Didn't actually find it, or at least didn't recognize it if I did, but after cleaning everything and putting it all back together again it worked just fine. A mystery. Finished the mowing at 6:25, dinner guests arriving—with a fir sapling as a gift—while I was putting the tractor away. They planted the tree while I was still in the shower, and suffered more blackfly damage than I did.[1]

The hour's cursing was followed by hours of smug self-satisfaction: a good start on the greenery encroachment, out there in the real world; a significant new botheration overcome, if not by brilliant insight then at least by dogged attentiveness; a tight schedule, however artificially so, adhered to. I could be a competent person still. It was enough to make me start looking around at things beyond my desk and saying hey, I can do that.

My handwriting improved.

"Like overtasked schoolboys, all my members and nerves and sinews petition Thought for a recess, and my very thigh-bones itch to slip away from under me, and run and join the mêlée," wrote Thoreau in 1841. "I exult in stark inanity, leering on nature and the soul. We think the gods reveal themselves only to sedate and musing gentlemen. But not so; the buffoon in the midst of his antics catches unobserved glimpses, which he treasures for the lonely hour. When I have been playing tomfool, I have been driven to exchange the old for a more liberal and catholic philosophy." Of course he was only twenty-three at the time.

---

1. As New Englanders come to know, the first blackfly bites of the season are virulent, sending raging torrents of itching coursing along the veins deep into the armpits and groin. That's groin, not loin. After half a dozen such physiological insults, however, one becomes almost immune. The bite leaves a welt, or, as they say in Texas, a whelp, and the blood trickles down, but it stops itching after twenty minutes or so, and if you can avoid scratching the top off so it becomes infected, it clears right up. What we have here is the wisdom of age.

Enough pieces of paper did arrive to allow me to buy lumber and hardware for the new dock, plus assorted paints and materials for a general sprucing up of the place. We painted, cleared brush, restored and mulched winter-ravaged flower beds. The bugs let up sufficiently that we began clocking serious deck time. After the long cold spring we finally began getting summer weekends, and made the most of them; the pond became warm enough for a quick plunge, although lolling wasn't yet on. I put away socks for the duration.

What I enjoyed most, bugs permitting, was sunbathing in the early evenings, when the sun was sufficient to heat cold bones but not to burn tissue-thin skin. I swore I could feel the winter skin begin to heal, relaxing metaphorical sphincters that had been clenched since the previous October. I'm not immune to the skin-cancer scare—I've been relieved of some small ones, having abused my skin lifeguarding in Texas sun in my youth—but being now both old and skinny, I crave sun more than I fear cancer. I accept the tradeoff. What the heck—statistically speaking, this skin has to last only another fifteen years anyway.

Baking in the evening sun, I notice I'm considerably bonier than a year ago. I haven't lost significant weight but I'm knobbier, more angular; my bones feel sharper, as if they want to poke through the flesh. It is vaguely startling, in a peculiar sense the most vivid glimpse of aging yet. It's another version of the change of dimension, of center of mass and the angles of joints, that makes aging like adolescence turned upside down. It's surely one source, along with sheer loss of strength, of geriatric clumsiness. Even my teeth are realigning themselves, making me learn other ways to chew.

It makes me realize how body-oriented—okay, body-obsessed—I've been all my life. The amusements I chose when younger—

swimming, diving, skiing, even car racing—were simply more ways of pleasuring that body. Cars and skiing in particular were ways of playing with the forces of gravity on the body, purely for sensual pleasure. It's why I began writing about physiology, trying to understand it: maybe there were ways to use my body more enjoyably.

I lie in the sun, wanting to go for a swim but resisting. Perhaps it will be too cold on my now toasty skin. I cinch up my resolution, walk on down to the pond and plunge in, glide and surface, and find its chilliness delightful. As I turn back for the dock a voice in my head whispers, "*Not* too old."

The solstice came on a Friday, dawning sultry. It was dock-building day. We'd planned a three-day solstice celebration—a private one— which would be highlighted, according to the forecast, by very hot, humid weather. By chance, or God's own showmanship, the solstice coincided with a full moon. Think of it: maximum light on the shortest night of the year, followed by maximum light on the longest day. Light and more light. I popped awake at 4:15, unable to get back to sleep for designing dock details in my head.

Years before, I'd built two docks in the pond, fifty meters apart to allow swimming laps between them. They had been badly designed, and after a few years sank to the bottom, irretrievable. Thereafter, for access to the pond, you waded in, knee-deep, on a submerged dock's ultraslick surface. This was unsatisfactory. For pilings, however, I'd used good sound pipe driven well into the bottom mud, which gave me a useful foundation on which to rebuild. We now used only one dock, out of convenience and custom, so I wouldn't need to replace both. The useful one would be eighteen feet long, four feet wide, standing in about four feet of water.

Mike had just finished refurbishing a utility trailer, replacing wood and rusted hardware, making it all shipshape again, and had written a glowing letter about the process: "Forty-eight delicious hours when the cares of the real world could be set aside to a higher purpose. Several hours of just looking at the sagging beast, in diagnosis of where the unaccustomed stresses had impacted the structure, and thoughtful evaluation of what might be required to effect a fix. . . ." He'd spent two days immersed in nuts and bolts, angles calculated, parts fitted, joints joined. I was insanely jealous.

Now I had my own very similar project at hand, and precisely the right frame of mind for accomplishing it. There followed four days of the most rewarding labor in living memory—four days, in effect, of nothing but spatial relationships: measuring, fitting, solving small problems. Solutions that were actually possible and could actually be made to work. Four days of standing crotch-deep in a cool pond in glorious summer sun, the sky aswirl with birds, the surrounding woods alive with action and growth. Full foliage, full birdlife, full greenery. Full summer. Outdoors, after a winter in jail.

Not exactly brain surgery: cross-members bolted to the pilings, stringers joining them and outlining the frame, planking for the entire assembly; 4x4s and 2x6s and bolts and lag screws. It was hard work, cutting to measure at the house and then schlepping the cut lumber—and several thousand small tools—the fifty yards to the pond to see if it fit. And back again, and back again. My carpentry is to real carpentry as pidgin English is to Shakespeare—me cut long fellow board nail somewhere mebbe not too short—but this time I'd located a supply of patience. Perhaps it was the surgery and attendant recovery period.

A lot of stooping and bending was required, and using small muscles for unaccustomed tasks. I got sore, banged myself up, here and there scraped my integument and bled a bit. What with climbing in and out of the water all day long, it was more practical, not to mention congenial, to wear as little as possible, even if hard on the skin.

I'd be tired enough by midafternoon to down tools and knock off for the day, which led inevitably to the invention of the No-Pants Cocktail Party (attendance limited to two).

It was that wonderful oxymoron, hard work as deep rest. I'd never understood so clearly how that kind of work uses a part of your mind totally different from what you use at your desk. (And in this case it resulted in a more satisfying finished product than some of my writings.) As a species we have come up with many devices for getting into the present tense—meditation, sports, large out-door experiences, even stretching exercises. (Never seems to hap-pen at a computer screen, does it?) These practices give the mind a rest. Your mind, strangely, doesn't *want* to rest. Perhaps it's the mind's preference not to rest that makes the computer screen so ad-dictive. Some people find giving the mind a rest to be frightening. Woody (Nature-and-I-are-two) Allen comes to mind.

It was a four-day rather than a three-day weekend because I worked too slowly, loving every minute of it as I did, and needed an extra day to get the dock done. When it was finished the best three months of the year still lay ahead of us.

"The Bermudians are hoping soon to have telegraphic communi-cation with the world," wrote Mark Twain, in "Some Rambling Notes." "But even after they shall have acquired this curse, it will still be a good country to go to for a vacation; for there are charm-ing little islets scattered about the inclosed sea where one could live secure from interruption. The telegraph boy would have to come in a boat, and one could easily kill him while he was making his land-ing."

Along about day four I did run right out of hammer strokes. It was during the final planking, all the interesting problems solved, nothing to do but cut boards to length, carry them down to the pond, and nail them in place. Four nails per board, fifty-five boards: for a real carpenter perhaps a couple of hours' work, but after about fifteen boards I hit the wall. My hammer strokes became more and more inaccurate—bouncing sideways off the nailheads, smashing dimples into the adjacent wood surface—and finally dragged to a halt. Finish this tomorrow, said my aching forearm.

It is not so surprising, as one gets older, to run out of the strength to complete a task. Strength is muscle, and we do lose muscle as we age—although whether the loss is a cause or a consequence of re-duced activity is up for grabs, as usual. Masters athletes, who con-tinue to train hard, lose strength more slowly, but lose it nonetheless. We lose grip strength. (Testosterone-replacement therapy may retard this loss in elderly men. Insert your own joke here.) Our muscles hang on to endurance better than they do to sheer strength. The largest losses are among the largest and fastest-working muscles, and most obvious at higher speeds of contraction. We lose more in the way of power than in strength.

Whatever the latter is: in tests individuals vary as much as 10 per-cent per day, irrespective of age. Psychological state seems to have a great deal to do with how much strength you can bring to bear. Low readings can come from unfamiliarity with the test devices, poor coordination, fear of injury. A good bit of the gain in training programs may come from familiarization, from simply reminding the body how to make effort. Some tests of the elderly show mys-terious improvement, which researchers suspect may come not from more strength but from loss of sensitivity in the hands, allow-ing the subject to handle the weights with less pain. Or less fear, same thing.

The aging muscle is stiffer at rest as well as in action, in part be-cause of structural changes, in part because the chemical transactions that make it work are slowed. We lose in the electrics as well as in the chemics: nerve conductance slows, and we are no longer as good at firing the muscle at will. We begin to lose that interesting capacity of the mind to tell which muscle to work and when.

Running out of hammer strokes was a result first of tying up with lactic acid, and second a pipsqueak, one-arm version of the marathoner's wall, the physiological lockup that hits the underprepared runner at about the twentieth mile. This is usually explained as running out of glycogen, the fuel the muscle runs on, but it might better be understood as running out of motor units. A motor unit is one motor nerve plus all the muscle fibers it branches into: as few as four or five fibers in, for example, the eye, as many as several hundred in the thigh. You contract a muscle by sending a message to its motor units. They will continue firing as long as they have fuel, are not injured, and are not choked with lactic acid and other wastes. Viable motor units are thus the currency of muscular effort; once fully spent with fatigue they shut down, temporarily unavailable for work. That's the wall you hit.

You never actually exhaust all your motor units, but only those you are accustomed to using. To keep going when you run out of viable motor units you must somehow find and recruit more, and just how we do that is one of physiology's sweeter mysteries.[2] The muscular movement that had been entirely automatic now must be willed. You don't do this by thinking about motor units, of course. In some unknowable part of the mind we hold a kind of personal library of available movement; we search through this and find something that vaguely resembles the moves we're in the process of losing. We try it; it sort of works; we continue for yet a while.

---

2. Fear, shock, stress may help: the legendary wisp of a housewife who lifts the burning car to free her baby is assumed to do so by somehow recruiting all her motor units.

Not surprisingly, then, a great deal of athletic training is devoted directly to motor units. Training prepares the accustomed motor units to function more quickly or strongly, or to last longer before wearing out, but it also accustoms more motor units to the task, to improve their accessibility to voluntary control. Training reduces the strength of signal needed to fire a given motor unit. We train to learn *how* to reach down for a little more. One trains the motor units by exhausting them, over and over again, and letting them recover. Only the very determined spend much of their training time recruiting new ones. It is too painful, too far down the well of exhaustion.

As we get older, or more sedentary, we need to be reminded how to recruit them. When I began working on the dock I would carry one 2x6 at a time; after a couple of days I was carrying two, sometimes three. I hadn't gotten appreciably stronger, I'd only relearned how to work, which included how to recruit the motor units the task required. The boards didn't feel any lighter, just less awkward. That also made it easier to stop worrying about hurting myself— which probably is always a mistake.

I had to be reminded because although I was using nowhere near maximum strength, I had grown considerably weaker over the preceding year. We lose muscle fiber faster than we lose motor neurons, so with age each neuron fires fewer fibers. Our intention enlists fewer recruits. More important than that numerical loss, however, was weakness from losing contact, in effect, with the strength that remained. It's there but you can't use it, can't fire it, a curious version of impotence. This is why it is important, I think, to make oneself quite tired now and then. It's the only way we have of reestablishing contact with a part of our powers as a human being, a part that if not yet quite lost has at least been hidden away from us by age.

We once had an aged cat who when you picked her up would vibrate in your hand like an electric shaver gone berserk. It was not purring, it was a muscular tremor, from going rigid at the prospect of movement. In my mother's seventies I noticed that when I took her hand to help her rise from a chair I'd feel that same vibration, a kind of muscular singing through her arm as she tensed. It happened whenever she tried to exert extra force, the muscles simply no longer used to that kind of work.

One distressing thing that is slipping away as we age is our comfort zone: the part of the physical world that we operate unthinkingly, with ease and grace and efficiency. That sphere of activity begins to shrink as surely as our connective tissue does. When I began doing physical work after a winter of sitting still, I would sometimes feel that same singing in my own stringy musculature. I found it deeply embarrassing, somehow—if only to myself, since no one else could know it was happening. It was the single greatest stimulus to resuming heavy activity: it could be damped out again, I knew, with a little work. And so it was.

In one study, frail elderly who were given weight training increased their muscle strength by an average of 66 percent. This apparently reflected mainly improved coordination, the study went on to say, since no significant increase of lean body mass was seen. (Science always has to have something to measure.) This "finding" is surprising, since coordination can't be measured, and therefore is not a useful scientific term. As far as science is concerned, coordination is a sort of gift from God. Perhaps it would be better to credit the improvement to muscular focus. That's what we oldsters must train for: usefulness; efficacy; the ability to bring muscle to bear. The problem isn't that you no longer have anything to bring, it's that you can't find it to bring it. You can't recruit it. You have to practice recruitment. In fact, that's specifically how practice works: without it you forget where those motor units are. You forget their location, their very address, in the computer sense of the term.

Motor units fascinate me so because they are accessible to the will. They are how the mind finds the muscle. Muscle is function. As I keep insisting, the only bad thing about aging is loss of function. We can resist aging, if we choose to resist it, on one level by improving our habits, by living healthier lives and all that. Those methods are largely preventive, however, before the fact: promises from the experts, a.k.a. pie in the sky.

The motor unit—the unit of muscular effort—gives you a way of putting your shoulder directly to the wheel of age—if not to roll it back, then at least to slow its progress. As one can rehab a knee injury, one can, with deliberate movement, rehab the injury known as age. Or at least that's the fitness-nut's argument.

As June's euphoria settled in, seemingly for a long stay, it occurred to me that aging is rather like being about one-tenth blind. Your vision may come back to 20-20—mine would, inexplicably, over the next couple of years—but there's a reduction in your peripheral vision, in speed of uptake, an increase in the time it takes for a new image to come clear. The same is going on with your hearing and the other senses. Until you take in the incoming message clearly you're a little confused, a little befuddled. It's like being a little bit drunk, a little sore in all the joints and muscles.

That's the disappointing news: you can get back a good deal of your strength and other gross categories of function, but you're going to lose the fine little edges, the connections, the interrelations. You get back the specifics but not the generalizations that connect them. On the other hand, with their loss you begin to understand better what the interrelations really are (or were). With conscious thought—and the confidence to take your time, which also accumulates with age—you can come to understand these things perhaps better than you ever did before in your life. But you can't pick them up in the moment. This makes you increasingly enamored of, or wistful for, time to mull, to think things over, to put them into place. To rank order, to assess, to weigh—when all your previous life you've thrived on rapid response.

A jock metaphor is irresistible: in a sense it's like being shifted from quarterback to coach. The player has to make the decision while the play is going on; the coach has to make the decision before the play starts. Becoming the coach, becoming a little older, just builds a little lag time into the process. (Your answers are supposed to be better—wiser—than the quarterback's; that's why they made you coach.) Successful aging requires screwing up your acuity so you don't need as much lag time. See old comedians, stepping on each other's lines: so much is implied by quickness of response. What it says is *youth.*

In the last thirty years we've put more and more emphasis on maintaining aerobic function, even in the very old. Now we're learning that maintenance of strength and flexibility (or, preferably, their increase) is equally important in holding on to volitional bodily function—and even, perhaps most important, cognitive function.

I can always use more of that, I think, stepping up my juggling practice. I'd been juggling for a few minutes each day before sitting down to my desk, thinking of it as a kind of wake-up call to my nerve endings—a loosen-upper, like the dancer's *barre.* Now when I run into a writing problem, when I can't quite get my mind around what I'm trying to say, when concentration fades, I step away from my desk and pick up the juggling balls. Clears the mind; answers tend to pop up.

I juggle until I've made a thousand passes, however many misses occur along the way. Occasionally I will make my thousand without a miss, but usually two or three restarts are necessary. The routine has taught me that I am a choke-artist: if I don't miss beforehand I will do so at 997, 999; as I get into the last twenty or so passes before the thousandth I tense up, get jerky, lose rhythm. I try to calm myself down, relax, go back to the easy-peasy flip-flop rhythm that got me through the first eight hundred or so, but cannot. I choke. Suddenly I am struggling like a fat man trying to get out of a wet suit. It's easier when there's music playing in the background. Rhythm, externally applied, seems to help.

A thousand passes, misses included, takes five to ten minutes, a longer break than I'd need to smoke a cigarette, which I used to do for much the same purpose. Juggling is considerably more satisfactory. By the time I return to my desk I've usually got a new handle on the problem that had me stopped.

Concentration also fades out and back in again as I juggle. It's interesting to watch that happen—which is one of the things that cause it to happen. Juggling is nothing more than pitching and catching. The misses occur on the catch. The best thing to think about, if you have to think about anything, is where you want the top of the arc of each pitch to be. You don't think "higher" or "lower" or "a little to the right," you just think of a spot in space, or look at the spot in space, where you want the ball to stop rising and start back down again. That's the only instruction your brain gives your hands, that imaginary spot, but your hands get it and act on it, throwing to it. All the practice is just to make them better at that. If the ball goes to the spot, it will be easy to catch. Your brain also instructs your hands where to make the catch, but the catching itself is almost subliminal, too automatic for instructions to apply. There isn't time. That's why that's where the misses are. Actually, the catch is the only place you *can* miss, even if your throw is wildly out of reach.

I have no idea whether this stupid little ritual had any effect on cognitive function at all, but I like to credit it with the recovery of my handwriting. It was probably more important as a minibreak, though, a way of keeping the hands and muscles busy while the mind is turned free. The mindfulness folks would have us surf the moment, and I wish I could do that better than I do, but when it's time to get my work done, staying in the moment is downright counterproductive. To notice how one's fingers work the keyboard, and how the little images march across the screen, puts a dead stop to cognitive function. Playing with juggling balls gave me some of the better thinking time of the day. Still does. [3]

I always wished Thoreau had been less reticent about the physical side of his life. In the journals he tells you what the weather was, whether he wore a thick coat or a thin one, when his boots got wet, but not much else, and not how any of that felt. You get no more detail of his physical life than you do of his sexuality. (Scholars naturally have combed him raw trying to dope out the latter. Freudians

---

3. Despite this endorsement, I can't help regarding the subject of juggling as a bit, well, silly. I was surprised, then, to learn that it has been the subject of at least one Ph.D. thesis, by Howard Austin at MIT. I learned this from *The Hand,* by Frank R. Wilson (New York: Pantheon, 1998). Maybe not so silly: "Juggling," Wilson points out, "with the considerable help of [master jugglers] Serge Percelly . . . and Marc Jeannerod, has taken us directly to the frontiers of research in neuroscience. It also confronts us with a premise about human learning that is so deeply embedded in educational theory and practice that it is almost never critically examined. It asks us to question the premise that intelligence is a purely mental phenomenon, that the mind can be educated without the participation of the body. Learning how to juggle . . . challenges the mind body dichotomy in an extremely interesting way."

would have him a mother-fixated, repressed homosexual. On a conscious level, even in his journals, he does come across as a fairly wretched prude: "The glory of the world is seen only by a chaste mind," and like that.)

I began a search of my own through the journals, although hardly of scholarly thoroughness, looking for acknowledgment or even awareness of his own physicality. When I did I discovered I hadn't been paying attention: with that specific goal in mind, some of his journal entries are a bit startling. "I never feel that I am inspired unless my body is also," he wrote in June of 1840. "It too spurns a tame and commonplace life. They are fatally mistaken who think, while they strive with their minds, that they may suffer their bodies to stagnate in luxury or sloth. The body is the first proselyte the Soul makes. Our life is but the Soul made known by its fruits, the body." My point exactly.

He is most effusive on the subject of swimming, or, as he characterized it, bathing: "I bathe me in the river. I lie down where it is shallow, amid the weeds over its sandy bottom; but it seems shrunken and parched; I find it difficult to get *wet* through. I would fain be the channel of a mountain brook. I bathe, and in a few hours I bathe again, not remembering that I was wetted before. When I come to the river, I take off my clothes and carry them over, then bathe and wash off the mud and continue my walk. I would fain take rivers in my walks end wise."

Always the ecstatic resurfaces: "In youth, before I lost any of my senses, I can remember that I was all alive, and inhabited my body with inexpressible satisfaction; both its weariness and its refreshment were sweet to me," he wrote in July of 1851. "This earth was the most glorious musical instrument, and I was audience to its strains. To have such sweet impressions made on us, such ecstasies begotten of the breezes! I can remember how I was astonished. . . .

The morning and the evening were sweet to me, and I led a life aloof from the society of men. . . . For years I marched as to a music in comparison with which the military music of the streets is noise and discord. I was daily intoxicated, and yet no man could call me intemperate. With all your science can you tell how it is, and when it is, that light comes into the soul?"

Which was pretty much the way I was feeling in late June, lying in the warm sun and contemplating what turned out to be an entirely satisfactory dock.

JULY: *The Machine Age and Me*

> How short the nights! The last traces of day have not
> disappeared much before 10 o'clock, or perchance 9.30, and
> before 3 a.m. you see them again in the east . . . leaving about
> five hours of solid night, the sun so soon coming round again.
> —Thoreau's journal,
> July 4, 1852

I step out barefoot into the blue-gold light of a perfect summer dusk, wearing the lightest, softest clothing I own, Mozart swelling from the house to accompany me as I stroll out to the compost bin. Okay, I'm carrying wet garbage, but I almost waft across the lawn anyway, an unfamiliar feeling for a fumble-footed sixty-five-year-old (minus four months). The sensual pleasure is only partially disturbed by a buzz-bombing deerfly, reminding me of the reality principle. (I am *not* in a TV commercial.) The thought pops into my head unbidden that what I want for the rest of my life is a direct continuation of the previous ten days. More than ten days: it's been that way around here since the moment my head was securely returned to the top of my neck.

My skin, however, seemed to have gotten a lot thinner over the inactive winter, another of aging's little jokes. Carpentry in particular had a way of demonstrating this. I'd be working away, minding my own business, and suddenly find blood smears on tools and work, from some unnoticed cut or scrape. In her seventies my mother acquired a rather ill-advised new puppy, and would take it out for early-morning, housebreaking walks; she'd always return sopping up blood, the rambunctious puppy's needle-sharp teeth and claws having shredded the elderly skin of her arms and ankles. She didn't mind. I didn't care when I was carpentering, except where bloodstains marred the wood. It didn't hurt much. It didn't matter.

Beneath the skin I seemed to be nicked and dinged in the same way, the thinning out duplicated internally. The bags that contain the working parts, and the strings that connect them, had grown more fragile. When you resume a physically active life after a long layoff, I quickly discovered, the heart and lungs come around a lot sooner than joints and muscles; wind and guts respond fairly quickly, but the stuff you pound on in order to resume heavy activity comes along more slowly. You must wait for structural cells to catch up with metabolic ones, structures being slower to change than fluids and their delivery systems.

It's frustrating: the essential you is ready for more action than the equipment you act with will quite allow. It's as if you've stockpiled a nice new carload of energy but can't get it out of the storage shed. I also noticed it was taking me a good deal longer to warm up sufficiently at a task before I could begin applying much force, and that force had to be applied in gingerly fashion. When I swam my shoulders complained for the first ten minutes or so; then they felt fine, and swimming became the usual dance of pleasure.

Lovingly restored old cars are a delight to look at but seldom pleasant to drive. No matter how thoroughly the restoration work is done, the car feels sloppy and loose in its controls, harsh and noisy. Finding exactly the right replacement bushings and grommets for the running gear, the little rubber snubs and internal bumpers that take up the harshness of metal against metal, is virtually impossible. Frame, suspension, and steering have lost the shock-absorption quality that was originally engineered into them. Even if you do find the exact matches for these small rubber parts, they'll be old, dried out, oxidized. The metaphor is apt: with age your bushings go bad.

Otherwise July's long days and good weather afflicted me severely with the opposite of winter's sitting-still problem. I had a good deal of trouble sticking to my desk, popping up restlessly at regular intervals to go out and circle the place, looking for work. I replaced a disintegrating low brick wall with solid benches, another mesmerizing four-day project. I painted things. I began to understand why some old guys have such clean garages, although mine wasn't there yet. I contemplated getting things organized for the Dumpster, for when I finally got around to that project, envisioning elaborate staging areas, piles of this kind of junk here, that kind over there.

The curious part of this restlessness was the new, unexpected, totally unearned supply of patience that accompanied it. It reminded me of my model airplane days, cutting out hundreds of tiny parts and gluing up complex structures one stick at a time. In those days there were no instant-setting cyanoacrylates; you had to wait for the old-fashioned glue to dry. Eventually you learned how long that took, and found a working pace that accommodated the delay. I never considered that training to be character-building, but I've known mature adults who never got it, and suffer for the lack. I certainly lost it myself for several decades, and paid the price. Age— and a hard collar—seemed to have brought it back. Some of it back.

A great deal of that patience was required when I decided to go ahead and acquire E-mail. We had resisted going on-line for a long time, throwing up the usual Luddite arguments, but finally decided it might be useful for research. Besides, friends were nagging at us, telling us E-mail was the greatest boost to personal communication since the invention of consonants. Patience was especially required because I had to learn Windows first, only about a decade behind the rest of Western civilization. I can't prove that age causes hardening of the software-learning arteries, but that seemed to be the case with me. Quite a few more hours of cursing ensued; days, in fact.

Once I had access to the Web it proved useless for the kind of research I generally did, at least to the extent I learned to explore it, and I abandoned it quickly enough. E-mail took a little longer. It was fun at first, and did stimulate me to stay in closer touch with a lot of people I'd been neglecting. A lot of people who had been neglecting me stopped doing so, which proved not so ideal. I am unfortunately unable to let a phone go unanswered, and E-mail was worse. It began to eat my life. When a technological foul-up by my service provider temporarily shut off the flow, it was such a relief that I used it as the excuse I needed. I took perverse pleasure in writing a real note on real paper to each of my E-mail correspondents, putting an actual postage stamp on it, and dropping it into the mail: sorry, but I hereby leap off the electronic universe.

More eloquent ranters than myself have dumped all over the Cyber Age, and I'm embarrassed to add to the din, but we oldsters are aborigines, dazzled by cybertrinkets from the invading Netniks, and I fear some of them may be laced with smallpox. The Web was no doubt an awesome utility before it too was taken over by advertising. I prefer not to pay someone for trying to sell me things I don't want. I am sufficiently whelmed with matters at hand. You electronicized folks go right on talking to one another, I'll just try to catch up with what I've already got on my plate.

At which point a magazine asked me to go do a quick little solo overnight canoe trip and write it up. There *is* a God, I muttered, and had my gear packed within the hour. Then I realized I was going at it all wrong. They wanted a reflective piece on the pleasures of canoeing, and I was mounting a blitzkrieg. I'd want as much solitude as possible, and it was Friday, weekend crowds on the way. A minor cool front was due, the weather looking to improve by Sunday. Shifting gears, I unpacked the car. Restlessly.

On a sparkling Sunday morning, then, I sneaked quietly out of town, canoe on car, grin on face. Screw the Sunday *Times,* I said, I'm out of here—but languidly, languidly: I was determined that Languid Man would make this trip. The magazine had suggested I find an appropriate place in the Berkshires, but I knew of none sufficiently wild, and opted for the Adirondacks, three hours away. The waters would be similar but the wildlife more abundant: a lake's a lake, but some are more congenial—i.e., deserted—than others. Chris and I had once spent a wet night on a nice little one in the Cedar River Flow, and I'd wanted for some time to go back and get a look at the place in daylight and sunshine.

Languid Man took over the driving. I passed a field where radio-controlled model airplanes were being put through their paces, and stopped to watch for a bit. I hadn't seen what those guys were up to in twenty years, and was excited at first, then disappointed. They'd solved the technology too well; the aircraft were too perfect, their pilots too skilled. There was a model helicopter doing aerobatics, flying upside down and backward, doing outside loops, maneuvers impossible in the real thing.[1] Obviously one could now make a

---

1. Former helicopter-pilot Mike informs me that modern, rigid-rotor choppers *can* do loops and rolls.

model airplane do anything one wanted, so what was the point? It was exactly as interesting as special effects in a movie: okay, so they can make anything look like anything. Who wants to go see that?

There were half a dozen cars in the parking lot where I was to embark, including one huge RV whose owner was repairing the previous night's bear damage. He'd put his plastic bags of garbage on top of the vehicle; there was a ladder at the rear, which the bear had proceeded to climb while the occupants slept—well, not exactly *slept*—inside. My hope was that the other cars belonged to day-tripping fishermen who weren't occupying the limited number of campsites. Languid Man unloaded in only a moderate haze of blackflies, put canoe in water, stored gear. How about one whole day, I proposed to myself, of not trying to get more? Canoes are good for that. Or, rather, what they'll get you more of is wildness, solitude, distance *in:* more of what was there before you came along, just as it was before you came along. A canoe will get you more of less.

All I wanted was a nice spot to set up camp, swim, lie on some rocks in the sun. Swim some more. Watch a standard-issue glorious sunset, maybe paddle the perimeter by the scheduled full moon. The cool front had brought with it a whippy breeze, however, and I shoved off into a stiff chop—at which point Languid Man jumped ship. My single-seat canoe is a semi-racer, ill-suited for loads in a crosswind. Canoeing is a gentle enough pastime when you're not going anywhere much and in no hurry, but in the face of wind and waves, languor does not serve. I was in for a piece of work.

The first campsite was nice but too close to the put-in—still in sight of the bear-scarred RV. The second, where Chris and I had spent the sodden night, was taken, ditto the third, the fourth unacceptable on grounds of filth. I spied a possibility on the opposite shore, three quarters of a mile away, and crossed, struggling with incipient whitecaps: a binocular-borne illusion, no campsites on that side at all. I'd have to cross back. By then I was well into a second hour of paddling, and swimming/lolling time was dwindling. Besides, the lake was getting shallower and weedier, and, well, brown. I was hot and sweaty but found the water uninviting. This was not what I envisioned. What had gone wrong here?

The wildlife didn't seem to mind. An osprey circled overhead; a lone fawn grazed the shoreline, only moderately alarmed by my approach. Once when I pulled into the shelter of the lee shore an otter let me get within twenty yards before rolling off his log with a careless splash. I spotted a pair of loons with chick, a mother merganser towing a string of babies: not rare or exotic species but in remarkable abundance. Good sign. The paddling continued irritatingly difficult, but I did at one point pause in a pleasant cove, look around me, and feel a small impulse to stand up in my canoe, wave my paddle at the sky, and shout, "I'm *working!*"

I saw one other canoe—two fishermen a mile away—and no one else. (The next human form I would see would be at the takeout, on the way home.) Recrossing the pond once more I finally found a decent spot, unloaded, and set up camp, attempting to resuscitate Languid Man. (Denied a swim, he tends to pout.) The work of paddling is always followed immediately by the work of setting up camp; not hard work, but continuous. Labor-intensive. Just to get something to eat becomes part of the workload, and all chores are to be finished before you sleep. It adds a certain focus to the day. I soldiered on but still managed to stop and look up from time to time. A hummingbird worked a nearby bush as I arranged my gear, and every few minutes some waterfowl or other passed by, usually quacking. Farrah the Fawn resumed grazing half a mile away. When I snapped a piece of firewood too loudly she looked up sharply, then bolted—and two more deer emerged farther down the shoreline. I was getting my money's worth out of my binoculars.

A fickle sky swung back and forth from sun to cloud to sun, my mood swinging with it. Funny how it'll do that. I chastised myself for my impatience at the day, for its resistance to measuring up to my patently overblown expectations. Gradually the gray did break up, allowing color back into the world. I discovered you can't actually see as well during the sunny periods anyway, everything shimmering too much, vibrating too hard. At least at my age: I couldn't focus my eyes tightly enough to hold the world still.

The wind dropped, the surface quieted. Languid Man stripped and waded out on a sandy bottom to mid-thigh and quietly soaked for a few moments—not exactly a swim, but it left me thoroughly refreshed. (Would I do it again at dawn? In a word, no.) Farrah reappeared. Fish were rising. Getting there had required nothing the least bit heroic, but I was perhaps more conscious than usual that I was sixty-five years old (minus four months) and sitting on a point of land accessible only by boat, some miles from another human being. On my own; responsible for myself. I hadn't paddled a boat in eleven months, and was tired in my arms, shoulders, back, tired all over but pleasantly so. Not to ill effect. No problem with my neck, my winter frailness: obviously I could paddle again. Our planning for a summer of canoe trips could be resumed.

The stillness magnified itself, becoming so quiet I could hear my clothes when I breathed. I got my sunset. A still lake at evening, surrounded by forest, is about as large a dose of peace, volumetrically speaking, as one can possibly absorb. This, I couldn't help thinking, completes my healing.

Earlier I'd put up the tent, tossed stuff inside, and gone on to other matters. It was our old tent, not the new one with the offensive L. L. Bean logo. When I finally turned in for the night, I discovered a pair of Chris's socks hanging in the interior. She'd hung them to dry during the last night of our last trip of the previous season, and we'd overlooked them when we decamped. They'd been stored away in the folded tent all winter long. A little nosegay of dirty socks, as a reminder of her absence. Solo is good but not necessarily best.

Some kind of frogs set up a clicking murmur all night long, sounding like a pot simmering on the back of a stove. Among the things I did not think about were mortality, aging, and being alone at night in the wilderness. A soft rain pattered the tent about three. I slept well. That moonlight paddle had been romantic fantasy anyway.

Dawn was gray, damp, still. As I sat with my coffee a perseverating loon began playing with its own echo, as if fine-tuning its sound. Or maybe, I thought, he is genetically driven to answer any call, and gets locked into a cycle he can't break. He makes the mistake of blurting out that first yodel, the echo comes back, and he is stuck here all day long, vocalizing away. Just like E-mail. Finally—anthropomorphic suspicions confirmed—he yelped once more, then dived before the echo could get back to him, to great relief all around. Why did I assume he was male?

Languid Man paddled out, cruising the lake, tranquilized; the conditions, as gentle as the previous day's had been stiff, impelled it. A small rain down did rain, for a little while, but without wind I didn't mind a bit. Hat-pin reeds ticked against the hull as I wafted along in silver light, exploring other coves, dawdling, not wanting to reach the end of the lake. Ever. It's odd how one pushes against this physical beauty, attempting somehow to break through it, into . . . what? Some kind of acceptance, I think. As if you're trying to get into nature's pants: this time you're somehow going to *score,* to make Mother Nature devote herself entirely to the satisfaction of your personal pleasures. As with most seductions, it almost always goes the other way. And that turns out to have been worth it anyway, and you go back again, and again, eagerly. As Thoreau—among others—has pointed out, there's always a barrier to being pulled into nature, to gaining admittance to it. But a canoe will get you closer.

To resume wilderness canoeing requires a certain amount of simple hardening-off of the flesh at the outset of each new season. The skin of the hands, for instance. This is oxymoronish, since a reasonable purpose for going to the woods is in effect to resensitize yourself: to refresh your appreciation of the natural world's physical vividness. Too bad you have to benumb yourself to accomplish that. There's a tough-guy tradition in these woodsy activities that has always struck me as the most counterproductive bullshit, yet it is only by being a bit tough about it—willing at the very least to endure discomfort—that you can get there and have all those fine, sensitizing experiences.

Zen Buddhism, at least to my limited understanding, seeks enlightenment through frustration. This technique is best demonstrated by the basic Zen adage "When chopping wood, just chop wood; when hauling water, just haul water." It's a Zen joke: the human animal cannot do that. We will haul water and worry about our taxes, chop wood and argue with our bosses, indulge in sexual fantasies, look forward to dinner. To be instructed to just chop wood, to be told in effect that all peace and happiness come from doing that and nothing more, is deliberately to be frustrated with an impossible task. The instruction itself is a Zen koan.

Impossible or not, it's worth working toward. The best way to do so, at least for me, is to go outdoors and sustain myself for a while. It is perhaps forgivable to put a personal twist on the wood/water metaphor: head for water, go into the woods.

Chatting with the middle-aged farmer who was taking care of our fields, I complimented him on the energy with which his late-adolescent sons were putting up hay. Well yes, he said, but they drove him crazy sometimes. He himself preferred doing things once. He wasn't sure they understood that principle.

Age does stimulate your interest in conservation of energy, as in dealing with daily chores. Camping solo was a vivid demonstration. It's hard enough when Chris and I both go, and we share the work as equally as possible; by oneself the labor is effectively doubled. You load gear into the car and the canoe on top of it, unload again at the put-in and reload gear into your boat, paddle to your destination, unload again. You stow canoe, erect shelter, gather firewood, assemble kitchen, make fire, cook, eat, clean up, prepare bedding, sack out. Swimming and other entertainments are inserted into the lulls. You repeat the next day, but in reverse, and repeat again if you're moving to a new campsite. You are *busy*—although you will always find time, barring storminess, for some kind of woodsy vespers. Whatever one's ceremonial predilection.

Labor is what it is, pure labor, a curious category of energy expenditure. We seem to miss labor when we don't have it. It may hurt while we're doing it, we spend a lifetime trying to avoid or reduce it, but when we don't have it to do our lives go awry. It is affirming; it tells us we are here, we can have an effect, we matter. Proof of this is at least implied in the peculiar development that work gets sweeter as you get older. And the rest it purchases gets sweeter yet.

It has to be work that you can do without killing yourself, can finish, can enjoy the result of. The psychologist Mihaly Csikszentmihalyi, whose specialty is flow states, takes these requirements further. You must be able to concentrate on it while you're doing it. Its goal must be clear. It must be absorbing enough to erase, for a while, your ordinary worries. It must give you a sense of control, of your own actions if not of the larger world. It must temporarily erase your sense of self (although its result may boost that sense).

And it must alter your sense of time, either stretching it out or making it go faster. When it meets these conditions, says Csikszent-mihalyi, "enjoyment, rather than pleasure, becomes the main source of rewards."

That last simple statement, the switch from pleasure to enjoy-ment, gives me a small jolt of understanding. It's where I got mixed up as a kid. Leisure was also involved. Kids don't call it leisure, of course, but "play," by which they mean freedom. Maybe I still think it isn't work if it doesn't hurt, and my concern with physical effort is the product of guilt. After all, I can play all day if I want—sit on my arse and toy with my mind, i.e., words. Maybe my body is point-ing out to me that this, too, can get boring. Also, of course, there's not time enough left to do all I'd like to do with the body, never mind what I'd like to do with the mind. Now that I think of it, that attitude seems to assume that the mind continues, which I'm not at all sure I believe.

What the law considers an attractive nuisance is exemplified by an unfenced swimming pool. Thus the body, if not quite in the legal sense: sure, it gives considerable pleasure, but it takes a great deal of maintenance, and can get you into a load of trouble—particularly if you don't give it some work to do. Biologically, when the body is no longer able to feed itself—in the essential go-get-the-food-and-get-it-into-the-gob sense—it is time to die. If you aren't doing the work that gets the food, how do you know when your time is up?

One must not get ideological about this, but in the animal king-dom, it might be noted, it is only the domesticated varieties—the ones we feed—that get fat.

The magazine piece was a rush job, but the writing had to be post-poned for photography: a pro from New York was coming to shoot me in the act of paddling. Nothing in the piece would be specific to the lake I was on, so the Berkshires, as venue of choice, could be reestablished at this point. You don't think all that stuff in magazines really happens the way it looks, do you?

At five in the evening, with two canoes on my car, I met the photographer, Rob Howard, to go scout locations. Chris's little ten-and-a-half-foot single-seater made a perfect chase boat; Rob was an experienced paddler, so we could shoot anywhere we found decent water, from just about any viewpoint. I did know an undeveloped pond nearby, which proved so perfect that he insisted on shooting well into dusk, just as a kind of warm-up.

I gathered him again at daybreak, and spent the rest of the morning paddling back and forth and around and around in a wild pond while he attempted to steal my soul with his camera. We'd lucked into a windless, clear blue-sky day, the pond was purely beautiful, and I really enjoy paddling a canoe. So did he. Posing is a horrifying enterprise, but I didn't mind a bit paddling back and forth, following Rob's instructions but also ignoring him, while he skittered around in pursuit of proper angles. We finally quit in midmorning and came back to the house, where we had a swim while Chris dished out raspberries and cream, then split a rather immodest cheddar and mushroom omelet. That too was a working day. Who needs retirement?

Of course a bit of hardening off is necessary for reimmersion in urban life, too. I suppose I can still get toughened up enough to be able to take the city, if it's really required, or for some reason is worth it. It's a trade-off: you shut down sensitivity to the noxious and hope that doesn't also shut down the enjoyment part. These damn nerve endings of mine are shutting down of their own accord far too fast anyway. I'm not keen on abandoning any more of them than necessary. I think my city days are pretty much behind me.

"One of the delights known to age, and beyond the grasp of youth," as J. B. Priestley put it, "is that of Not Going."

Occasionally, on my overnight and also when I was paddling for the photographer, I found myself pulling back in my mind, as if into an imaginary spaceship, and getting a glimpse of the wriggling lump of meat that was me, drifting about down there on the water's surface. From a distance, even an imaginary one, it looked rather like part of the unfolding of a comic novel.

I wish I could remember to pull back that way more often. It illuminates the notion of soloing. Going out into the woods and spending a night by yourself is not about being alone but rather the opposite: escaping aloneness. You are only alone if you retain self-awareness; at the best of times soloing wipes that completely away. If no one else is there to be aware of you, you cease to exist as a separate self. It's a great relief.

"The writer's volume of accomplishment depends precisely on the ability to sit alone in a room," said Susan Sontag, but it never struck me that way. I am not that heroic. I'm not alone when I'm at my desk, pushing bits of light across the screen, trying to freeze moments in a different medium. I'm not present to be alone. There's nothing there but the words, the elusive ideas trying to force their way into accessibility. I don't show up until I get hungry and shut off the machine to go get lunch. Then, if Chris isn't there, I'm alone.

At times the writing trade is nothing more than selling experiences, selling moments. This has never struck me as exactly a noble endeavor. You get to go do something—spend a lovely time on a lake in the Adirondacks, for example—and report back. Reporting back, unfortunately, has a way of tainting the experience. It forces you to take notes, tuck away moments for later, run words by in your head. Reporting back feeds the monkey. Feeds me, too, and therefore I can't complain, but I sometimes think I'd prefer it quieter in my head. Sometimes I'd like to keep the Adirondacks as a private deal, between me and my nerve endings. Reporting back makes it no longer solo, which frankly is the best part.

Look at me, selling soloing, when I'm the guy who's always bitching about being sold to. I wish being a writer did not so often mean trying to make people want things. Maybe *that's* what I mean by retirement.

Ralph Waldo Emerson on sitting for a daguerreotype: "And in your zeal not to blur the image, did you keep every finger in its place with such energy that your hands became clenched as for fight or despair, and in your resolution to keep your face still, did you feel every moment more rigid; the brows contracted into a Tartarean frown, and the eyes fixed as they are fixed in a fit, in madness, or in death?"

My restlessness goes away at sundown. I help it along with alcohol, which may or may not be a shameful practice. (Suggested bumper sticker: ONE DRINK AT A TIME.) I even take alcohol along on canoe trips, where it is unnecessary (as if it were ever necessary). That might be considered even more shameful. We didn't take alcohol when we first started canoeing, assuming a kind of Spartan rigor was required. Alertness is necessary in the woods, where your safety is dependent on your wits and your capability of responding. Most boating accidents involve booze. Our worst experiences have involved not weather or wildlife but drunken boaters. But as we became more comfortable at going canoeing, we began to allow ourselves a few luxuries. Better rain gear, softer air mattresses; an evening drink.

At sunset, when stillness begins to settle in, a little taste does not seem a cardinal sin, in wilderness or out. A bad habit, perhaps. It's certainly a habit. When I flick off the computer for the day and head downstairs, I can taste the gin that awaits me. It carries a good measure of solace, frankly, as well as putting a quietly celebratory stamp on the end of the active part of the day. I don't know which I love more, the solace or the celebration. When I was younger, solace wasn't involved. Maybe the solace is for the aging.

I do not love the packed feeling in the head that alcohol brings, the low-grade pressure that says I've had enough: loaded, as they say, or, in the thirties, tight. It's an appropriate euphemism: that's how your head feels. My father would get "tight," and the trouble would begin. I also fear alcohol, for cause. I've had warnings enough. He died at forty-one, his health and first marriage both wrecked by booze. I remember harrowing trips to the bootlegger in dry Oklahoma City, when I was ten or eleven. Once he was so drunk he burned the end of his nose with the car's cigarette lighter, trying to light up while he was driving. How we survived without a wreck I'll never know. For days he had a round brown scab on the end of his nose. It made me so angry that I took the same cigarette lighter and burned a pattern of circles into the mohair door panel. He was furious, but too drunk to punish me.

Jud fell prey to alcohol in his later years, according to his widow, Marty, complete with bottles stashed in secret hiding places. (He was ashamed, clearly: we both got that message sharply enough.) On our last visit he was on opiates and forbidden alcohol, but at that stage his care was only palliative, and one evening his doctor gave permission for a small ceremonial drink with me, the visiting brother. Marty brought a half-pint of brandy to the hospital room, and we each sipped an ounce or so. I finished mine first and she offered me more. No, Jud said in his drug-bleary state, he can't have any more of that. There's another bottle in the car, Marty lied. His own future supply assured, my dying brother then permitted me a second drink. It was a peculiar little-brother moment for me, being nearly sixty years old at the time.

I hadn't associated problem drinking with aging until I walked into the late stages of an alumni cocktail party at a local inn and had trouble making my way through the roomful of tottering, elderly drunks, clinging to one another for support. They were a well-dressed, clearly affluent, successful-looking group. They weren't my alumni—I was a stranger, simply looking to get dinner—but it struck me that they were too old to drink that way, that it shouldn't be allowed. And was shocked at myself for the prohibitive thought.

The experience had a clarifying effect on my social drinking, I hope, which it needed. When I was younger I did more than my share, celebrating drink, bragging about it. In our family, despite our history, drinking was supposed to be funny. "A crow can't fly on one wing," my stepfather would say, urging another round on guests. For years I drank too much on most occasions, trying to make things funnier than they really were. Drunkenness *was* funny, at one time. Then it stopped being so, a societal tradition coming to an end about the same time Dean Martin did. Foster Brooks is out of work. You don't see drunk acts anymore.

The individual goes through a similar transition, I think. You go from acting drunker than you actually are, because it's funny, to acting more sober than you actually are, because it isn't funny anymore. That's the breakover point, if you like to drink but are lucky. We've all known the unlucky ones.

In youth I fell for the common misconception that drinking led to good times, actually looking forward to cocktail parties, which have now become a form of torture. I'm sure I paid a social price, although I was usually oblivious to that. I used drink as a social lubricant until I began to realize that relationships formed with its assistance had a way of turning unsatisfactory when sober. None of the warning signs of alcoholism applied, except perhaps that I was usually looking forward to the next time. And behaved like a jerk.

The elders I know seem mostly to drift away from alcohol, whether from simply losing the taste for it or from finding its attendant confusions and other costs too high. I've read that some of the elderly, particularly widows living alone, tend to get in trouble with the stuff. Myself, I would certainly dread having to quit it completely. "Giving up booze," says Wilfrid Sheed, "felt at first like nothing so much as sitting in a great art gallery and watching the paintings being removed one by one until there was nothing left up there but bare white walls."

Nowadays I look forward to the first drink, enjoy the second, and for the rest of the evening what I look forward to is bed. But the first, the sundowner, is important. "Even sensual pleasures survive," says Pierre, in his ninety-fourth year. "In late afternoon, traditional hour of adultery in French novels, I do not lack resource. Then three and a half ounces of Scotch is the orgasm of old age."

"I love my bed," said Mike in a recent letter. Oh how I do too, how we all come to that. Maybe as we get older we get too tired to get drunk. When you're young, sleep is something you can do when you get old. And boy, don't you ever.

Slow down, my body keeps telling me. Languid Man was born of this discovery: the best way to have a good time is not by drinking alcohol but by slowing down. Slowing down is also better for you, and for the rest of the world as well, a concept that has caught the attention of the deep thinkers. I am deluged with literature on the subject. Speeding up the flow of water through the landscape, which we do by clear-cutting, paving, and filling wetlands, increases flooding, reduces water quality, and degrades aquatic habitats. (We spend billions to reduce flood-plain damage, but it has risen by 50 percent in the past fifteen years.)

Strip development, outsourcing, and dependence on the automobile speed money out of the community, destroying older downtowns and wreaking other havoc. The fewer times a dollar is spent in the local economy before it goes outside, the higher the level of poverty and unemployment. Speeding the flow of data has us swimming in information but drowning for lack of knowledge (a useful distinction), to say nothing of what used to be referred to as wisdom. It is as if we think we could compose more beautiful music by cramming in more notes. "There is a secret bond between slowness and memory, between speed and forgetting," says Milan Kundera, in *Slowness*. The older you get, the more you are interested in remembering.

I love the Patrick O'Brian sea novels, reading them obsessively. Plot-wise, everything in them turns on information acquired too late, in the wrong order. "Not a moment to lose" is a running gag line, the British navy's slogan. In the age of sail, in all our history to that point, the fastest delivery of information was by horseback. The machine age was in large part driven by our efforts to improve on that poor device, and the electronic age entirely so.[2] Maybe that's why I am so fond of the canoe.

I am sympathetic to the pressure, however, and in most cases a willing participant (or victim). After all, I type as fast as I possibly can. I can't get it all done, everything I think I should get done, and speed would help. Thoreau couldn't finish his Natural History of Everything in part because he couldn't be everywhere at once—he couldn't know what was going on every day with every plant and

2. These observations are cribbed from "Speed," by David W. Orr, in *Conservation Biology*, February 1998; and "Fast Forward," by Mark Kingwell, in *Harper's*, May 1998.

animal in Concord. I don't much like the cocky young Thoreau, or the negative, holier-than-thou one that so often comes through, but my heart aches for the middle-aged man struggling to accommodate all knowledge, to observe everything, to get it all down—never quite admitting he was bewildered by the size of his task.

Is it me wanting to slow down or is it my aging nervous system? Is it the slowness of uptake, of reaction time? The TV ad-maker brags about cramming a hundred and forty-two cuts into a thirty-second commercial. To the young this means more information, to the old it means a great deal less. The ad-makers happily admit they don't want you to understand anything (or, God help us, examine anything, such as the product), they just want you to feel something, some identification: the product as an attractive but perfectly vague entity. Personally, all my vague entities are pretty much in place. Why would I want more?

I'd like to make a nice philosophical argument against this mad acceleration, but I suspect my personal motive is really fatigue. The Cyber Age is passing me by. As with demographics, I'm aging out of this one, too. It's undoubtedly a fascinating cultural phenomenon, but I can't summon the energy to keep up. It's all electrons to me, and it's the mechanical age that I hate to give up on: that time when we could understand how things worked and fix them when they broke. I don't want to give up on that world. It's also the one where physiology still counts for something.

Watch it, the author is trying to commit wisdom. It's a terrible temptation. After all, wisdom is allegedly an attribute of age, and if the age part is happening to me, don't I get the other to go along with it? I'd love to be able to think of myself as wise, but that would require ignoring the evidence.

I hanker after wisdom instead, but have to outsource it, too, as our current anti-language culture might put it. I suppose that's the attraction to Thoreau. He was not stingy with advice, some of which sounds like wisdom and probably is. It was a quality he valued, perhaps too highly: "I am sane only when I have risen above my common sense, when I do not take the foolish view of things which is commonly taken, when I do not live for the low ends for which men commonly live. Wisdom is not common."

He sprinkles aphorisms throughout his journals, from the very beginning. "Value and effort are as much coincident as weight and a tendency to fall," he wrote in 1840, before his twenty-third birthday. "It is the faith with which we take medicine that cures us," in 1852. "The too exquisitely cultured I avoid as I do the theatre. Their life lacks reality. They offer me wine instead of water. They are surrounded by things that can be bought." At one point he strings out a kind of homeboy's list of aphorisms:

> The highest condition of art is artlessness.
> Truth is always paradoxical.
> He will get to the goal first who stands stillest.
> By sufferance you may escape suffering.
> He who resists not at all will never surrender.
> When a dog runs at you, whistle for him.
> Stand outside the wall, and no harm can reach you. The

danger is that you be walled in with it.

Jud, being a poet, was in the wisdom business. He used to say, among other things, that no one ever has bad intentions, which seemed like wisdom to me at the time. I have my own little list, which I think of as my personal principles of happiness and am always revising. The most recent one is that everyone's right. That comes after don't sell so hard, and stop trying to get more. Another one occurs to me: few people realize how irritating wisdom is. Proffered wisdom.

One of the tasks of aging, perhaps the wisest thing we can do, is to shuck off as many as possible of our illusions, our wishful thinking, our defensiveness. Clear up all that youthful baggage (that's what the Dumpster is for). There's a certain last-chance aspect to this time, a final opportunity to change. An almost frightening freedom is implied in the opportunity. Chris and I were kicking this idea around, intrigued by its possibilities. There's a threat implied also, Chris pointed out: change now, or risk dying the same jerk you were when you were sixteen.

Yes, I responded at the time, one of my goals is to become, finally, a former jerk. Immediately I hear a Greek chorus intoning, "We'll be the judge of that."

AUGUST: *Going Orthopedic*

"I am struck again by the perfect correspondence of a day—say an August day—and the year," wrote Thoreau in 1853. "I think that a perfect parallel may be drawn between the seasons of the day and of the year. Perhaps after middle age man ceases to be interested in the morning and in the spring."

The analogy of the day and the year certainly rings true, even pleasurably so, but he had it wrong about mornings and spring. Perhaps he didn't live long enough to learn that while springtime can be a kind of luxurious torture in middle age, the mornings get better—and come earlier—the longer you live. At least on the evidence so far.

On the afternoon of the next to last day of July, as I was just sinking into a little postlunch snooze, Chris came into the room in a noticeably jolly mood—"merry," as she would characterize it later—

and handed me a fax that had just arrived. "I think you'll like this," she said. Merriment justified: it was word that another book, one that was already written, had sold. The money would come in small batches, wouldn't start arriving for several months, and would not make a down payment on a single yacht, but that didn't make it any less welcome. And it was as unexpected as if someone had left a shoebox of small bills in my car while I was in the post office.

The news left us somewhat giddy, immediately planning much-needed repairs to the place. We still had an environmentally threatening in-ground oil tank that needed replacing. The previous winter snowplows had removed most of our driveway. Now we could get cracking on the Dumpster project. Chris said she might even consider replacing the living room chair that was held together with duct tape. She hated to give it up, though, because it drove her visiting family nuts, and one mustn't let opportunities like that slip away.

I can't remember what, if anything, I was wearing at the time the news arrived, but it was certainly sufficient occasion for another pants-optional cocktail party. With, on this occasion, champagne. In fact we declared a weekend, although the news arrived on a Wednesday.

I tend to forget that the subject of nudity makes some people uncomfortable. Nudity's visual aspect is definitely a problem, one that grows worse with age, since we oldsters are not at all pretty. The visual part has never been the point, however. Seeing others naked or being seen in that state are equal violations, equally offensive. There's no need or intent ever to inflict it on others. (This assumes that Chris is by now inured to the sight. I hope.) I have no interest in it as a group activity—as in nudist *colony*, for God's sake. No exhibitionism allowed.

Actually, it's rather like solo canoe-camping: it becomes comfortable exactly to the degree that self-awareness is lost. If you go on a solo, or pursue any other wilderness activity, in order to be seen, you won't have a very good time; in fact to the extent you see other people at all you forfeit pleasure. I happen not to like clothing, most of which I find uncomfortable, and prefer wearing as little as temperatures allow. Living on a dead-end rural road and working at home, I find dispensing with the entire issue, weather permitting, to be not only a time-saver but a great clarifier, which age causes me to appreciate more every day. Besides, if word gets around it tends to discourage drop-in visitors. Underneath my clothes I'm naked all the time anyway. It helps to keep that in mind.

Clothing becomes a problem as we age. Many elders cling to a level of formality that is out of character with what we do and who we are. I assume this is not so much from pride as to avoid disgrace—and disgrace, or at least embarrassment, is never farther than an unnoticed food stain away. The shopping aisles are full of the elderly wearing sour, dirt-rimmed polyester, obviously adopted for ease of care but, through sheer inattention, gone tattered with wear and impervious to any known cleaning methods.

But oldster formality—jackets and neckties on men, dresses on women—must also be driven by a confusion, or reluctance, about style. (The aging woman: gafferette? gafferina? gaffereuse?) How *are* we supposed to look when we're not dressed to the nines? However eccentric, i.e., comfortable, we may be in private, there's a certain expectation of us in public. Chris, discussing this, remarked that there's nothing sadder than an old man in jeans. As I wear jeans nine months of the year, this hurt my feelings. I'd wear something else, I told her, if I could find any other form of trousers I could stand. By that I meant it was a comfort issue, but on reflection came to wonder what kind of pants an old man could wear that would not be sad. Sad as an old man's pants: at least she'd given me a handy new simile.

I had not yet given much thought to aging's visuals, an excruciating subject. If you are not yet sad as an old man's pants, you will be, in five years, or ten, or whenever. And whenever it happens it will be too soon. Aging's unavoidable leitmotif: too soon, too soon. Journalist Martha Gellhorn, in correspondence at age eighty-four: "I have become ugly. You may be surprised that at my age this both horrifies me and startles me. My idea of the bad part of old age was just that; getting ugly. I never thought at all about the inevitable decay of the body and what that could mean. I only thought about my face. Now it's plain hideous. . . . I am sure that vanity (physical) never dies in either men or women; all that happens is you feel unacceptable because there is nothing left to have vanity about."

Okay, so when it comes to nudity, vanity is not the point. (Vanity arises when clothing selection begins.) But freedom definitely is. Nothing on earth makes me feel freer and more comfortably myself than exposure of skin to air. I think it's more the sheer privacy of the state. Nobody's business but my own.

Sunset on our west-facing deck in August invariably reminds me of our year without media, of the conceit of sailing the house one circuit around the sun. It is very like sitting on the fantail of a ship, watching the day recede as the house plunges ever eastward into the gentle night. The west thus represents the past, the east, where the new day comes from, the future—which now that I think of it is a bit backward, historically, for the North American continent.

In the Patrick O'Brian novel *H.M.S. Surprise,* the ship's surgeon and its captain are enjoying the view from the masthead. The doctor asks the captain if he had ever considered "the ship thus seen as a figure of the present—the untouched sea before it as the future—the bow-wave as the moment of perception, of immediate existence?" I think about that a good deal when we are canoeing.

It had been three years since we pursued that media-free whim, but I was older then, although only from inactivity. This summer had become entirely different. I still had a few tender areas, but essentially I was repaired, returned to normal: better than normal, since I'd also begun to round into shape again. Chris perceived it as virtually a twenty-year shift: from an apparent age of about seventy to perhaps fifty. Mid-fifties, anyway. I composed an imaginary letter to my surgeons: maybe we should go ahead and do that other vertebra, I would say, and take me to the mid-thirties? More likely I'd wait until the mid-eighties—physically if not chronologically—and then get knocked back to my sixties. Sixty-four, I was discovering, was not a bad age at all.[1]

Not that I'd escaped the strong sense I might go orthopedic again at any time. From middle age on, orthopedism is always hanging over you. You can push on into it—into sheer structural breakdown—at any point. It's always there, looming, but it isn't necessarily a bad thing. It keeps you from being really foolish. It's a lot better to know that if you push too hard you're going to have a torn muscle or a sprung tendon than to fear that if you push too hard you're going to have an infarction and fall dead. One important part of exercise, psychologically anyway, is to have something against which you can safely push.

When you're young and obviously immortal you have nothing really to push against, except perhaps your competitors, and the rules of the game, the restrictions of whichever discipline you're operating under. You can't push against yourself because you don't have any limits, or can't really conceive of them. The great athletes

1. As I was writing this an eighty-five-year-old friend asked me what I was working on. A book about turning sixty-five, I told her. "Oh, sixty-five," she said, "I remember that. That was a good age."

are probably the ones who conceive of themselves early on as having limits, and learn to work within—and against—those limits. They learn to manage them.

Any discipline, any craft, is ultimately bounded by a kind of wall, representing the limits of possibility. It is this wall against which the craftsman works. To exceed it is to destroy the work; to approach it too cautiously, to stop short, is to settle for the second-rate. The best result comes from working as close to it as possible, pushing closer and closer, leaving a finer and finer margin. When you get it right you move the wall back a bit. New possibilities emerge.

My swimming continued to go well, if softly, gently: a thrice-weekly contribution to my sense of recovery and well-being. After a rewarding but still frustrating several weeks of not being able to go fast enough, I began using workout fins, which let me go faster with what seemed like the same expenditure of effort. Cheating, in other words—but, well, speed thrills. My shoulders, elbows, even my wrists didn't seem to like the new loadings, but swimming with fins unloaded those structures and loaded legs and lungs instead, which didn't mind a bit. Fins also turned each workout into a gentle dance—the mental equivalent of a session of Tai Chi at dawn on a Chinese morning in about, oh, A.D. 620.

In fact, swimming came along so well it began to make me wonder if there wasn't a little more to be had along those lines. Perhaps it was time to resume running, after what had turned out to be an unconscionably long layoff. Swim one day, run the next: why wouldn't that be ideal? I gave it a whirl. The first run was a painful thirty minutes, never mind the distance, down the hill and back up again; of the thirty minutes I actually ran perhaps twelve. Getting myself *able* to run again would take some time, I realized, and realized it more graphically the next day, when my legs felt as if they'd been beaten with rubber hoses. It would take a good ten days to work through that damage.

I have been accused of having a high pain threshold, which is sheer nonsense, as anyone who has heard my lifetime of whining can attest. All my life I've gotten shockingly sore from undertaking a new physical task. Sometimes I almost think it's a unique, unidentified disease, a special case. (And who among us isn't a special case?) Maturation has brought only a slight modification of the tendency to do too much too soon, saving me occasionally from being a tottering cripple the next day.

Thus management of the body becomes a game, the object of which is to keep yourself on the verge of orthopedism, in order to avoid going systemic. Systemic is the part of aging you don't want any part of. Going orthopedic hurts, but going systemic feels *bad*. How would you rather feel, hurt or sick? It's an important distinction. You can hurt without feeling bad. Actually, with age you mostly hurt all the time, but it turns out to be of little consequence. It's just the price you pay. It brings the daily news: you're alive.

The soreness is always precisely specific: what gets sore is *exactly* what you used. It's a sign you've used that part and it needs to recover. It will do so, and be stronger. You can use it harder next time. Each time you get sore and recover you move the wall back a bit. You do want to be able to use yourself, don't you?

But it is not infinite, this improvement. How do you deal with the end of improvement? That's the quandary of aging in a nutshell.

In mid-August, in holiday mood, we shut up the house, loaded our big canoe on the car, and headed for Ontario's French River, point of entry for Georgian Bay. We'd been longing to go back there since we were introduced to the place six years before, by Mike and Jo, and had since considered it the best place we'd ever been in a canoe.

It took a long day's drive—through unceasing rain—to get to North Bay, for last-minute supplies and a last indoor night. Despite a slightly surreal beginning—the Oscar Mayer Weeniemobile was parked next to our car at the motel—a couple of hours' drive around the north shore of Lake Nipissing, on a brisk and brilliant morning, brought us to Hartley Bay, our put-in point. We chose that entry because it avoids a not terribly entertaining thirteen miles of paddling before the good part begins. The French River is essentially a straight-line, east-west crack in the Precambrian Shield— the great dome of granite on which most of Canada sits—that eventually turns south and heads for Lake Huron. The straight part cuts through cottage country, with fishermen, outboards, the occasional Jet Ski,[2] and other anathemata to canoeists. Worse, its water is an unappealing tannin-brown.

Once it makes its turn, however, it enters the area where the southern edge of the dome fractures, like tempered plate glass, into several thousand islands. (Local tourist promotions claim thirty thousand.) The French River then splits into several channels and begins turning from brown to a brilliant dark green, which grows lighter and lighter in color, and ever more transparent, as you approach the bay. The final hue is such a distinctive shade Chris and I refer to it as Georgian Bay green. As it reaches the bay it gives onto what seems an infinite supply of sparkling clear-water passageways between softly rounded smooth granite islands. You camp anywhere you find a flat spot big enough to hold a tent. The water is potable,

---

2. Trademark-registered. Or generically, as the hard-pressed industry flacks like to call them, personal watercraft. My fellow canoeists and I are contemplating starting a Jet Ski Assassination League.

and in August has been known to warm sufficiently to permit the immersion of human bodies. The islands are what we came for.

Paddling again, in tandem, in a fully loaded canoe, was the usual delight and the usual burden: we both love moving along in a good boat, but neither of us was in shape for several uninterrupted hours of this pleasure. We opted therefore for an easy first day, settling on a remembered spot called Crombie Bay. The surrounding country dazzled us with pink rock, red pines, and purple loosestrife, interspersed with little bays and coves filled with brilliant green reeds and startlingly bright cardinal flowers. Opposite our campsite, three hundred yards away across the water, was a pink and yellow wall of granite, among whose crags and crevices white seagulls and black ravens made aerial sport. At sunset the wind dropped, and we were able to stop bustling and sit still for a while. It is curiously intense country to look at. The mix of woods, water, and terrain is beautifully balanced, the scale large. Each of the elements in that mix provides a bright and well-defined example of its kind: hard-edged scenery, presenting itself with a stunning clarity. I still find it astonishing to get to such a spot and be allowed to sit there and take it in. It makes me realize, once again, how much of my time I spend being insufficiently grateful.

The next morning's paddle started with a search for the Old Voyageurs' Channel, a magical passageway used by the early-eighteenth-century fur traders, part of the great route connecting Montreal with the Great Lakes and beyond. We'd been enraptured by it on our previous visit, a narrow, twisting conduit, pink granite walls ten to twenty feet high and close enough at times to touch with a paddle on either side. Within it you're out of the wind, the water still. It is narrow enough to force you to glide through slowly, picking your way. When you talk to your partner you find yourself speaking very softly.

On our previous visit we'd been led by much better navigators than we proved to be, a failing that would bedevil us for the next several days. After two or three hours of almost aimless paddling, interspersed with long consultations with topo maps, we did finally find our way in. It was as beguiling as it had been the first time, but shorter than we remembered—and completely devoid of camp-sites, when we'd been hoping to spend at least a day and a night in the midst of its attractions. So we paddled on, emerging into the larger main channel in conjunction with a sudden downpour, pre-cluding a lunch stop: we couldn't see far enough or well enough to make a landing, and the prospect of sitting in an increasingly wet canoe, trying to make and eat wet sandwiches, did not appeal.

The rain increased. We were by then among the scattered islands of the bay proper, looking at first for shelter, then, giving up on that, for any place we could pitch a tent and make our own. Our rain gear was good, but we were soon more than damp around the edges, and the canoe had become a cistern, collecting enough rain-water to soak our packs. The situation was becoming a bit frighten-ing. Finally we scrambled onto a marginal stone platform where a couple of withered trees provided at least a hint of shelter, got the tent erected in the still-pouring rain, and tumbled inside to cram down a sodden cold lunch. Everything was sopping except, luckily, sleeping bags and spare clothing.

So we hunkered. The rain finally slacked off in late afternoon, only to be followed by shrieking winds. Our situation was the very definition of the term "windbound": waves so high there was no way we could even load the canoe, never mind paddle it anywhere safely. There was also no point, in that wind and the accompanying intermittent rain, in trying to make any kind of formal camp. We dragged the food bag up to the door of the tent, concocted a cold supper, and settled in to wait it out.

So, a hell of a fine canoe trip—and a true test of patience, although both of us were by then sufficiently wrecked not to be ill-disposed toward just lying still for a while. At 7:10, just when we'd ordinarily have expected to watch a nice calm sunset, the next violent thunderstorm came rolling in. It's funny how often, when your only shelter is a tent, you are treated to a thunderstorm. It's a very different experience than being in a nice dry house. Intense. Intense country seems to attract intense weather to go with it. Maybe, we thought, it's the scale: it's *larger* weather. We named it the Land of Rude Surprises, and reminded ourselves once again that the good places always come at a price.

At about midnight we were startled by an unaccustomed silence, and realized the rain had stopped: full moon and bright stars overhead, back to sleep with spirits rising. We awoke to fog, however, and were rained on again before we finished breakfast. Packed up wet clothes, tent, and gear, and set out, in sporadic spitting rain, in search of a remembered island that offered a footprint at least a little larger than the diameter of our tent, and the possibility of erecting a tarp for sheltered cooking and eating.

Couldn't find it. Never did find it. Paddled up and down various channels, in heavy winds and spitting rain, essentially lost, for three hours or so. Discussed, as we paddled, bagging the whole affair, heading home. Finally landed on an unpromising island that would at least give us solid ground on which to get some lunch, realizing we were by then quite tired and would soon need shelter again. As if in a lull between battles, we assessed our wounds. Chris had a groin pull and a wrenched knee, plus an assortment of abrasions on her feet, making her disinclined to move around very much. My right hand was swollen half again the size of my left, so sore I could hardly tie knots—some kind of bursitis kicking up, I surmised. It quit raining. The island turned out to be a little more spacious than it had first appeared. Chris made a bountiful steak-and-potato lunch—the previous night's uneaten dinner—while I spread out wet tent, sodden clothes, and sleeping bags to dry.

The sun came out, albeit with continuing blustery winds. We both dozed, and woke up feeling better. We risked a swim—not *entirely* frigid—and warmed ourselves in the strengthening sun. Upon exploration the campsite turned out to offer real possibilities. Perhaps we might take a rest day. We both were, or had been, terribly tired—approaching Edge City, equanimity-wise—which helped with the decision. At that point I slowly and thoroughly anointed my entire body with sunblock, stretched out on warm granite, and suggested that we might perhaps stay a couple of days, since we were there and set up and all. There are sensual pleasures to be had in those circumstances—sights, sounds, textures, pleasures of the skin and muscle—but they do tend to have a touch of pain to them. *Harsh* pleasures, not subtle ones. The moon that night, when I got up to check, was as full as my bladder.

Our rest day was a maddening, teasing one, however, the clear dawn followed by a high overcast that never quite broke, all day long. When all we wanted to do was swim and sun. We spent most of it stretched out on warm granite—clothed—with binoculars pasted to our eyes. I made a list: loons, gulls, terns, crows, ravens, cormorants, goldfinches, buteos, buzzards, ducks, ospreys, whitethroats. A confusing fall warbler or two. Ducks, I realized for the first time, fly as if on a strafing run, always point A to point B, no dillydallying.

The accumulated fatigue of the previous two days began to lift, assisted by serial naps. The evening sky finally broke heartbreakingly free into golden sunlight and warmth at 7:05, after we'd eaten supper. Almost warm enough for a comfortable swim. By then I'd even begun to stop resenting the necessary thirty-six round trips from one end of the campsite to the other just to get things put away for bedtime. Sweet bedtime. At our age there's no sitting around the campfire telling stories, roasting marshmallows. Chris always brings candles, but we seldom light them. Sweet, sweet bedtime. Old folks gone camping.

Dawn was perfect if chilly, clear-skied. While we were making breakfast we heard a strange loud screeching, which we thought at first was from some kind of very large bird, perhaps a heron or crane in distress. Then we saw a round black head with big, round, Disneyish ears swimming across the channel to the next island to our north: a black bear cub, squalling its heart out, presumably for missing Mom, as it swam. Would Mom perhaps be on our own island? we wondered. Behind us, so we were between her and cub? After a quick search the cub gave up on that island, blundered back into the channel, crossed to the other side, and disappeared northward, still squalling.

Our food supply gave us two more nights, at least one of which we were determined to spend at a place Jo and Mike call the Citadel, a long day's paddle away. Our various sorenesses didn't seem to preclude paddling, and even permitted a gingerly breaking of camp, so we had a perfectly lovely paddle back inland, although we overshot the Old Voyageurs' Channel once again—those things look different from the other end, you know—and blew an extra hour and a half trying to find ourselves. During that search we were startled to come across a sow bear with two cubs, again swimming across a channel between islands. In all our previous canoe-camping we'd chosen island campsites when we could find them, assuming that islands made bear precautions unnecessary. Now we'd seen four bears in one day, all of them island-hopping. We would revise our site-selection parameters.

There is little portaging in French River canoeing, except by choice, but one small lift-over does block the Old Voyageurs' Channel. It's known as La Petite Faucille ("Little Sickle"), and requires only that you carry gear and canoe ten feet across a rocky ridge to the next water. The day had grown gloriously hot by the time we got there, making for a delicious, almost ceremonial skinny-dip. The weather held—maybe we'd given up on the Bay too early?—but the subsequent paddle was into a headwind and a stiff chop, and went on forever. Curiously, my swollen hand wasn't affected by the pull of paddling—perhaps because I paddle on the right and could dip it into cool water at every stroke[3]—but otherwise we were both wore plumb out, as they say in Texas, with a couple of hours to go to the Citadel. At a late lunch in a swampy little bay with rather chummier insect life than we quite enjoyed—after five and a half hours of paddling—we designated ourselves certified wimps, and forswore perseveration. Perhaps it was because we noticed on the map that our quite satisfactory first night's campsite at Crombie Bay was only one more headland beyond.

We slept well, despite our newly raised bear-consciousness, and treated ourselves to a luxurious breakfast. A leisurely decampment put us on the water at 8:45, under an empty blue sky and windless warm conditions. As we started out, a line of southbound geese—it was, after all, late August, and we were quite far north—went whipping across the sky like the tail of a kite. The Citadel turned out to be two and a half hours of very warm paddling away, making us glad we hadn't tried to make it the day before. But, blessedly, it was not only unoccupied but well supplied with firewood.

It is a curious campsite, atop a granite ridge thirty feet or more above the waterline, which is probably why it is usually available. It looks and in some ways is remarkably inconvenient. There's only a

---

3. Also, I was paddling in the bow, which is less taxing; Chris in the stern was doing all the steering.

small, somewhat precarious ledge for beaching your canoe, and you have to haul your camping gear up the steep rock face. To fetch water or go for a swim requires scrambling up and down that same pitch. After a few trips one becomes a thoughtful planner. But on top there's a good deal of tent room, there's a lower ledge with a convenient fire ring and cooking area, and you have a fabulous 270-degree view: a veritable lake to the east, and the arms of two large rivers, the French and the Pickerel, on each side. It is back in cottage country—there's fisherman traffic and recreational boating going on about you—but you are invisible in your aerie, with a watery world of activity at your feet but complete privacy.

The weather held. We spent the day sauntering up and down to swim, then frying on our rock like lizards in the sun: such a splendid day in such a splendid place that we forgot to be tired. Finally, pelts sated, we rigged a tarp for shade, under which we ate and drank sinfully, attempting to finish off all our supplies except for the next morning's breakfast. Snoozed and swam and sunned, and got the sunset that was owed us, an eternally long sunset in the company, for me, of the single person with whom I can talk about anything on earth. She seemed to like it too. "This," Chris said, in the summer evening, "is the completest thing."

Then home again safe and sound, effectively recreated. At the take-out a group of college boys had been loading their canoes for the trip in. What had happened in the world while we were away? I asked. By any chance had Bob Hope or Frank Sinatra died? (On a similar occasion we'd missed the media flap over Sammy Davis, Jr.) Nope, the college boys said; *Rats!* I responded. They paddled off trailing peals of laughter. We were rained on all the way home.

I sent Mike a summary report of our trip, as is our reciprocal custom; after all, they had introduced us not only to the French River but also to canoe camping, and we share information for future use. Mike responded with a chart demonstrating, from my report, that despite our claims we couldn't possibly have had a good time.

Okay, I answered, but newspapers don't print stories about all the planes that *didn't* crash. What was missing from his chart, because I'd neglected to tell him, was an enjoyable overnight stop in the Adirondacks on the way in, in good weather and with good friends; sufficient acknowledgment of our simultaneous historical trance just from being in the Old Voyageurs' Channel (both ways); the fierce beauty of the bay islands, even in rain; our detailed discussions about the true meaning of the word "exposure"; how well we ate, every meal, once we got out of the rain; how if you're so bad a navigator that you don't recognize places you've already seen, then you're always seeing totally new territory, i.e., it's never boring; how there were no bugs to speak of; and how much we enjoyed paddling again, even while lost. What an incredible machine the canoe is, what pleasure there is in making it take you to beautiful places all day long. How much we like to do this. See, I said, I just told you the grumpy parts. We'd go back tomorrow. As a matter of fact we'd be in better shape for it if we *did* go back tomorrow.

The attractions of nakedness—okay, *my* attraction to nakedness—formed early. I am now six foot three, but still vividly remember being small enough to sit on the back of the just-drained bathtub and slide down the wet surface, banking the curves, to swirl to a stop at the drain. Bathtub as playground equipment. It is now almost inconceivable to me that this current lank, clanking, pendular, barely manageable mass of a body was ever that tiny, but I can recall just what it felt like. Didn't we all do that? Wasn't it fun?

I've been disingenuous, however, in the matter of visuals. My hope that Chris is inured to the sight of my naked body is rather contradicted by the fact that I am not yet inured to hers, after thirty-one years, and doubtless never will be. Yes, I confess, there is something sexual about it. But it is not necessarily so, not always. Would it seem too perverse to admit that once when she was away, and I got some other remarkably good piece of news about my work, that I put down the phone, stepped immediately out onto the deck, and, naked as a jaybird, danced while I conducted the entire slow movement of Mozart's violin concerto in D, which happened to be playing at the time? Laughing like a maniac all the while?[4]

Why canoeing is good for you when you're old: as we stopped on a lakeside rock on the first day and began digging lunch out of various packs, I found myself thinking, Oh, right, nothing will be *convenient* for the next several days. A great deal of what we would be doing on those days was directly aimed at reducing, or attempting to reduce, that inconvenience. These efforts in themselves have a certain entertainment value. The rest of our energies, however, would be devoted to the larger project of getting safely into a beautiful wild place, and securing survival in, and if possible enjoyment, thereof. This is good for an old person.

I realized it as I was sitting in the sun after two hard days' paddling, when I began to feel as if I'd become a great ape, with arms eight feet long, a back three feet wide, muscles positively on fire with recovery; sore, but with the good kind of soreness that stretches right out. It occurred to me then that it is worthwhile to take your corpus into the woods, where it will quickly remind you that you are a contraption of levers and sinews, moved by those

4. "David, it will be recalled, danced naked before the Ark of the Lord."—Aubrey Menen, *The Mystics.*

clever gadgets the muscles. Move you will, and ache they will, as inevitably as sweat. They are reminding you that nothing is convenient; you are reminding them that they haven't been used in quite this way for a while, and their own working parts, down at the cellular level, are certainly rusty. Shockingly so. All of these two-way lessons are entertaining as hell, on some platonic level or other. They take your mind off the pain. The state you get into is the one we used to call "bone weary," back when we loved language more than science. It is refreshing, in an acheful way. Canoe camping is hard work, but restful hard work. I always forget that.

We'd planned for a summer full of canoe trips, but would only manage to make the one. Debriefing each other afterward, we were still in shock at the workload, which we'd remembered imperfectly from the last trip, nine months before. In future we would have to train up for that. We'd sworn we would train for the French River, too, but hadn't gotten around to it.

As a result, all the problems—other than the weather itself, which is always a given—were of connective tissue and of fatigue. Chris's wounds were the small pulls and tears, usually assumed to be to muscle but in fact always to connective tissue, that are only to be expected from unaccustomed, repeated, heavy loading in awkward positions—and hauling heavy gear into and out of a canoe and up and down steep rock faces certainly qualifies. Her sore back was almost entirely from digging cooking gear out of a tall food bag, a bad piece of equipment that we would quickly replace. My swollen hand, perhaps better characterized as water on the wrist, was probably just from the repeated rolling of sleeping pads and sleeping bags to stow them in stuff sacks—not terribly hard work, but sufficient to irritate the joints and allow the resulting fluid to leak from the joint capsule. Chris's wounds healed a little more quickly than mine, perhaps because she is ten years younger, but all were nearly forgotten by the Citadel, and completely gone by the time we were home.[5]

If in preparation for future canoe trips we followed some training program that prepared those particular weak spots, the next line of collapse would surely follow. The same general principle would apply to any scheme aimed at defeating the general fatigue that wiped us out the first day or so. The only conceivable training program for going canoeing is going canoeing, as our generally fine state at the end of the trip amply demonstrated. The solution is to go do it, and put up with the pain, bitching as you must, each trip preparing you for the next.

Unfortunately, it is relatively impossible to maintain the specificity of this kind of training for reasons of climate: the places where we want to do it are available for less than three months of the year (and are even relatively bug-free perhaps half that). To cut down that nine-month gap would mean starting earlier in May and going later into November, which would entail much greater exposure—and exposure gets quite specifically more dangerous as you age.

So: we're going to be foreclosed from canoeing eventually—and, weirdly enough, it'll be failing connective tissue that does it. Injuries threaten one's ability to get out safely. Injuries can't be avoided, not if you're going to get to the good places. You just try to keep them minor.

In other words, or until then, it's a piece of cake, once you're willing to accept certain pain levels. And that was the way you did it when you were younger, wasn't it? Except the pain levels somehow weren't as painful?

How long, then, can we continue doing this? I don't know. It will be a desolating loss. Usually I can come up with some sort of age-

---

5. This just in: not the one on her great toe, Chris points out. Funny how I remember my wounds better than hers.

related compensation for losses like this, but not for this one. Except perhaps that then we won't have to go out and hurt ourselves like that anymore. When I was younger I never thought I might not do such things forever. Now I think it all the time. It's amazing how that sweetens the experience.

A reporter was interviewing one of the now elderly Nicholas Brothers, a hyperacrobatic duo from the golden age of movie tap dancing. They were known for stunts like leaping off pianos and landing in a full split, never missing a beat. One brother, Feyard, was by then in a nursing home. The other, Harold, was asked, not altogether seriously, could he still dance like that? "No, I can't do that anymore," he said. "I don't want to do that anymore. To tell you the truth, it *hurt*."

"August, royal and rich. Green corn now, and melons have begun. That month, surely is distinguished when melons ripen. July could not do it. What a moist, fertile heat now! I see naked viburnum berries beginning to turn. Their whiteness faintly blushing" (Thoreau's journal, August 1853).

We settled quickly and comfortably back into our daily routine—routine being another of aging's warm baths. The same habits of dailiness that you thought would drive you nuts when you were younger are now sprinkled with delights. You begin to learn that there's nothing wrong with a routinized life so long as you're not bored. It is an enormously productive way to live—and living a productive life, and using yourself well, are among the greatest pleasures available. What greater aid to making it through the night could there be than knowing, by your own honest appraisal, that you are making good use of yourself. *Have* you done enough today?

Productively routinized or not, I found myself very much aware that late August was upon us. It is a season that does things to the back of one's throat—which, I notice, sweetens what you see when you look at the woods. There's no reason, at least that I can think of, why your throat shouldn't ache similarly in the spring, but mine does not. In college one of our English lectures was interrupted by the sound of trumpets from the auditorium down the hall, rehearsing for an Easter oratorio. The professor, who fancied himself something of an aphorist, paused, listened for a moment, and said, "How's this: if you understand the difference between bells at Christmas and trumpets at Easter, you're ready for heaven." I'm not entirely sure I do, but the notion certainly lodged in my mind.

"What means this sense of lateness that so comes over one now," Thoreau wrote that same August of 1853, "as if the rest of the year were down-hill, and if we had not performed anything before, we should not now? The season of flowers or of promise may be said to be over, and now is the season of fruits; but where is our fruit? The night of the year is approaching. What have we done with our talent? . . . The year is full of warnings of its shortness, as is life. The sound of so many insects and the sight of so many flowers affect us so,—the creak of the cricket and the sight of the prunella and autumnal dandelion. They say, 'For the night cometh in which no man may work.' "

SEPTEMBER: *The Chronicles of Hypochondria*

Now, about the first of September, you will see flocks of small birds
forming compact and distinct masses, as if they were not only
animated by one spirit but actually held together by some invisible
fluid or film, and will hear the sound of their wings rippling or
fanning the air as they flow through it, flying, the whole mass,
ricochet like a single bird,—or as they flow over the fence. Their
mind must operate faster than man's, in proportion as their bodies do.

—Thoreau's journal,

1851

In early September we drove to Nova Scotia to visit Mike and
Jo, whose approach to retirement was to buy land there and build a
house on it. We wanted to see the place, celebrate its completion,
and perhaps do a bit of retirement scouting for ourselves—not to
mention celebrating our thirty-first wedding anniversary. We'd
camped out on the land with them the year before, and were eager
to see how woodlot had been transmuted into domicile.

Their new hamlet consists of a store and a lobster shack wrapped
around a deep inlet, dependably drained twice a day by the famous
Bay of Fundy tides. Waking early on our first morning there, in their
airy, brilliantly simple new house, I strolled the mile or so—excuse
me, the few kilometers—to the wharf and back, enjoying the bright
September dawn and the birdlife. Coffee was up when I got back.

By the time breakfast was done I discovered an egg-sized knot behind my right knee. Didn't hurt, didn't make me limp or cramp my style, but a definite presence. Weird.

Mike is an ardent birder, Chris equally so, which fairly well set the agenda for our visit. We drove into nearby Port Williams to walk the series of dikes with which Acadian settlers had reclaimed a good deal of land in the Minas Basin two hundred years before—a sinuous three or four miles of easy strolling, unfortunately not terribly bird-filled on that particular afternoon. By dinnertime the knot behind my knee had disappeared but my leg was swollen from the knee down. The next day we made an expedition to Brier Island, a birder's paradise: another few miles, wandering the shoreline; leg about the same, swollen but not really discomfiting.

Our hosts' view to the northeast included a spectacular towering cliff, miles in the distance, called Cape Split. I couldn't take my eyes off it. Could we get closer? Yes, said Jo, it's a park, you can walk out onto it; a long walk, most of it climbing through fairly ordinary local forest, but it does end in a fabulous view of the bay. Chris and I set out to see the sights.

Jo's description was dead-on; the hike in, or rather up, bordered on the tedious but the reward was enormous: a grassy knob dropping off vertically on three sides several hundred feet to the sea, separated from an equally tall, isolated stack—the split in Cape Split—by a windy gulf. The famous tides, ripping over shoals on two sides, boiled up whitewater. In fact the entire surface of the sea, as you looked down on it, was shifting rapidly west on one side of the cape, east on the other. Seabirds soared; clouds raced overhead. It was as spectacular a spot, for sheer magnitude—and motion—as I could recall, and it immediately made me dizzily ill.

I'd had one previous attack of vertigo in my life, rock climbing in Colorado thirty-five years before, not while climbing but after I'd gained an almost perfectly flat summit. Determined to look over the edge, I found myself dropping to my knees and then my stomach as I crawled toward it, and lay spread-eagled on the surface when I finally looked down, feeling as if the rock itself was somehow going to fall out from under me.

It never happened again. I spent decades thereafter skiing, sliding down the very steep slopes of very tall mountains and riding rickety lifts to get there, with only minor uneasiness. I'd always liked high places—even, if there was sufficient water below, jumping off them. I was no longer comfortable working on tall ladders, but otherwise had little problem with heights. But I couldn't sit still on Cape Split, couldn't stay out there, and dragged Chris back down the trail before she was quite ready to go. Once back in the shelter of the woods—out of sight of all that swirling sea and sky—I was fine. Weird again.

The walk down was quite tiring, and by the time we got back to the car, after a roughly nine-mile round trip, my swollen leg no longer wanted to bend sufficiently to let me sit down. Perhaps I'd been a bit foolish to come; certainly the bout of vertigo had taken the fun out of it. That night—after a dinner of poached Digby scallops that brought tears of pleasure to our eyes—I kept thinking of Richard Nixon's phlebitis, about which I knew nothing but remembered that it had gravely worried his doctors. He'd been forced to spend long periods with his feet up, for fear a blood clot would break loose and migrate to lungs or brain. Dire.

The next morning I found a medical dictionary and frightened myself further with the specter of phlebitis. Nova Scotia was lovely, but we were due to leave for home: was it safe to travel? The pleasant young physician in the local emergency ward said he didn't know what my problem was but it was not phlebitis. Go ahead, drive home, but see your own doctor when you get there.

By the time I did the swelling was gone. Dr. X didn't put a name on it either, but didn't find it worrisome. It never returned. Baker's cyst, perhaps? You could call it that, said Dr. Z during a later checkup; fluid leaking from the joint capsule, anyway. Probably the same general mechanism that caused my swollen hand on the French River. Of no consequence. So why did I seem to be springing a leak in a new place every time I turned around? None of the three doctors actually used the word "age," but I heard it anyway.

I didn't ask about the vertigo, but learned later that it's a common complaint with aging, a product of a diminished sense of balance. "Older people have particular difficulty in balancing under conditions of sensory conflict (for example, when walking near a stream of fast-moving vehicles)," says physiologist Roy J. Shephard, perhaps explaining why all that swirling wind and water unnerved me so. We're supposed to compensate for it with better judgment. Humph.

Home again, I picked up the juggling balls for the first time in three weeks. My decidedly limited skills hadn't deteriorated, but I was shocked at how quickly my arms and shoulders got tired—just as I'd been shocked that swimming and running hadn't prepared me for the work of canoeing, never mind a little casual hiking. Despite writing about the subject for thirty years, I still get caught out by the fact that being in shape for one kind of physical effort does not prepare you for the next. It is a cardinal principle of athletic training, known in the trade as specificity. You train only the part you use. That's why it gets sore so precisely. (And as ski teacher Denise McCluggage wisely points out, when you practice something, you practice only what you *are* doing, not what you think you're doing.)

"Cross-training" has in recent years become the fitness movement's new toy. It is an outgrowth of the triathlon boom, based originally on the antispecific, and erroneous, notion that fitness is fitness, and training at, say, swimming would improve your performance in running or cycling, or both. It works, in a way, but not by repealing the iron law of specificity. What it does is reduce the frequency of breakdown. Triathloners, and fitness enthusiasts in general, are by nature overzealous people. They come to love training so much that they do it until something breaks down. What breaks, of course, is connective tissue.

The cause of this, too, is specificity, which works two ways: if you load a given tissue too hard for too long, with insufficient recovery time, it fails, just as Selye predicted. The more narrowly you load it, the more quickly it reaches its point of failure. Spreading one's efforts over various fitness disciplines also spreads it over more and different parts of your connective tissue, relieving this specificity of loading. Keep the training varied and you can train more without breaking down.

Almost, but not quite, free lunch. The gains from cross-training, from a purely fitness point of view, are mostly nonstructural, i.e., systemic. Structural gain, if any, probably comes from rest—as in resting one set of muscles and their connective tissue while working others. Being able to work the aerobic system harder does improve the aerobic system. If what is limiting your performance in cycling is specifically your aerobic system, then perhaps swimming or running can help reduce that limitation. For serious competitive athletes, no possible gain is going to be overlooked. And sure enough, with the increase in cross-training came some new discoveries: being stronger in the upper body actually helps you run faster, for a somewhat surprising example. You use the arms to drive yourself up hills, to counterbalance the effort with your legs, to help initiate movements with more force.

Coaches used to fear that athletes would become "muscle-bound," a concept now as out of date as the notion of second wind.

There seems to be no sport at which being stronger is not an advantage, which is why you now see bulging deltoids on basketball players and Popeye forearms on baseball players, even on golfers. Serious athletes now, universally, include weight training in their regimens. Serious athletes don't miss a trick.

The fitness marketeers will tell you that exercising thirty minutes a day three times a week will keep you fit. That, however, is only the aerobic part—the heart and lungs—and it is systemic fitness. Everything depends on how one defines fitness, but a 3 × 30-minute regimen will give you only the barest maintenance level of it.

The fitness marketeers would also have you believe—and I have been guilty of preaching—that aging can be held off indefinitely. This more or less loony notion comes from a body of research showing that athletes who continue to train sufficiently do not lose certain measurable physical capacities, even into their seventh and eighth decades. Note "sufficiently," and "certain" capacities. Measurements such as aerobic capacity may be maintained, but measurements such as time for a ten-kilometer run—that is, *results*—cannot. "Sufficient" training requires both volume and intensity—intensity actually seems to be more important than volume in holding off the effects of aging—and the sad truth is that both eventually come a cropper on structural integrity. Much as the gaffer-athlete may want to, you cannot train that much or that hard forever. The spirit indeed may be willing, but it is the connective tissue that is weak.

If this wasn't irreversibly, ineluctably true, the ranks of professional athletes would be filled with at least the middle-aged. After all, they started out as the most skilled athletes in the world, and have access to the best training and the best coaching, no expense spared. (And the money is better than they'll likely ever make again.) Why would they give up? In fact, the trend is in this direction—we already see forty-year-old starting quarterbacks and pitchers—and in fact you *can* bring back an aging, sedentary body, a long way back. But you cannot freeze elite-level capabilities. You can maintain a system or two—if you keep up the intensity—but there's no way you can maintain all of them. You can't hold on. You can only delay, and give ground grudgingly. Or not so grudgingly.

Alpinists refer to the region above eight thousand meters—roughly 24,000 feet—as the death zone: to remain there without supplementary oxygen is to begin, inexorably, to deteriorate. Even with adequate hydration, nutrition, and rest, your body is consuming itself. You are being foreclosed. Eventually you reach a point at which the energy demands simply of breathing require you to operate at your maximum aerobic capacity. Any further effort plunges you deeper into an oxygen debt that quickly becomes irrecoverable. You exhaust yourself just staying alive.

"My residue of energy is taxed to the limit," says ninety-four-year-old Pierre, "by simply not letting my days die before I do." The metaphor is inescapable; what age does is drag the death zone down the mountainside. In the very old the body can become so detrained that to lie quietly in bed is to operate at its maximum aerobic threshold. Death might perhaps be regarded as the moment when the organism's demands exceed that threshold. Breathing itself becomes hard enough work to use up more energy than the metabolism can recover.

The medical profession, required to label things, would hold that there is no such thing as death from "natural causes." If there were, this would be it: when breathing itself becomes as much work as, say, running a marathon. It's a gruesome notion, but it helps to imagine what a sweet relief it must be, in that state, finally to stop. To let go.

What we have here is one of aging's bleaker jokes. You have to work just to keep the systems working. You lose it (life itself) if you don't continue to do the work. You may have thought that someday you might be through with work. That's what "retirement" was supposed to represent, wasn't it? But you aren't through with work. You never are, never will be. One standard cliché about retirement is that if you stop work you die. It turns out to be true in a much deeper sense than I ever realized.

I'd kept up my fine-motor fitness program (juggling), but let the gross-motor equivalent—the weight-lifting program, launched with such simpleminded enthusiasm the previous January—go to hell. It was stupid to quit. A little more strength always comes in handy, not just in athletic endeavor, not to go do anything heroic with, but just to get through the day a little more easily. It's dirt simple: the stronger you are, the smaller percentage of your capacity you have to use for a given task. Therefore the later you will get tired. Since sitting still is the problem, and is precipitated largely by getting tired, being stronger is the best defense. Unless you become fond of getting tired, in which case weaker is better. The other thing is, if you don't get tired so soon you get to complete more, and completion becomes very important as you get older. One might even say you develop a completion complex; a completion obsession.

And strength, according to the authorities, is the one capacity that you can to a remarkable degree get back. One study of oldsters who were put on a weight-lifting regime showed an increase of muscle strength, on average, of 174 percent, and of walking speed of 50 percent. (Speed can be more important than we realize: a majority of the elderly cannot get across the street while the "walk" sign is still blinking.) We've been gung-ho for aerobic exercise and better nutrition for years, to very good effect in public health, but recent studies show neither is sufficient to protect the aging body. A healthy old age requires strength. Without regular, progressive resistance exercise, a.k.a. work, your strength will simply desert you.

Neither vertigo nor swollen leg kept me from enjoying our Nova Scotia trip. They colored it, but they didn't keep me from it. Not yet. Not yet.

There's no need to feel sorry for ourselves that we don't have too many more canoe trips ahead of us. When they get too hard we'll give them up, probably with some relief. Ruefully. Judging when the relief is more important than the reward is very like judging when to have elective surgery: how much pain will you put up with for the pleasure of doing this? It's an appropriate metaphor for the whole aging business, because it is exactly how you'll let things go. You can swear all you want that you'll never let anything go, but you're going to. Get ready for it.

One capacity I've given up with great good cheer is the all-nighter. I can remember when that kind of effort used to be almost fun, in an exhausting and irritating way. So was driving all night, a memory that now stirs the internal equivalent of a horse laugh. Now mental energy runs out as surely as the physical does, and earlier. I think I'm still able to work as hard mentally or physically as I ever did, but it's only in bursts. One new skill I seem to have developed is noticing when I've run out of gas.

Sometimes. It's not always easy to pull back far enough to see that my effectiveness has temporarily gone south. Sometimes I can't see that I've gone stone stupid until I'm faced with physical evidence. It takes an event, the mental equivalent of a jab in the ribs. The phone call is for Chris; "Sure," I say, "just a moment," and hang up the phone before going to fetch her.

No all-nighters allowed, anyway; the idea of pulling one is now absurd. It is another example of age's natural conservatism: I allow more lead time now—and use it more wisely. I also recognize what a self-serving piece of horse hockey it was, all those years when we really didn't get going until the deadline was on us—because, we insisted, we worked better under pressure.

September brought school buses clogging the back roads, a regular reminder that the year had now resumed. The first cold fronts of September cleared the air, giving brighter and sharper mornings than deep summer ever allows. With the declining sun come longer shadows, overdramatizing everything. Even at high noon the shadows are a little off, skewed. In September light suddenly, every sunny day, it's a little later than you think. It's as if an urgency chip has been surgically implanted in your brain. So why don't the long shadows of springtime get our attention the way those of September do?

I was having trouble settling back down to work, a reentry problem. I fought against giving up the deck, soaking up all the sun I could against the coming winter dark, toasting my thin dry skin. (When what it really needed was poaching. That's what swimming's for: rehydration, externally applied.) I'd sit in the sun and read, and feel my mood swing as the sun dodged in and out of the early-fall cumulus clouds, almost as if the emotional content of the page changed with the level of light.

Once you notice that happening, Seasonal Affective Disorder loses much of its mystery. When the sun goes behind a cloud and some tiny psychic part of you sighs with disappointment—and grins at the warmth and light when the sun reappears—it's fairly obvious that the change of light is dumping subtle splashes of brain chemicals into the system. In the fall you just get too much of the darker brew, and the load goes toxic. I don't know why science doesn't consult me on these matters.

When I first began hearing about SAD, and found its symptoms familiar, I sought the technological fix. I mounted a battery of full-spectrum fluorescent lamps on my office ceiling, and would get up at 5:00 A.M. and go lie there, staring up at them, like a member of some goddamn cult, for half an hour or so. By thus restoring the missing daylight one was alleged to reset one's biological clock. I thought it helped a good deal. When that got too boring I'd still go in at five and turn on the bright lights, then just work at my desk for a couple of hours. It still seemed to help. Then I began forgetting to turn the lights on. Now I seem to be able to deal with the affliction, at least at my pipsqueak level, simply by getting up early, which I love doing more every passing year.

Not long ago scientists reported that they'd managed to reset biological clocks by shining a bright light on the back of the knee. As Dave Barry would say, I am not making this up. The theory is that you don't need the light through your eyes, you just need it shining on your *blood*—even through your skin, unbelievably enough—and while the eyeball is a good place for that to happen, with a nice blood supply and all, so is the back of the knee. So undoubtedly would be the testicles, if they weren't hanging in the shade that way. Wouldn't that be an amusing way to take a light treatment.

It would still need to take place at the correct time, however, which perhaps explains why sunbathing in midafternoon soothed but failed to cheer me up. Anyway, brain chemicals are a handy cop-out. We used to blame everything on either weakness or damned meanness; now it's pollen, air pollution, environmental poisons, or brain chemicals. What a relief: you can be weak and mean and still get off scot-free.

We had an extended drought, the pond dropping to the lowest level in memory, a three-foot lane of newly exposed mud marking its borders. Walking barefoot across the lawn was like stepping on French-fried onion rings. The first frost came on the twenty-fourth, not terribly early but I wasn't ready for it. The air went out of the year. Forced indoors, I grudgingly gave up shorts, then T-shirts, and finally bare feet, cursing as I pulled on socks again, for the first time since mid-May. Socks, those little T-shirts for the feet. I had at some point inexplicably acquired a couple of pairs of those extra-thin white cotton ones, old guys' socks, and looked in horror as I pulled them up over what were becoming ever spindlier shanks. They were the sort of socks that should be worn by eighty-year-olds with the top of their shirts buttoned up tight. Sad as an old man's pants.

Out of some indefinable psychic funk I then decided I was sick of my beard, which I'd worn with only a couple of interruptions for thirty years, and shaved it off. Three days of daily shaving demonstrated that in the slick mode one spends a great deal more time staring into mirrors than in the fuzzy one. That means you get sick of what you see a lot quicker. I let my beard grow in again.

To look for rationality behind one's actions at this time of year is a pointless exercise, I think. A little research would surely turn up not a few historical disasters launched by saddened individuals in the fall of the year. It's when the stock market crashes. The world itself is mad, people nuts, making too many phone calls, asking pointless questions, raising irresolvable issues, scurrying around like ants trying to get all those dead bugs and cookie crumbs and little balls of unidentifiable feces stored safely down there in the hole before the light dies and the snow flies.

Make that so-called Seasonal Affective Disorder, another imaginary ailment like Chronic Fatigue Syndrome and Multiple Chemical Sensitivity: "imaginary" because we haven't found the microbes yet. Only we neurotic twitches suffer. I'm not at all sure SAD is a real phenomenon, or just something the magazines dredge up each fall to have something to write about. I can't tell because my own "case" is quite low-grade. I have found it a helpful explanation, though, for why, along about September, I begin brooding about fatal diseases and mass famine and global warming and my humiliatingly high level of personal guilt.

Behaviors follow. I hate behaviors, particularly when I'm the one who is demonstrating them. "If I could wholly cease to be ashamed of myself, I think that all my days would be fair," Thoreau once wrote. One September.

Shaving off my beard was a behavior, a purely hormonal one, very likely testosterone-related: testosterone poisoning, or as a urologist I know jokingly calls it, "deadly semen back-up." No such thing exists, we are assured. If that's true, what is it that makes us males so cranky?

It has not gone unnoticed that many of the physiological changes we associate with normal aging in the male—loss of muscle mass and strength, increased body fat, osteoporosis, lack of energy and generalized weakness—are also characteristic of testosterone deficiency. After about age thirty, testosterone production begins to drop off at 1 to 2 percent per year. Free testosterone, that portion unbound to body proteins—floating free in the blood, causing behaviors—dwindles even more sharply. Some of us then face a second tier of symptoms: difficulty in concentration, forgetfulness, insomnia, sagging libido, occasional impotence. These aggravations can also be reversed, to an extent, with testosterone-replacement therapy.

This is the argument that there is such a thing as male menopause—*viropause* in England, *andropause* in Europe, androgen being the general term for male hormones. (Or ADAM, for Androgen Deficiency in Aging Males; imagine the giggling when someone came up with that acronym.) If women can replace their dwindling supplies of estrogen to alleviate the very real distresses of menopause, why shouldn't we males alleviate the perhaps subtler but equally real distresses of our own physiological aging?

I think hormone-replacement therapy in women is an entirely good thing. Chris has been on estrogen for some time, to utterly good effect. It has made both our lives better. I am not so sure about hormone replacement in men. There is some sexism in this attitude that I can't quite unpeel. I don't think I'd consider it for myself, although it's clear that my production of the stuff has fallen off. I'd like the increase in strength and energy, and wouldn't mind having a stiffer member, but the rest of what I remember of higher testosterone levels—mostly the behaviors associated with it—I'd just as soon do without.

There are additional caveats to fiddling with hormones. Testosterone "replacement" when testosterone levels are not low is useless to dangerous, and ineffective for sexual dysfunction if that problem has other causes. There's also the suspicion that high testosterone levels predispose for prostate cancer, and replacement therapy might increase that risk. Similar concerns—about breast cancer—surround estrogen-replacement therapy for women. Human growth hormone levels are also often low in aging males (and females), and replacement can have restorative effects similar to those of testosterone. But this therapy can have bad side effects, is useless if blood levels are normal, and is quite expensive.

On the other hand, vigorous exercise stimulates the production of both testosterone and human growth hormone in both sexes, with none of the risks and a slew of other benefits. I'm not inclined to seek testosterone replacement from pills, for the aforementioned behavioral reasons, among other things, but I'm not above trying to make it happen naturally with some form of resistance training or equivalent. Hint to the hormonally deprived: testosterone is produced only by the testes and only during deep or slow-wave sleep. Deep sleep declines with age because of an unexplained decrease in production of melatonin. (Most endocrinologists regard the melatonin products on the market as useless if not actively dangerous.) Another way of achieving deep sleep is by wearing yourself out with hard work.

I have so far been reticent on the subject of sex, not to protect my own privacy but because talking about it unavoidably violates the privacy of someone else, which I do not in any way want to do. (The exception would of course be the solo version, which is *truly* uninteresting.) However, I can think of no topic of deeper interest to aging males. It's also a subject of enormous poignancy, almost too painful to think about. Pierre, medically castrated years ago to slow his prostate cancer, reports that while the function is gone, the sexual thoughts continue. So does a seventy-year-old magazine-writer friend who is impotent from MS. They consider this unfair. I have to agree, having suffered every kind of sexual failure myself except for the libidinal one.

OLDER PEOPLE ENJOY SEX, SURVEY SAYS, reads the most idiotic headline of the decade, in *The New York Times.* The National Council on Aging, which is commissioned to spend good money on such matters, reports that 39 percent of us are satisfied with the amount of sex we're having, and 39 percent of us would like more, both of which cases I find true of myself. Include me in that 78 percent. Yes, he said, yes.

The survey also found that more than 70 percent of us find sex as or more satisfying than it was in our forties, which I am also happy to confirm. But it is different. The survey did not address these details. It is no longer, for example, hot and wet, or as hot and wet as it was, which I sometimes think I miss—except that when sex was hot and wet it was also quick, and now it never is. I certainly don't miss the quickness. Now it is slow and inventive and generous, sweet and soft, a far cry from what used to be characterized, accurately enough, as rutting. It is restful and restorative, rather than demanding and debilitating. It has become a dreamy, tender, mutual celebration of the flesh. Youth has the language all wrong. Sex is not something you "get," it's a gift. You give and are given it.

For many males it is this softness (pun intended) that seems to be the rub (ditto). As women and a good portion of the medical profession like to point out, we do tend to think with our penises. Women do not, in my opinion, think with their vaginas. The human species has a brain on top, and an antibrain somewhere in the middle, appended either above or below, depending on the sex, by a couple of little agents provocateurs. Women may think with their ovaries; men, however, do not think with their testicles. If we did we might be better off, although we might also have more of a population problem than we already do.

Thinking with your penis means the goal is the orgasm, not the ejaculation. Ejaculation is a more or less unfortunate side effect.[1] With age our penises, when they do become erect, no longer become as large or as rigid as they used to. Some of us find this change distressing and difficult to accommodate, since a good deal of our sexual mythology is tied up in size and stiffness.[2] One study actually

---

1. After radical prostatectomy some males regain sexual function, but the orgasms they experience are "dry." Candidates for this surgery are assured by their urologists that this is as pleasurable as the old way. Their urologists, one must assume, still have working prostates. Perhaps sixty-five-year-old men should seek sixty-five-year-old urologists.
2. The beloved nature writer George Washington Sears, pen name Nessmuk, writing to a friend in 1879 at the age of fifty-seven: age, he said, was ". . . stiffening me up where I wish to be limber, and limbering me where I most desire to be stiff. That last touch near killed me."

postulates that men die, as a norm, twenty years after becoming impotent.

If we do come to accommodate it, it is perhaps because we begin to understand that this is the mythology of penis-as-tool—a familiar enough characterization in gutter slang—or even as weapon.[3] Ah, but to reach an age that would prefer to eschew behaviors is also to begin finally to wonder who—of either sex—would get pleasure from such a thing, from such a use. It's hard to imagine a more inappropriate attitude, in those moments when the very last thing on earth you're interested in is combat.

The truism about men is that we're afraid or even incapable of talking about our feelings. It's probably valid, in both the nerve-ending sense and the Barbra Streisand sense. Having a high pain threshold, for example, carries with it a certain moral approbation, although that's probably true for either sex, as both disapprove of whining. But men famously do not talk about these intimate details, not with their women or other men but also not with doctors. We're notorious for refusing to seek medical help. We seem to think it's not manly.

In the case of testosterone replacement, look how the question curls itself into a conundrum. It is somehow less manly to admit you need to feel more manly. Wouldn't it be more manly, after all, to accept responsibility for addressing one's needs? Or would it be more manly to accept that you don't need to feel so manly anymore, in the clichéd sense of the term? Manliness itself seems to be the problem. Why do we have so much greater need to be manly than women do to be womanly? Is our manliness in fact the delicate flower that Norman Mailer has always claimed?

3. Certainly the Pentagon seems to see it that way, recently tossing fifty million extra dollars into the annual military budget for the purchase of Viagra. Thus military, or engineering, thinking: address the plumbing, not the plant. One can't help thinking that testosterone pills—bolstering the fighting spirit rather than the weaponry—might provide more bang for the buck.

If we are lucky, what we finally begin to understand is that when sex was hot and wet it was driven by emotions that no longer answer. That we often found we regretted. If there was ever the *tristum* part of the deal, that was when it was.

I have no idea how I would be thinking about this if I were still out there in the meat market. I might even be looking for Viagra. Viagra, I gather, brings a return to the hot and wet—and brief. The pharmaceutical companies were quick to realize that men didn't find nine bucks a pop too stiff (sorry) a price to pay. Insert here (sorry) old jokes about never paying for it; how much'll you pay for upgrading the equipment you use for it?

But to reiterate, it's the quick part that's easiest to give up. Having a good time, I discover—at sex or anything else—is most dependably achieved, as mentioned, by slowing down. (I have mentioned this, haven't I? Old guys' memory isn't all that dependable, you know. Did I tell you the one about . . . ?) Slowing down allows you to start doing things for the thing itself. Once you get the hang of that, a lot of aging becomes just an amusing thing that is happening to you. It is also tragic, but only if you take it personally, and yourself seriously. Aging, being temporary, is a comedy. This too (you, your precious self) shall pass.

Comedy is temporary, tragedy is permanent. Comedy is the news, tragedy is history. Whoops, more of that wisdom crap. "You know you're getting old when, after taking a leak, you shake your dick and dust comes out" (George Carlin).

Thinking back about my solo canoe trip, I noticed I remembered a good deal more of the paddle in and the paddle out than usual for a canoe trip—more, for example, than I remembered of our more recent French River adventure. When you're alone your adrenaline level is a little higher. You're more alert. It makes you see more, remember more. Memory, too, must be a chemical matter.

The meditative disciplines teach that happiness lies in getting out of the past and future and into the present. To do so takes an act of forgetting. The struggle to remember—the pain, the pressure to remember, that increases with age—is an attempt to hang on to your own personality, your ego-identity. Memory is clinging, attachment; much frowned upon, at least in some circles.

In the supermarket parking lot I see a nicely dressed woman of about my own age standing beside a car, keys in hand, staring into space with a perfectly empty expression on her face. She is quite obviously lost. I consider going to her aid, but don't want to embarrass her. I sit watching for what seems like minutes until she finally collects herself, gets in, and drives away. I give an involuntary shudder.

Chris does my names for me, I jokingly say when I can't come up with one. My memory for them is increasingly poor. I get a little stab of panic when I'm expected to come up with one, particularly if I'm talking to a stranger. I suspect it's a bad habit in processing material, not yet anyway an organic failing. My retrieval mechanism, my search function, is rusty. My reaction to all current experience is, I'll process this later (and sometimes, unfortunately, that's when I'll get around to feeling it, too). This makes me a bad listener.

Chris had an uncle whose wife predeceased him. Everyone thought he was a perfectly functional elderly man, but at his wife's death he immediately went to pieces, exposed: she'd been covering for him, smoothing over his lapses, for years. I resolve not to let Chris do my names for me anymore, but she still comes up with them more quickly than I can. Sometimes. It depends, to a shocking degree, on how interested I am in the subject.

Often when I wake from a deep sleep I struggle for a moment, trying to place myself: what day is it, what comes next? I doubt this

is age; it used to happen more severely when I was a business trav-
eler, waking in hotel rooms and struggling to recollect where I was.
A friend describes having it happen to him when he was wide
awake, riding in a hotel elevator: what lobby awaited, in what city,
when the doors finally opened?

As an adolescent I used to get lost regularly off diving boards. I'd
be cutting some fancy but familiar aerial dido, and, in mid-dive, lose
my place: Where was the water? Which way was up? Then there was
nothing to do but curl into a tight ball and wait for the impact, not
knowing from which side it was going to come. We divers joked
about it among ourselves; happens to everybody.

I once wrecked a nice racing car by getting lost on the track. It
was a road course in California; I was doing a magazine piece about
Carroll Shelby's school for racing drivers. I'd had a couple of days of
instruction, going through one turn at higher and higher speeds
until I had it down pat, then going on to the next. Finally the instructors set me to driving the entire course, a couple of miles and
a dozen or so turns per lap. I came into one high-speed curve in a
fog of inattention, and could no longer remember which turn it was
or how fast it could be taken. Panicking, I locked up the brakes and
slid into a pile of hay bales, even though I'd been well below the
maximum speed for that corner. The instructors photographed me
standing beside the wrecked car, a rubber cone marker on my head
as a dunce cap, unhurt but with a thin smile of humiliation on my
face. I still have the photograph somewhere, but prefer not to look
at it.

When you get lost, what seems to happen is that you temporarily lose the capacity to direct your attention. Or, when you attempt
to direct your attention to a specific, intentional thing, you draw a
blank. To reorient yourself requires memory, of where you are and
what you're doing. The fright comes when you see what it's like

when that connection is no longer there. Getting lost is a glimpse of what Alzheimer's might be like. It must be a terribly frightening condition.

Most of us think of Alzheimer's as the ultimate horror, but I suspect that's wrong: ALS, Lou Gehrig's disease, must be worse, leaving mental function intact, so you can do nothing for yourself and yet are still perfectly conscious of every particle and detail of your debility. These things are not easy to think about. It doesn't do to brood on them, but some preparation would seem to be in order. One tries to be a little bit prepared, to reduce if not avoid the shock. As we get older we spend a lot of effort avoiding shock. We fear shock more than pain. (Pain we know about.) We fear the future, for cause.

Everyone is going to have a health crisis eventually; the object is to have fewer, later, shorter ones. The best would last a couple of seconds. I'd nominate ALS as the worst. We could come up with a Dread Scale. We are statistically assured of an eventual fatal disease, probably heart or cancer. One does what one can to avoid both, but it behooves us to be ready for the diagnosis when it comes. Jud, for example, was not.

When I try to imagine my own end I see a naked, shivering body being rushed onto a stainless-steel table. Probably an operating room. Attendants are scurrying, there's a hint of panic in the air. The panic, I'm fairly sure, is mine, not theirs; I am only another incipient stiff. See what I mean about September?

Fortunately, it helps—a little—to know that we are all being made crazy *innocently,* by serotonins and ilk, not by moral failings. The grocery bagger at the end of the aisle you mistakenly chose? The one who takes you step by step through her surprisingly gaudy ten-year employment record, including failures of each of the respective bosses to fully appreciate her contribution? She's only undergoing a dopamine surge. The nine days you deliberate on whether or not to enter your entire middle name or only the initial on your Social Security application form—the one you'd like to finish filling out before November rolls around—is not a failure of the intellect but of norepinephrine uptake, right there in the synapses. Knowing this, you can cut yourself a little slack. Sure, the world is turning into a lifeless frozen cinder, but that's not *your* fault. Besides, on January 5—with the horrible depression of New Year's Eve out of the way—it will all be okay again, won't it? The light coming back and all?

"I find the water suddenly cold," wrote Thoreau—in September 1851—"and that the bathing days are over."

OCTOBER: *Uneven Ground*

So, says I to myself, why not come indoors, then?

"October answers to that period in the life of man when he is no longer dependent on his transient moods," wrote Thoreau in 1853, "when all his experience ripens into wisdom, but every root, branch, leaf of him glows with maturity. What he has been and done in his spring and summer appears. He bears fruit."

Henry was a wise old thirty-six at the time.

I pulled myself out of the pool with an exaggerated grunt, and the lifeguard, in her early twenties, gave a little giggle. "That's just the sound of old bones talking," I explained. "Mine must be old too," she said; "I make the same noises."

Once joked about, the sound was lodged in my consciousness. I began to notice how Pawnee, who was not to last the coming winter, gave out with the same groans as she rose or lay down, almost every time she changed position. Watching her decline rubbed my nose in the denial business. If aging is all in your head, what had gone wrong with Pawnee? It seemed unlikely that her deterioration was just from fantasizing that she'd gotten older. I might have been a poor observer, but to tell the truth she didn't seem to have that much imagination.

Aging skeletons do want to sing out after you've been using them hard—or, contrarily, not hard enough. They have no mechanism for it, however, so the nerve signals dance from frame to spinal cord to lungs and voice box, which help you out in your efforts by emitting groans and yelps and in extreme cases even quiet little shrieks. Fairly gloomy songs: bones are not given to laughter.

Update from Mike: "I've recently been taking note of what I see in the mirror, and what meets the eye as I examine the plant. I am coming to believe that I've aged a lot in the last two years. For instance, I simply cannot make myself get out and run, or even walk vigorously, even though I'm getting a large gut and feeling logy. My hair is thinning very quickly at the front and the barber spends a fair amount of time clipping hair from my ear 'ole and eyebrows. Lines in my face are deepening. Sense of taste is diminishing. Skin on my forearms could have been taken off a lizard. Profusion of liver spots on the back of my hands. Elbows more pointy than ever. Cute bum is entirely gone; old man's slats have replaced it. Foot of an old man. Yet, inside this wreck there beats the heart of a what? A sixty-six-year-old on some days and a twenty-four-year-old on others."

"I share your shock at age's recent ravages," I wrote back, "and raise you a despoliation or two. Since summer—since surgery—my skeleton has somehow gotten sharper. The bones seem to dig at me from the inside out. I am unsteadier on my feet—which, as you mention, are turning into huge, unfeeling, swollen lumps—and often now must pause to stabilize myself when I stand up. Alcohol in the evenings is of no assistance here whatsoever.

"The sagging flesh on my upper eyelids threatens to obstruct vision, even when I have the energy to hold my eyes open, a window of time that shrinks daily. The bags below are big enough to flap when I run, annoying me. My waistline seems to fluctuate a couple of inches every week, with no appreciable change in weight; when it's on the up cycle I must loosen belt and zipper—on any pair of pants I own—to be comfortable when seated, yet when I stand up the same pants, now zipped, threaten to slide to the floor. I suspect my bum is still cute, however, although I can't turn my neck far enough to check it out."

Preparing for a recent canoe trip, I found myself short of bourbon, which goes down better than gin after you've run out of ice. I didn't want to buy another bottle just to add a couple of inches to the flask I usually take, so I topped it up with scotch. Augmented with Canadian lake water, it tasted just fine. I don't much care what flavor alcohol comes in, I just want its dark poison, its reminder of risk and death.

Subtle flavors are obviously wasted on me. I love good food but will never get serious about it. If it tastes too good I just want to eat too much of it. In restaurants I generally order fish; it's not my favorite, but I really don't care. Fish is allegedly healthy, we don't have it that often at home, what the hell. I'm usually hungry enough that everything tastes good.

(My attitudes are less severe, however, or at least more hopeful, than my friend Bruce's. "Eating," he writes. "It doesn't matter. Tastes good, tastes bad, but only for a few fleeting moments and in any event you have to do it and will be doing it all over again in a few hours and at least 65,000 times in the average life, and even voles and snails do it, and I recall that Buñuel movie where he reverses eating and elimination as social rituals—*The Discreet Charm of the Bourgeoisie*—and snort.

"But then I realize that you could just as well say all the above about having sex.")

I am conscious of diet but not to the extent of doing much about it. I get the occasional flash of foreboding—is this the pat of butter that finally closes off that coronary artery?—but am easily confused. Margarine, they now say, is worse than butter. Low-salt diets are either dangerous or so beneficial they allow the elderly to get off medication, take your pick. Lowering cholesterol increases risk of suicide, accidents, and murder. Eggs are okay again, this week. Yogurt doesn't promote longevity after all, diet drugs damage the heart, most chicken is tainted with salmonella. Recommended vitamin D dosages are too low (and sun screens prevent the body from manufacturing it). Nobody gets enough calcium. The new fat substitutes leach nutrients out of the body even when they don't cause diarrhea. Alcohol increases the risk of breast cancer. Incidents of food poisoning are on the rise. What are you going to do? (It helps to stop reading magazines.)

Chris and I tried a vegetarian diet for a while, back in the brown-rice sixties. The experiment worked—tasty food and plenty of it—but didn't take: too much trouble, and in fact it made us obsessive about food, preparing too much, always worrying if we were getting enough. Nowadays we eat more meat than we should, but then the portions recommended by the food police would reduce meat to a garnish anyway. I never mention it to vegetarian friends—well, seldom, anyway—but one Scandinavian study found direct correlation between the hemoglobin level in the blood and the number of teeth in the head, real or artificial. Simply put, the more teeth people have, the more meat they tend to eat. I need my hemoglobin, I have use for it. Besides, if you get old enough, cholesterol stops being a problem. So does fat. Now *there's* a benefit of aging. Will people think more of you if you're imperially slim? Who's looking? That's it, that's the secret: *no one's looking.* You're invisible when you're old.

Besides, diets don't work—a bit of news the publishing industry has been determinedly squelching for most of this century. (Or maybe it's the public: books have been written that point this out, but nobody buys them. We prefer to believe.) A full-time nutrition-ist at your elbow, gram scale in hand, can't tell you within three hundred calories a day how much you're actually eating—and miss-ing by that much can put thirty pounds on you in a year.

The nutritionists would put us old folks on low-salt diets. This does not come from thinking about how people actually eat. Salt acts as a lubricant, stimulating the flow of saliva, which age other-wise dries up. A dry gullet doesn't help you enjoy food either, never mind the Heimlich maneuvers: saliva is required to make the taste buds work. I know of a quite elderly woman who is dying of con-gestive heart failure, whom the authorities have put on a salt-free diet. She hates it, hates her food. So now she's dying of congestive heart failure and slow starvation. Maybe she'll live a few months longer; hungry, it'll seem a lot longer than that.

Decades before running became a national pastime, a friend of mine was running five miles a day. He bragged about this to his doc-tor. "That just means you're going to die of cancer," said his warmly sympathetic personal physician. *What?* Sure, said the doc, you're ei-ther going to die of heart disease or cancer; all that exercise just re-moves the first option. My friend died of leukemia (at, as it happens, sixty-five). I always think of this when I hear about low-salt diets: it's so you can die of cancer, right?

I think we have to hang on to our pleasures; natural processes are taking them away rapidly enough. I am very much in favor of pure sensation for the aging, particularly including myself. I don't think we should stint on sensual kicks: flavors, substances, sights and sounds, sexual practices, sybaritic body care. Let us celebrate our nerve endings while we can.

But I find—another of aging's little jokes—that for sustained pleasure value, few sensory trips actually measure up to going to bed really tired. Fortunately, age will oblige in this regard. Age will assist you generously, unstintingly, in this self-indulgence. Gaffer Savings Time, Chris calls it: God resets your clock. Going to bed and getting up early is neither willful nor noble, it is laid on from the outside and there is nothing you can do about it. And it becomes an exquisite luxury.

A few years ago we went to the Caribbean with a couple young enough to be our offspring. All had a fine time, but the schedule had to be adjusted. In the beginning they tried to get up early enough to join us for breakfast, and a couple of times we stayed up late enough to join them for dinner—never mind anything so unimaginable as "night life"—but both couples quickly abandoned all that as unnatural. We met for lunch; our social afternoons were just great.

Every now and then, but not as often as I'd really like, Languid Man does the dishes. It is a lovely, restful way to go at chores, at the little repetitive tasks at most of which, most of the time, I scurry as fast as I can. It's not easy to bring to those tasks the proper combination of energy and patience, to give oneself permission to slow down and get things right. Unfortunately, slowing down at chores drives other people crazy—especially if you make sure that the way you go at it implies a little moral lesson. Maybe another book: *How to Be an Irritating Old Man.*

Setting out deliberately to become fussy is probably a bit perverse, but it has a growing appeal. It's what might be called the completion craze: there is great reassurance in getting one more thing very thoroughly, very completely *done*. Getting one's world in order. ("Retired," Chris mutters, every time we happen to drive past an open garage the interior of which is noticeably neat, or an exceedingly meticulous lawn.) One begins to entertain a kind of philosophical speculation on repeatable versus completable chores.

It's really just a process of moving on, switching generations, the very thing we vowed never to do. I used to be on other people's bumpers; now they are on mine. How loudly we used to yell about Vietnam, and couldn't believe they didn't hear us; how loudly they are yelling now, about whatever, and how easy it is for us to ignore them. Tongue dumbbells, and other body piercings. The only thing I notice now is the volume.

Speaking of which, last year I bought Chris a mute button for her birthday. I had to buy a new TV to get one, the old set having been manufactured in 1976. It turned out to be the best $250 investment in electronic gadgetry I'd made since my first computer, in 1980. The word "Mute" is already worn off the remote control. My visiting grandchildren couldn't understand why we don't have a car radio. "I don't like noise," I said. "I DO!" shouted the four-year-old instantly; "I DO!" chimed in his nine-year-old sister.

Recent research indicates osteoporosis may occur even in the ossicles, the tiny bones of the middle ear. If those bones lose density, they may not transmit sound as well, a finding that has implications for aging's traditional deafness. There's a wonderful use-it-or-lose-it metaphor here. Audiologists are constantly sent cases, usually male and usually nagged into getting tested by their wives, who turn out to have perfect hearing. What does the doctor recommend? Listen to your wife, says the doctor. Load up those little bones in the middle ear—use 'em or lose 'em—or you *will* go deaf.

It's a nasty loss.[1,2,3] Therefore it's worth fighting any way you can. The first step is probably learning to pay a different kind of attention. This, too, is a matter of energy, which age is also stealing from you. Maybe the best way to fight it is not to pursue hearing itself but more energy. More, higher levels of energy. How do you do this? Hint: work.

In October, as an experiment, I stopped wearing a wristwatch. With a clock in the car and in almost every room in the house, it struck me as rather pointless to have something like jewelry dangling around my wrist. I'd abandoned rings and other adornments years ago, but had always worn a watch. Chris won't wear one, hates them in fact. I was curious to see what going without would be like.

Not much different, as it happens, and after a month I put mine back on again. Going without it didn't make me crazy but didn't add anything either. I felt no more or less constricted, not suddenly freed from the tyranny of time but also no more bound to it. It was mildly inconvenient. I occasionally like to time things. Putting it back on didn't significantly encumber me. Actually I liked it. Maybe, I thought, I'd start adorning myself.

Then I decided to consider it my retirement watch. It was a $19 Timex I bought in 1992, after losing its $30 predecessor while struggling with a swamped canoe in swift water. It has served me

---

1. Deafness has to be the most irritating ailment of the old. Both speaker and listener inevitably get exasperated with each other. It is the most trying part of socializing with one's elders. And it leads to withdrawal from social and even physical activity.

2. There are other exasperations. In her later years, when my mother couldn't come up with a name, she'd get angry at her listener. "Oh, *you* know who I mean," she'd say, implying that it was just damned meanness that kept you from supplying her with the name she wanted.

3. My thanks to Dr. Oliver Sacks, who has so elegantly demonstrated the efficacy of serial footnotes in stringing together otherwise unrelated ideas.

just fine ever since. Maybe it was time for me to retire. Nobody else was going to give me an official retirement watch, I'd made sure of that.

Mike had hung on to a couple of consulting contracts when he'd given up full-time employment, but was beginning to get exasperated with their demands. They required a good deal of travel and some extremely boring responsibilities. Why don't you just retire? I suggested, and then got completely swept up with the idea myself.

Look, I pointed out (i.e., lectured): "retirement" is a psychological change, not a financial one. (He'd officially retired from the Canadian Navy several years before, but had quickly gone on to civilian employment.) I suggested that he might notice little difference in his life except, with luck, a slightly more cavalier attitude toward his responsibilities. It would just be a change of mind-set. He would still be trying to make the best possible use of the day, do what needed to be done, think of new things that needed to be done. The only difference would be that *he'd own his own time*—and if he claimed he was retired, he'd be able to be a little more eccentric about how he spent it. Maybe even a lot more eccentric.

He'd certainly filled his life sufficiently before retirement, I argued, and there was no reason not to do the same now; he'd just be relieved of the unpleasant parts. Why not let retirement mean only that he'd stop doing the things he didn't like to do? Or that he at least had the right to choose when—or even whether—to do them?

By then I realized I was lecturing to myself. I really had retired years ago, when I began making the little joke about just kicking back and writing books, but I'd never quite figured out how to settle into it. I'd never acquired the mind-set. I'd always suffered from the gold-watch notion: the struggle over, feet up, the hammock and the gin and tonic. But that required the other part, desk and secretary, an office party, putting your stuff in a box and carrying it out to the car: some formalizing ritual.

I didn't need that. So I declared it for myself. I am now retired, I told Mike; whew! Jesus, you don't know what a relief it is. I'm out of it, over with. Don't have to keep up anymore. I can now devote full time to being a foolish old man, quietly amusing myself without, within limits, bothering anyone. This is a role I can get into. As a matter of fact it opens up whole new worlds of possibilities. Can't wait to fill in one of those boxes marked "occupation." Problem is, when you're retired you don't *apply* for things much anymore.

He seemed to like the idea. Subsequent letters mentioned a continuing, growing euphoria. Ditto at this end. Maybe it works. Maybe it's a myth anyway, this retirement business. "I think it's a ruse, an economic scheme that's been perpetrated on the nation," says Bard Lindeman, in *Be an Outrageous Old Man*. "I wouldn't be surprised if this failed social experiment, in its present form, didn't last another generation."

Others have pointed out that retirement was not invented as a reward for past labors anyway, but as a social necessity, a way of opening up jobs. Personally, I refuse to feel guilty about continuing to work. It's not as if I'm keeping some young-punk writer out of a job. Okay, sure, there are too many writers, too many books being printed, but for me to stop writing them isn't going to help that situation. Anyway, when Social Security kicks in—when I can afford to take it, in five more years (plus a couple of weeks)—I go on the writer's equivalent of the farm price-support system. The government will in effect be paying me not to write so much. It'll save some trees, too.

But I really have to watch the lecturing, especially to Mike, who has two years on me. Almost any utterance that wants to come out of my mouth these days, if I am not very careful, is a grab for a position of some kind of moral authority. Would-be moral authority. Unfortunately, part of me thinks I've earned it. Another part recognizes it as the most poisonous single aspect of the aging mentality. It's more of that proffered wisdom.

It startles me to realize that most of my male friends are older than I. I find it harder to make any kind of real contact with younger men. I was callow too long, worked too hard to get over it. I don't like callowness, even sentimentally. I'm never sure, even as I approach sixty-five, that I am not still callow, and that gripes my ass. One of my problems with Jud was that he wouldn't let me not be callow.

All available advice says that an important key to successful aging is to maintain social connection: a support group of acquaintances, for mental stimulation as well as actual help in times of need. It is an aspect of aging that I have seriously neglected. I have no talent for maintaining friendships that aren't based on work or shared special interests. Can I be funny and warm enough, helpful or just plain interesting enough, to hold another's interest, to take up his time, without some external link? I don't think so. I suspect most males have this problem. Thus we are thrown back on family, and everyone knows how that works out. The ugly truth is that most men bore each other stiff. This may well be because we don't know how to get at those parts of our lives that we would find truly interesting. Most of those parts—sexuality, power, fear, emotional states—are customarily regarded by men as shameful. Women seem not to have this problem.

Maybe I expect younger men to be callow, and don't want to be disappointed. They seldom are, past the age of thirty or so. Clearly, I don't work hard enough at my friendships with them. What seems to interfere is a difference in the level of wanting. It's worth asking: what do you want? It gets harder to answer as you get older. The answer gets subtler and subtler.

My son Marty visited, and I asked him for help with a computer problem, which is his professional field. He whirled through it, solving it with utter, tactful competence, while I stood behind him hanging by my fingernails, unable even to follow what he was doing. How nice that was to see, my son so much better at something than I am, a relief from the default assumption, between fathers and sons, that seniority is all. A relief to me to see him so much better than I at something; God, I hope it's a relief for him too. Or maybe he never had the same self-doubts I always had.

Not that many years ago this would've been threatening, I suppose. I've become peculiarly aware of the feeling that masculinity, maybe even gender, is beginning now to slip away—not in my sex life, just in my take on the world. What is sliding away is the male point of view, the male interpretation. I hope.

I have an anatomist friend—the only person I know who has dissected a rhinoceros—who reads more widely than just about anyone, and peppers me with sources. He sent a copy of A. Alvarez's *Feeding the Rat,* a profile of British mountain climber Mo Anthoine. In the last pages Anthoine gets talking about when he might quit going on the difficult, dangerous climbs. Perhaps someday he'll be satisfied with the easy stuff, he says, but ". . . every year you need to flush out your system and do a bit of suffering. It does you a power of good. I think it's because there is always a question mark about how you would perform. . . . If you deliberately put yourself in difficult situations, then you get a pretty good idea of how you are going. That's why I like feeding the rat. It's a sort of annual checkup on myself. The rat is you, really. It's the other you, and it's being fed by the you that you think you are. And they are often very different people. But when they come close to each other, that's smashing, that is. Then the rat's had a good meal and you come away feeling terrific. . . . But to snuff it without knowing who you are and what you are capable of, I can't think of anything sadder than that."

I've always found this kind of talk simultaneously fascinating and disturbing—distrusting it, distrusting the self-administered testosterone check, even while, occasionally, performing it. (My own rat, if I ever had one, is now a somewhat geriatric gerbil.) I'd be first to admit a certain pleasure after the fact in finding one's capabilities are still there, in finding you *can* do the next thing. What I don't want anymore is the head-to-head, individual stuff. Mano a mano. Swim-racing in middle age fully exorcised that demon, I guess. I don't even want to go head-to-head against myself.

Anthoine speaks of suffering, which is only one half of the rat-food equation. The other I'd have to call daredeviltry, as in the traditional redneck's last words: "Y'all watch this." (George Bush and skydiving come to mind.) Risk sports, the analysts call them: all these people doing all these crazy things, some of which I used to do, albeit on a decidedly dilettantish level. That impulse was entirely testosterone-induced, I think, although for all I know there are as many female bungee jumpers as male. (That's testosterone in the metaphorical rather than the clinical sense.)[4] I was for too many years a would-be acrobat—what a curious term—and, as mentioned, am surely alive and at least ambulatory today only because even skateboards were invented after I was past the age of seduction. I suppose that age passed when I realized that none of the resulting thrills was lasting, edifying, or in any way useful. Besides, by

4. Snowmobilers, unable to wait for snow, now go drag racing on grass, achieving speeds of over 100 mph. Of course, as Chris points out, acceleration makes you stupid. I don't know why science hasn't measured this. But then so does sex, as millennia of infatuations, and behaviors, have demonstrated. What we have here is the Lout Factor. Most of us have been one, in some version or another. Even women.

then I'd broken a few bones. If I got anything at all out of those experiences, it was only a kind of quivering appreciation for my continuing existence. People say they do those things for the "rush." The rush I remember is inseparable from the one you'd get from vomiting on the hostess's best tablecloth.

And now I am so very glad to let that rat die.

Okay, actually I was manipulated into the retirement business by the government. Exactly one month before my sixty-fifth birthday, per the feds' explicit instruction, I went in and signed my name to the Social Security rolls. I could not say to the authorities that I was retiring, nor could I begin drawing any money—there was no way I could get by on that measly pension, and if I continued to earn anything like a decent living I'd have to pay it back anyway—but I was also eligible for Medicare, which assistance I definitely could use. I kept trying to infuse the transaction with some kind of larger symbolic meaning, but it was just paperwork. A very nice lady, but nothing ceremonial. People, she implied, do it all the time.

We received very good news from surgeon Fritz, of the mysterious amyloid deposits. He was still managing most days to put in eight hours or more at the operating table, before returning to his gardening and landscaping, mowing and snowplowing. When he walked he needed a rest, albeit a very brief one, as frequently as every few dozen yards, he said, but he continued. He had been told early in his diagnosis to avoid strenuous exertion, which caused the usual microtrauma to the heart muscle, ordinarily replaced by new, stronger muscle; in his case, however, the damaged tissue would be replaced with amyloid. He therefore wasn't out seeking exercise, but living the life he wanted to live, to the degree that he could, and accepting the result. He and his wife, Janet, who is seventy-seven, have always made better use of themselves than anyone we've ever known. Janet has given clear expression to their mutual attitude toward these matters, crocheting a sampler attributed to, of all people, Rosalind Russell:

> *Seal my lips on aches and pains.*
> *They are increasing and the love*
> *Of rehearsing them is becoming*
> *Much sweeter as years go by.*

And here I've gone and written a whole book ignoring that very good advice.

Otherwise I seemed to spend October driving around the valley with a handful of credit cards, stocking up against the coming disruption. At any moment, we knew from past experience, lightbulbs and faucet washers would begin giving up the ghost, and the whole houseful of assorted appliances begin coughing and stuttering and keeping us awake at night with the certainty of imminent failure. Happens every fall. (When you're forty, twenty years is an eternity. When you're sixty-five, it's about the life of a really good appliance—one of a seemingly endless series you've been repairing and replacing all your life.)

Time anyway for the storm windows, getting the hoses and garden furniture in, the car winterized, the deck—literally—cleared. Flannel sheets on the bed, firewood stacked. October is the great month in New England. All of the clichés apply. November will bring bittersweet and melancholy, but October is all glory, all tribute, all celebration of the great swell of life that erupted out of the previous winter and found its fruition in the fall.

It's glorious even if everything is dying. Actually, I'm not quite past the October of my life, am I? I quickly do the math. Taking

Thoreau's year-as-life-span metaphor, a month is equal to 6.6 years (80 divided by 12), a day to two tenths of a month (6.6 divided by 30). At sixty-five, then (minus a couple of weeks), it is now, oh, October 28 of my life span. If, that is, I am going to die statistically, on the equivalent of December 31. I am past the 80 percent point. Ouch. How does one think, then? How do you manage, how do you handle it, what do you think about, when less than 20 percent of your life remains?

When I was a small boy, perhaps ten, and in the grip of some bitter grievance against the world, I got down my stepfather's pistol from the closet where he thought it was hidden, put the muzzle in my mouth, and pulled the trigger. The safety was on. By the time I'd figured out how to release it my impulse to kill myself had safely run its course. Mechanical problems have always served me that way. But isn't it amazing how naive parents can be about firearms and children?

Childish snits aside, suicide never stopped seeming to me to be the rational option. I think it's a common attitude, if infrequently expressed. Carolyn Heilbrun lays it out quite simply in *The Last Gift of Time:* "Having supposed the sixties would be downhill all the way, I had long held a determination to commit suicide at seventy. . . . Quit while you're ahead was, and is, my motto." She chooses not to, of course: "I find it powerfully reassuring now to think of life as 'borrowed time.' Each day one can say to oneself: I can always die; do I choose death or life? I daily choose life the more earnestly because it is a choice."

Our society has recently experienced a wave of what must be described as grim enthusiasm for that kind of opting out—the Hemlock Society, Dr. Kevorkian, Oregon's assisted-suicide referendum.

I've watched each of these developments with a secret little *frisson* of guilty interest. Yes, that might prove useful. I can see that; I might want that myself. Yet I've never been suicidal. I have from time to time consoled myself with the thought that I only have to continue this farce for however many years more. I've had images occur to me, while driving, of fiery crashes into bridge abutments, and similar disasters. I've even figured out how one might go about running the hose from the exhaust pipe into the passenger compartment (use duct tape). But I've never given the deed itself a moment's consideration. An option, that's all. If and when.

Increasingly, however, I find that whole option business to be the thinking of a younger person. My aging cohort used to baffle me in this regard, and while I never quite had the courage to ask any of them why they did not kill themselves, I did once manage to get the ever-realistic Pierre to discuss the general subject. "The days are long now," he had written. "I am often at a loss to fill them. Even reading sometimes palls. . . . If Keats in his wonderfully productive twenties could be 'half in love with easeful death,' how not in one's superfluous nineties? So says the mind. But it is not the mind that moves us in matters of life and death.

"Schopenhauer was right in this regard. He grasped the truth that the eternal element in man is not intellect but will. The intellect may counsel easeful death, but the will is bent on living. So it was with Schopenhauer. His low opinion of life did not prevent him from living beyond three score and ten." And so it is with Pierre, who dutifully attends to his health.

His Schopenhauer had confused me, however, and I wrote him back. I'd always understood will as something imposed on the organism by intent; wasn't Schopenhauer describing something closer to a biological force? If will alone would do the trick you could commit suicide by holding your breath. Suicide is only possible by putting the will in service of the intellect. If will says Survive no matter what the intellect says, I asked, isn't that the biological argument?

Pierre answered, suavely as usual: "Maybe it is because we have more options on this side of the Atlantic than the older and more crowded nations of Europe that we are inclined to think of the will as free to make choices in a pluralistic world (William James) or a pragmatic one (John Dewey). For Schopenhauer the will is not free. The will to live is biological compulsion. He likens human life to a planet that would fall into the sun if it ceased to hurry forward.

"We don't have to believe him, but he is still the most readable of philosophers. This, for instance: 'Those few who are comparatively happy, or seem so, are decoy birds.' Let us be decoy birds."

I'm not sure which I need, Pierre or Schopenhauer, to understand the case of a friend with ALS. He'd been a bull of a man, a former minister, a college president at thirty-two who rode his motorcycle to work, as lively a man as I'd ever known. When the disease took his voice he acquired a computer to speak for him, and gave public speeches with it. Gradually he became totally paralyzed. He had assured friends he would opt out when he wanted to—and seemed to feel he would have the medical support to do so. He lived two years on a respirator, able to move nothing but his eyes: his only means of communication to look away for no, to look at you for yes. When he finally died, of pneumonia, he was still saying yes. Kevorkian, I now realize, serves a level of despair much deeper than I can quite conceive.

One of the more rueful amusements of age is watching yourself turn into only a slight variation of every other poor schlub who ever lived. We spend our youth and our adulthood earnestly working at separating ourselves from the ruck, trying to establish our special-ness, our uniqueness. That certainly was my driving force. I could never heed psychological advice, for example: it was too general, and I was too specific. I lived by that motto of the young, Do not un-derstand me too quickly; I am a much more complex and interest-ing individual than you can possibly know. There are mysteries about me that you cannot possibly comprehend.

Maybe it was time for the oh-please-understand-me stage—or, rather, age. My aphorist brother used to say, "The Devil is complex-ity and God is simplicity—or maybe it's the other way around." Age wants to strip me of complexity. I am being reeled back in. Every-man is swallowing me up.

If I really sucked it up, it occurs to me, I could perhaps continue to be what I have rather fatuously considered to be that highly indi-vidualized person. I might hold out at the game for another five years, maybe ten. But the stunning truth is that being that fellow is no longer all that much fun. Maybe it never was. The individualism act wears thin, not as entertaining as it used to be even for myself. And, once again, it is the body that does it: I am far too special a per-son to have a swollen prostate, a bum neck, fading eyesight. That's what happens to all those others, those old people. Whom I am swiftly joining.

As you cease, with age, to be an individual to yourself, you even more dramatically cease to be one to society. That's where it hap-pens first. Your body and your society conspire to demonstrate that you are in fact Everyman after all. Actually most of us, I suppose, continue thinking of ourselves as individuals in private, but the public individual doesn't bear exposure. Isn't worth the trouble. Yeats's foolish, passionate old man is an embarrassment to us all—and will go to his grave aching in ways he doesn't necessarily need to ache.

Autumn thoughts, perhaps a natural product when you're deep into the battening-down season. I'd about got my little hole packed full, another chink or two to pull in behind me—which I hoped to do as daylight saving gave a sigh and departed, and dark started arriving in early afternoon. I didn't mind. I still had half of Thoreau to read, and the firewood in. Birthday coming up; after this one, I planned to go to school on Heilbrun. The trick is to begin thinking "Any day now." After sixty-five, a gift. I wanted to live that way. It was a statistical certainty that on my hundred and twenty-fifth birthday I would be dead. Maybe I could work backward from there.

In fact, my birthday wish for myself was that things would go along just about the way they were for the duration, whatever that turned out to be. Meanwhile, time's a-wasting: I was serious this time, I was going to call the Dumpster guy. Drop one in the driveway for the coming month. November would be a good time to clean all the crap out of this place. That was a weight-lifting program I could get behind.

Temporarily stuck on a writing problem, on a bright midmorning in late October, I gave up the desk and set out to walk our hillside loop. Our land is a nature preserve, open to passage, to strangers, to rustication; the only thing we don't allow on it is recreational killing. I'd run or walked it more days than not since we moved here eighteen years ago—one year, with the help of snowshoes, I got around it two times a day, programmatically, on all but about ten days of the year—but somehow this past summer it had gone neglected. Blackflies and mosquitoes will do that to you. With the turn of the foliage, however, the woods had called themselves to our attention again, and Chris and I had done the loop the previous week, a long slow walk through October glory. We vowed at the time to make it a habit, but you know how those vows go.

This time I took along a small pruning saw. The trail needed maintenance, and there was an infestation of fox grape at the height of land that was driving me crazy. Wild grape is pretty enough when it's green, and it feeds the birds, but it also strangles and pulls down healthy trees into tangled knots of ingrown jungle. I'd been hacking away at the vines, off and on, ever since we moved here. A forester told me I was wasting my time—the only way to get rid of them is by poisoning the roots—but we'd never summoned that level of aggression. Still, I couldn't resist sawing them off at ground level, at least when my level of ambition, or frustration, was sufficiently high.

Enough foliage was down to allow me to see deeply into the woods, to see the contour of the land, now covered with the orange-red velvet of fallen leaves. Unimaginably, in another couple of weeks all that mulch would be an even, dull tan. I walked and pruned, removing deadfalls, opening up the trail to flow. I know every step of that trail, know it the way your tongue knows the inside of your mouth, but the greenery that surrounds it keeps coming up with small surprises. The previous winter had dropped a couple of large trees across the path, too big for me to remove, so I began cutting bypasses. The grape infestation was worse than I expected, some vines four inches thick. Sawing through them with my small saw was hot work. I took off my sweatshirt, had to stop from time to time to mop my face. I got tired enough to stagger a bit, on the uneven ground, as I worked from vine to vine. It made me feel old, lurching across the forest floor. I'd noticed the same unsteadiness in the woods on our canoe trip. If I did something like this every day, I thought, I'd improve my balance, be better able to deal with future unevenness. If I didn't, I'd spend weeks at a time on nothing but pavement or solid floors. You can't turn on your heel in a carpeted room.

Not that I wasn't getting the same warnings when I moved too fast, trotted up stairs, shifted furniture: inattention combined with slowing reflexes now and then giving me a small scare. I'd stumble, catch myself—a little less gracefully than I seem to remember doing in the past—and a little warning bell would go off in my head. Watch it. You're going to have to be more careful. Years ago I asked a fellow middle-aged swim racer what losses he regretted with age. "Agility," he answered immediately. I hadn't thought of it before, but it was exactly true for me, too. Being careful is an almost foreign concept. How strange to acquire a whole new set of concerns (safety, security), and how much stranger to let go of so many old friends in that category. It wasn't me, exactly, this doddering hulk I was turning into—but I was beginning to understand that it was closer to me than any of the other people I'd felt it necessary to be over the previous six decades. Everyman indeed.

My staggering unsteadiness started me bitching to myself about our impending loss of canoe trips, about goddamned age. I resorted to reason. After all, I'd started the year barely mobile. I had surgery and recovered splendidly, at least to my own standards. We'd gotten in a major canoe trip, one of our most demanding, and I'd had another minor outing or two: plenty of paddling, plenty of time on water. I'd really enjoyed building the dock. Actually, it had been the most gloriously active summer in memory, in part because I was determined to make up for recent losses, in part because I was feeling strong enough and energetic enough to get out and do things. A hell of a year. Insufficiently grateful.

Cutting grape vines is like eating cocktail peanuts; one leads on to the next, and it's hard to stop. I began to slow down, spending less energy thrashing around, more time selecting the next to cut—

identifying the problem, removing it, pulling it out of its tangle, putting it someplace out of the way so I didn't trip over it. Not quite Languid Man but, at least for a little while, no longer the Anxious Fool either. Thinking about canoeing, and loss, and healing as I went, drifting off in a cocoon of daydreaming, all the while working hard, using muscle and enjoying it, getting tired and wondering why I didn't stop. Assessing in my usual paranoid/hypochondria-cal/neurasthenic fashion the specifics, but realizing that, no, no damage was occurring, I was not going orthopedic. I could continue. Not quite spitting on my hands, but then this was a more satisfying task than shoveling and raking. More cerebral, or perhaps reflective; actual decisions were involved. Engaging, that's what it was. In fact it was lovely work to do, and I was enjoying it. Deeply.

The loop is a thirty-minute walk; I got back to the house an hour and a half later, arms and shoulders aching, all tired out, filthy, scratched and bitten, and generally feeling better than I had in about three years. Made lunch, then had a little nap, sleeping like a concrete bridge abutment. (Producing melatonin like crazy, I liked to presume.) Woke up stiff, amazed, content. Cutting brush, I realized, was the perfect work for me, at my age, at this time of year. Hell, with gloves—and, in a pinch, snowshoes—I could do it all winter long. An hour a day: get out, get it done, keep pecking away at it. Great for the arms and shoulders, for balance, for sheer strength. I could think of at least four other areas, in the woods immediately adjacent to the house, that could use brushing out. Open them up to strolling, turn boondock into glade.

Whatever I cut would sprout again in a few years. By the time I had worked my way through the fifth glade, the first would be about ready for redoing. Just like painting the Golden Gate Bridge. Maybe I'd found my Golden Gate. Suddenly I was wealthy—again—beyond measure. After all, as Camus pointed out, Sisyphus was essentially a happy man.

About the Author

JOHN JEROME, a former young person, now sometimes claims to be retired, but can't prove it. He has in the past raced in cars, on skis, and in swimming pools, but now lives as slowly as possible in far-western New England and writes books. He is a former magazine editor and advertising copywriter and columnist for *Esquire* and *Outside* magazines. Previous books include *Truck, The Sweet Spot in Time, Stone Work,* and *Blue Rooms.*

ABOUT THE TYPE

This book was set in Perpetua, a typeface designed by the English artist Eric Gill, and cut by The Monotype Corporation between 1928 and 1930. Perpetua is a contemporary face of original design, without any direct historical antecedents. The shapes of the roman letters are derived from the techniques of stonecutting. The larger display sizes are extremely elegant and form a most distinguished series of inscriptional letters.

Printed in the United States
by Baker & Taylor Publisher Services